Silent Music

Currents in Latin American and Iberian Music

Walter Clark, Series Editor

Nor-tec Rifa!
Electronic Dance Music from Tijuana to the World
Alejandro L. Madrid

From Serra to Sancho:
Music and Pageantry in the California Missions
Craig H. Russell

Colonial Counterpoint:
Music in Early Modern Manila
D. R. M. Irving

Silent Music

Medieval Song and the Construction of History in Eighteenth-Century Spain

BY SUSAN BOYNTON

UNIVERSITY PRESS

Oxford University Press, Inc., publishes works that further
Oxford University's objective of excellence
in research, scholarship, and education.

Oxford   New York
Auckland   Cape Town   Dar es Salaam   Hong Kong   Karachi
Kuala Lumpur   Madrid   Melbourne   Mexico City   Nairobi
New Delhi   Shanghai   Taipei   Toronto

With offices in
Argentina   Austria   Brazil   Chile   Czech Republic   France   Greece
Guatemala   Hungary   Italy   Japan Poland   Portugal   Singapore
South Korea   Switzerland   Thailand   Turkey   Ukraine   Vietnam

Copyright © 2011 by Oxford University Press

Published by Oxford University Press, Inc.
198 Madison Avenue, New York, New York 10016

www.oup.com

Oxford is a registered trademark of Oxford University Press

All rights reserved. No part of this publication may be reproduced,
stored in a retrieval system, or transmitted, in any form or by any means,
electronic, mechanical, photocopying, recording, or otherwise,
without the prior permission of Oxford University Press.

Library of Congress Cataloging-in-Publication Data
Boynton, Susan, 1966–
Silent music : medieval song and the construction of history in
eighteenth-century Spain / by Susan Boynton.
    p.   cm.
Includes bibliographical references and index.
ISBN 978-0-19-975459-5 (hardcover : alk. paper)
1. Paleography, Musical—Spain. 2. Music—500–1400—Manuscripts—Spain.
3. Music—500–1400—History and criticism. 4. Enlightenment—Spain—Influence.
5. Neumes. I. Title.
ML431.B69   2011
780.946—dc22   2011002533

Publication of this book was funded by the Margarita Hanson Fund of the American Musicological Society
and the Publications Endowment of the American Musicological Society, supported through the
National Endowment for the Humanities.

1 3 5 7 9 8 6 4 2

Printed in the United States of America
on acid-free paper

R0440195417

MUSIC INFORMATION CENTER
VISUAL & PERFORMING ARTS
CHICAGO PUBLIC LIBRARY
400 SOUTH STATE STREET
CHICAGO, IL 60605

CONTENTS

LIST OF ILLUSTRATIONS

ACKNOWLEDGMENTS

The research for this book was initially funded by summer research fellow-ships from Columbia University and the National Endowment for the Hu-manities. My writing was supported in 2007–08 by an ACLS Fellowship from the American Council of Learned Societies and by a membership in the School of Historical Studies, Institute for Advanced Study (Princeton), which was made possible by the National Endowment for the Humanities through its Fellowship Programs at Independent Research Institutions. I am particularly grateful to Caroline Walker Bynum, Giles Constable, and Marian Zelazny for their many kindnesses to me and my family during our year at the Institute. I thank Suzanne Ryan of Oxford University Press for her sustained interest in the project, and Walter Clark for welcoming the book into his series.

It goes without saying that a book about an archivist originated in the archives, and I owe a special debt of gratitude to the outstanding librarians and archivists who have aided my work with alacrity, patience, and goodwill for the past ten years. The initial discovery that generated the book project was made possible through access to medieval manuscripts at the Hispanic Society of America granted by John O'Neill, Librarian of the Hispanic Soci-ety. My work in the Hispanic Society's collection began with the preparation of an exhibition of liturgical manuscripts organized by Consuelo Dutschke, Curator of Medieval and Renaissance Manuscripts at the Rare Book and Man-uscript Library, Columbia University. Both of these distinguished scholar-librari-ans have continued to be of invaluable assistance and have kindly granted my requests for reproductions and permissions. Pamela Graham, Latin American/ Iberian Studies Librarian and Director of the Area Studies/Global Resources Library Program at Columbia University, has swiftly and graciously obtained every publication I have ever requested, no matter how obscure or costly the item might be. Karen Downing in the Library of the School of Historical Studies at the Institute for Advanced Study (Princeton) went far beyond the call of duty to help me with an essential and difficult interlibrary loan item at a crucial time. Elizabeth Davis and Nicholas Patterson of the Music and Arts Library, Columbia University, are the serene, efficacious guardian angels whose dedication to their work has ensured the best possible library support for my research and teaching for the past ten years. Seth Kasten and Michael Boddy of the Burke Library at Union Theological Seminary have facilitated my consultation of many rare eighteenth-century books essential to this project. For access to the library and archive of Toledo Cathedral and permission to take photographs there, I am grateful to Angel Fernández Collado, Archivist of Toledo Cathedral, and Ramón Gonzálvez Ruiz, Archivist Emeritus, as well as to their staff. I also wish to acknowledge collectively the staff of the libraries at the Hispanic Society of America, the Biblioteca Nacional de España, the Biblioteca de la Real Academia de la Historia, the Biblioteca del Palacio Real, and the Real Biblioteca de El Escorial.

I would like to express my heartfelt thanks for the help and advice provided by many colleagues and friends. Elizabeth del Alamo, Constancio del Alamo, Michael Agnew, Sonia Agnew, Susana Zapke, Juan Carlos Ruiz Souza, Manuel Pedro Ferreira, and Ellen Gray offered bibliographies, introductions, invitations, advice, hospitality, translations, and crucial explanations. Elizabeth A. R. Brown was the tireless editor of my first publication on this subject and has encouraged me ever since, and Ronald Surtz patiently corrected mistakes in a more recent work. Eduardo Henrik Aubert, Sam Barrett, William Barcham, Màrius Bernadó, Anthony J. Cardenas, Frederic Clark, Almudena Cros, Isabelle Cochelin, Joseph Dyer, Ellen Gray, Patricia Grieve, Louis Hamilton, Richard Hitchcock, Colum Hourihane, Peter Linehan, Nathan J. Martin, Tom Nickson, Michael Noone, Ana María Ochoa, Stephen Parkinson, Nils Holger Petersen, Catherine Puglisi, Louise Rice, Martín Ríos Saloma, Juan Carlos Ruiz Asensio, Martha Schaffer, Robin Thomas, Catherine Whistler, and David Wulstan generously shared information and made helpful suggestions. My research assistants, Sean Hallowell, Karen Hiles, Jane Huber, Lauren Mancia, Liam Moore, and Jill Schackner, made valuable contributions at various stages of the work. Liam Moore corrected many of the translations and helped me with secondary literature. Julia Grella O'Connell's expert editing improved the book manuscript at a time when I had become deaf to its cadences.

My parents, Alice and Stuart Boynton, have helped in many ways, including providing a subvention for the cost of the color illustrations. My husband,

Jens Ulff-Møller, has helped me with countless aspects of this project from the outset. Finally I would like to thank Burriel and Palomares for bringing me into a scholarly world that, despite its remoteness in time, was familiar to me as a fellow library rat. Because I share their passionate interest in the minutest details of medieval manuscripts, I relished the many hours spent perusing Burriel's papers and comparing Palomares's copies to the originals. In 1756, when Burriel finally had to abandon his lofty goals for the Commission on the Archives, he lamented that no one in the future would be able to make sense of his unpublished notes. Despite his bitter disappointment at leaving so many projects unfinished (a feeling with which all scholars are surely familiar), I hope he would be glad to know that his efforts were not wasted—that, to the contrary, his findings remain pertinent and instructive even today.

In October 2001, while studying an uncatalogued manuscript in preparation for an exhibition at the Hispanic Society of America in New York, I made an unexpected discovery. The neumes in the manuscript suggested an origin in northern Spain in the eleventh century, but as far as I knew, no Iberian liturgical codex of this date was preserved in a North American library. On a second visit I compared the notation in the Hispanic Society manuscript to that in another manuscript that seemed similar; for this purpose I used a copy at second remove, published in the dissertation of Clyde Brockett, who had laboriously hand-copied all the notation in an eighteenth-century handwritten copy of a lost manuscript (Toledo, Biblioteca Capitular, 33.2).[1] After a brief comparison of the medieval manuscript to the modern copy, I realized that the book in front of me was the lost original. This small volume, which I localized to the abbey of San Millan de la Cogolla, contains offices for Saint Martin, Saint Emilianus, and the Assumption of the Virgin Mary.[2] Further investigation confirmed my conclusions: the manuscript that is now B2916 in the library of the Hispanic Society of America was last seen in Toledo Cathedral in the late nineteenth century. While the medieval manuscript was missing, its contents were known only through the eighteenth-century copy, which provides a remarkably accurate record of the text and, more surprisingly, of the neumes in their precise configurations. The copy has been used in many musicological studies of the Old Hispanic chant tradition published in the twentieth century.[3] Indeed without this copy it would not have been possible to identify the missing manuscript conclusively as the book now in New York.

The precision of the copy raised a host of new questions. Why was it made? Reproducing medieval manuscripts in any manner was not common in the eighteenth century, and few in Spain were studying liturgical books at the time, much less their musical notation. This was an extremely unusual instance of a thorough and painstaking effort to reproduce medieval neumes by hand.

Exploring the circumstances surrounding the copy, I found that it was created in Toledo for an ambitious program of research undertaken by a tenacious Jesuit, Andrés Marcos Burriel (1719–62), in association with the noted calligrapher Francisco Xavier de Santiago y Palomares (1728–96). In the early 1750s they studied Toledo Cathedral's medieval manuscripts as part of a government-sponsored survey of ecclesiastical archives. The results of their labors constitute a significant yet unpublished body of evidence on the historical construction of the Middle Ages in the age of absolutism. Central to the vision of history shared by these two men were medieval liturgy and music, which they wove deftly into their respective narratives of events. For Burriel and Palomares sacred music was an essential component of a Spanish national identity that persisted from the early Middle Ages to the present. The particular notion of transhistorical "Spanishness" they espoused is best understood against the background of shifting cultural influences in Bourbon Spain during the first half of the eighteenth century.

Royal Patronage and Hispanism in Bourbon Spain

The death in 1700 of Charles II, the last of the Habsburg rulers of Spain, left no natural heir to the Spanish throne. The resulting War of Succession (1701–14) ended with the installation of the Bourbon dynasty in Spain, beginning with Philip V (1701–46), grandson of Louis XIV.[4] Philip's court was shaped by French taste but also dominated by his second wife, Isabella Farnese (Elisabeth of Parma, 1692–1766), and her Italian courtiers.[5] Philip's patronage of the arts and letters included the establishment of learned societies on the model of the French *académies*, and he founded the Royal Library in 1712, the Royal Academy of the Spanish Language in 1713, and the Royal Academy of History in 1737.[6]

Many of the artistic and intellectual projects initiated by the government of Philip's successor, Ferdinand VI (1746–59), were also indebted to French models of cultural policy, but it is fair to say that Ferdinand's accession to the throne initiated a new era with regard to the question of national identity. In spite of his family ties to France and Italy, he insisted that Spain remain neutral during periods of armed conflict, which earned him the reputation of a pacific monarch.[7] The foremost initiatives associated with Ferdinand's government are the reform of commerce, taxation, agriculture, and the navy, all accomplished principally by the Marques de la Ensenada, Cenón de Somodevilla (1702–81). Since 1743 Ensenada had served the crown not only as secretary of state and superintendent of revenues, but also as secretary of finance, war, the navy, and the Indies.[8] Contemporaries saw the marriage of these public endeavors with patronage of the arts as integral to the emergence of a new Spanish national ethos.[9] The linkage appears, for example, in a well-known work of official art, Antonio González Ruiz's 1752 portrait of Ferdinand for the Royal Academy of Fine Arts, which depicted the king as Protector of Agriculture, Commerce, and the Fine Arts.[10] Ferdinand's founding of the Royal Academy of Fine Arts (the Real Academia de Bellas Artes de San Fernando) manifested his interest in promoting the idea of a national past in the arts; as Catherine Whistler points out, "The new academy could provide an instant symbol of the spirit of Ferdinand's hispanophile reign—just as, for instance, Philip V's French confessor was replaced in 1747 by a Spanish Jesuit as a 'national' appointment."[11] Indeed it had been a political decision of the new secretary of state, José de Carvajal y Lancaster (1698–1754), to supplant the French Jesuit Lefèvre with the Jesuit Francisco de Rávago (1685–1763).[12]

Nevertheless an increased emphasis on Spanishness (or "hispanism," *hispanismo*) did not amount to a rejection of influences from abroad. Instead it yielded novel forms of stylistic hybridity, such as those in the works of the Italian composer Domenico Scarlatti (1685–1757), who had come to the Spanish Court as the music teacher of Barbara de Braganza (1711–58) while she was still the princess of Asturias. Although identifying them with precision has sometimes proved elusive, Iberian influences and references are thought to shape Scarlatti's keyboard compositions.[13] Likewise the cultivation of opera during the reigns of Philip V and Ferdinand VI yielded a distinctive synthesis of Spanish and Italian elements that could be described as a new national tradition.[14] Both the Spaniard José de Nebra (1702–68) and the Frenchman Francisco Courcelle (1705–78; raised in Parma, he was known in Spain as Corselli), composed operas for Madrid as well as liturgical music for the court chapel; Courcelle was the *maestro de capilla* in the court chapel beginning in 1738, and Nebra was the organist (from 1724) and deputy *maestro de capilla*.[15]

Under the direction of the renowned Italian castrato Carlo Broschi (known as Farinelli), whom Philip V had brought to the Court in 1737, opera in the Madrid court theater and the Aranjuez palace reached unprecedented heights.[16] The castrato was given even greater authority by Ferdinand VI and came to function as much as a producer and artistic director as a singer. Between 1747 and 1758 Farinelli oversaw an extraordinary range of entertainments both at the court theater in Madrid and at the palace in Aranjuez and simultaneously became so influential at court as to be a de facto government minister, with a particular involvement in Spain's foreign affairs.[17] This conflation of the spheres of politics and art was mirrored on the Spanish stage, where, owing to the representational qualities of opera, political meanings were never far below the surface. According to Rainer Kleinertz, the advent of Spanish opera in the Italian style, as well as that of Italian operas (sung either in Spanish translation or in the original Italian), is best understood in the context of dynastic succession, a subject that greatly preoccupied Philip V. Philip's support for Spanish culture (including music theater) reflected his desire to legitimize his own rule in the wake of the War of Succession.[18]

Although most sacred music was set to Latin texts, the *villancico*, a Castilian vernacular genre often characterized by a pastoral flavor, was also performed in the liturgy on certain feasts, especially Christmas and Epiphany.[19] In the course of the eighteenth century the villancico increasingly incorporated Italianate structural elements such as recitatives and arias, features that became standard after 1720. Many villancicos were in effect Spanish cantatas, their form exemplifying the hybridity that characterized so much Iberian music in the eighteenth century. The villancico's Spanish character, however, now associated primarily with texts in Castilian, did not always work to its advantage. In a letter written to her father on Epiphany in 1747, Barbara de Braganza referred to the performance of villancicos during Matins in the royal chapel in Madrid, characterizing the mixture of these "Castilianisms" (*castelhanadas*) with the liturgy as inappropriate and even ridiculous, and added that she would seek to prohibit them if possible. She states her preference for responsories composed earlier by "the Frenchman" (presumably referring to Courcelle), but she notes that the singers did not want to perform these Latin liturgical compositions because they were "old."[20] It is noteworthy that Barbara de Braganza wanted to ban villancicos from the liturgy as early as 1747; after 1750 they were no longer performed in the royal chapel, perhaps due to her influence, although they continued to be performed elsewhere.[21] Thus because of its use of Castilian texts, the villancico, although musically and formally Italianized, displeased the musically discerning Barbara. The example of the villancico is instructive because it complicates the idea of the Bourbon Court's *hispanismo* at midcentury. The hispanization of culture was a subtle process, in which the blending of diverse national traditions prevailed over the promotion of strictly Iberian forms.

The Royal Commission on the Archives

It was in this context of a heightened cultural nationalism informed by an awareness and appreciation of French and Italian cultural forms that the government of Ferdinand VI founded the Royal Commission on the Archives in 1749.[22] The initial purpose of the Commission was to locate and transcribe medieval archival documents for use in ongoing negotiations with the Vatican over royal control of benefices, a prerogative known as the *patronato real*. The origins of the patronato real have been traced to 1486, when Pope Innocent VIII granted Isabella of Castile and Ferdinand of Aragón patronage over ecclesiastical appointments in the kingdom of Granada. Although in theory this privilege merely guaranteed the Spanish throne the right to present candidates to the pope for approval, in practice it was used, beginning in 1523, as a means by which kings could in effect appoint bishops of their choosing to bishoprics throughout Spain.[23] The patronato real thus became a powerful tool by which the regalists in the government of Ferdinand VI aimed to discontinue the papal curia's powers to fill vacant benefices and to give lucrative dispensations in dominions under the Spanish crown.[24] The Royal Commission on the Archives ordered a search in Spanish ecclesiastical archives for documents of royal foundation and donation that would demonstrate to the Roman curia the sovereignty of the Spanish monarchy.[25] Thus the framework of the Commission was determined entirely by political objectives, the foremost consideration being the primacy of the national church over Rome.

The government's sponsorship of the Commission was essential to the success of this endeavor; an earlier experiment, initiated by a scholar rather than by a minister of Ferdinand VI, had failed for lack of support at court. In 1747 Pedro Clemente de Aróstegui (1692–1760) wrote to Carvajal to propose a new academy of church history, to be based in Rome. The purpose of this institution was to renew the study of Spanish history by bringing together a group of scholars who could make use of the documents in the Vatican Archives, thereby strengthening Spaniards' knowledge of their historical relationship to the Holy See. By 1750, however, the project had failed, precipitating the founding of the Royal Commission on the Archives.[26]

Carvajal appointed as director of the Commission the Jesuit Andrés Marcos Burriel (1719–62), who had begun his academic career as a teacher of grammar at the Jesuit College in Toledo in 1742–44; his intellectual distinction had brought him in 1745 to the Imperial College in Madrid, where he became part of the extended network of the court. As *director supernumerario* of the Seminary of Nobles (a position he held in 1746–47), Burriel established a reputation as an effective administrator. In the course of reforming the seminary, which had been in financial crisis, he cemented his existing relationships with influential courtiers, including the most powerful minister in the government, the Marques de la Ensenada, whose nephew was a student in the seminary.[27] During this time one of the ways Burriel ingratiated himself with those in power was by writing a *zarzuela* for the students to perform before the new king and queen. The terms in which Burriel describes this zarzuela in a letter of 1747 suggests that he wrote a libretto rather than a musical score; there is no other evidence that he was an accomplished practical musician.[28] As the term "zarzuela" generally designated a musical comedy or light opera with spoken dialogue,[29] one can speculate that Burriel wrote a rhymed text set to music by others or sung to preexisting music.

In 1747 Burriel became a professor of philosophy at the prestigious University of Alcalá. In the years that followed, stimulated by the exchange of ideas with friends such as Gregorio Mayans y Siscar, Burriel developed an ambitious plan for a broad-based renewal of Spanish culture by improving the resources for research and teaching in Spain.[30] In 1749 he prepared to go on mission to the New World as an act of thanksgiving for his recovery from a serious illness suffered the year before. At the same time he was asked by the procurator general of the Indies, Pedro Ignacio Altamirano, to revise a history of Baja California written by a fellow Jesuit, Miguel Venegas. When Burriel's departure was imminent, he was detained by Rávago because of his value to the government's historical and archival projects and was appointed director of the Commission on the Archives, a position in which he would inventory the medieval manuscripts of Toledo Cathedral while continuing his research on the history of the Spanish colonies in the New World. Completing Venegas's work was a complex project that occupied Burriel almost continuously until 1757, when the text was published as the *Noticia de la California*.[31]

The Commission on the Archives began its work in Toledo in October 1750. According to the letter by which Carvajal presented Burriel and his colleagues to the canons of Toledo Cathedral, the aim of the project was to write a new ecclesiastical history of Spain.[32] Embracing this mandate, Burriel developed a wide-ranging research program encompassing not only the requisite archival inventories and transcriptions, but also medieval manuscripts of canon law, patristic literature, theology, and liturgy. He saw the liturgical books in Visigothic script as key artifacts of the Hispanic past that not only exhibited a distinctive Spanish character, but also represented the continuity of belief over the centuries. His account of the liturgy contributed to the nationalist cultural discourse cultivated by the Spanish Court, thereby implicitly buttressing its political claims. Burriel's focus on the Old Hispanic liturgy emerged from the larger project of the Commission.[33]

Aided by assistants, and in collaboration with the philologist Francisco Pérez Bayer, Burriel set out to transcribe and inventory the privileges preserved in the archives of Toledo Cathedral. The copying and transcription of liturgical books in the library began soon afterward. Approximately one year after the team's arrival in Toledo, the inventories, transcriptions, and copies of those documents in the cathedral archive most essential to the negotiations had already been completed in large part.[34] Beginning in the autumn of 1751 Burriel and his colleagues increasingly focused on the medieval manuscripts of literature, history, theology, patristics, and canon law in the cathedral library, transcribing and collating texts in preparation for publication. As aids to their research, Palomares and several other scribes produced copies that exhibit an unprecedented degree of accuracy.

Palomares's extraordinary calligraphic skills played a crucial role in the work of the Commission.[35] Born in Toledo, he grew up under the influence of his father, an intellectual omnivore steeped in the spirit of antiquarianism; a letter written by Burriel in 1745 describes Palomares's father as erudite, though not university-educated, and fascinated by early scripts and antiquities.[36] The younger Francisco Palomares probably learned his calligraphic and paleographic skills from his father, whose help with inscriptions, seals, and documents was acknowledged by Burriel and Mayans in the mid- to late 1740s, as well as by Enrique Flórez in two early volumes of his *España Sagrada*.[37] Palomares's treatise on the Visigothic script, written twenty years later, included two illustrations copied from liturgical fragments in Visigothic script owned by his father.[38]

Between 1752 and 1755 Burriel's team produced numerous volumes of collations, commentaries, and transcriptions from medieval liturgical manuscripts, many accompanied by single-page copies that Palomares drew to illustrate pages from the originals. Although Palomares signed only a few of the copies, he probably produced many of the transcriptions as well. Under Burriel's guidance Palomares made expert copies not only of texts but also of the ornately contoured neumes in the early chant manuscripts. In a few cases he created copies that included drawings of all or nearly all the original musical notation. Such products appear to have been intended only for study, or in some instances for presentation to a patron.[39] Unlike other copies of early music manuscripts from the same period, Palomares's copies were apparently not made with an eye to reconstruction or performance.[40] However, copying music by hand was still a central means of transmission in eighteenth-century Spain, and chant choir books were still produced in manuscript. In 1751, for instance, copies of the chant books in use at Toledo Cathedral were commissioned by Ferdinand VI for the Royal Chapel in Madrid.[41] Choir books produced for the Royal Chapel were decorated in 1752–58 by one of the great still-life painters of the period, Luis Egidio Meléndez (1716–80).[42]

Although both Burriel and Palomares took an evident interest in music, neither apparently was an accomplished musician. As a Jesuit Burriel did not sing the hours of the Divine Office in choir; his own experience of the music of the liturgy was as a listener. For Burriel and Palomares, creating exact copies of the liturgical sources was a way of recording their contents and an essential step in the process of comparing multiple manuscripts. In this regard they differed fundamentally from later historians, who studied medieval music as a tradition that could be made to live again in the present.[43] The methods employed by Burriel and Palomares—paleographic analysis, historical criticism, textual criticism, and exact copying—had never before been applied to the Old Hispanic liturgical books in Toledo Cathedral and remained unusual for the study of Iberian liturgical sources until the twentieth century. As we will see in the Introduction, one of the reasons for this neglect was the complex liturgical history of Toledo.

Notes

1. Brockett, *Antiphons*, 227–53. The copy, which is contained in Madrid, Biblioteca Nacional, MS 13060, is discussed in chapter 2.

2. See the description in Boynton, "A Lost Mozarabic Liturgical Manuscript," 189–219.

3. For instance, it was used in Randel, *The Responsorial Psalm Tones*.

4. For the cultural and musical ramifications of this succession, see, most recently, Ceballos, "Scarlatti and María Bárbara," 197–205.

5. On Philip's reign, see Kamen, *Philip V of Spain*.

6. Today's Real Academia Española was originally the Real Academia de la Lengua. On the academies in general, see Aguilar Piñal, "Las Academias," 151–93.

7. The description of Ferdinand's reign as peaceful is the central theme of the interdisciplinary exploration of the period in the exhibition catalogue *Un reinado bajo el signo de la paz*.

8. Lynch, *Bourbon Spain*, 160. On reform under the Bourbons in the second half of the eighteenth century see most recently Noel, "In the House of Reform."

9. See Schulz, "Spaces of Enlightenment," 189–227.

10. Whistler, "On the Margins in Madrid," 77.

11. Zanardi, "Preservation and Promotion," 304; Whistler, "On the Margins in Madrid," 80.

12. Lynch, *Bourbon Spain*, 160.

13. For a recent reassessment of the role of Iberian musical influence on Scarlatti's sonatas, see Sutcliffe, *The Keyboard Sonatas*, 107–22. On their relation to Barbara de Braganza, see Ceballos, "Scarlatti and María Bárbara," 197–205.

14. See Carreras, "From Literes to Nebra," 7–16; Carreras, "Entre la zarzuela y la ópera de corte," 49–77; Leza and Knighton, "Metastasio," 623–31.

15. On Courcelle, see Strohm, "Francesco Corselli's Operas for Madrid," 79–106. On the service of José de Nebra in the court chapels of Philip V and Ferdinand VI see Álvarez, *José de Nebra Blasco*, especially 31–32 and 56–76.

16. For a synthesis of the role of Farinelli and of opera at the court of Ferdinand VI, see Torrione, "La sociedad de Corte," 165–95. A recent discussion of the arrival of Farinelli and other Italian virtuosi at the court can be found in Nicolás Morales, *L'artiste de cour dans l'Espagne du XVIIIe siècle: Étude de la communauté des musiciens au service de Philippe V (1700–1746)* (Madrid: Casa de Velázquez, 2007), 238–47.

17. A complete record of his achievements is contained in the manuscript *Descripcion del estado actual del Real Theatro del Buen Retiro: De las funciones hechas en el desde el año de 1747 hasta el presente . . . (1758)*, preserved in the Biblioteca del Palacio Real in Madrid. For the most recent discussion of Farinelli's international political role, with references to earlier studies, see J. Clark, "Farinelli," 321–33.

18. Kleinertz, "Ruler-Acclamation," 235–51. See also Kleinertz, "Music Theatre in Spain," 402–19.

19. Ramos López, "*Pastorelas*," 283–306.

20. See *Correspondência de D. João V e D. Bárbara de Bragança*, 453. I am grateful to Ellen Gray for her help in translating this passage.

21. Torrente, "Italianate Sections," 72–79.

22. On the Commission, see Díaz, "El reconocimiento," 131–70.

23. This summary is based on Barton, *A History of Spain*, 99. On the history of the patronato real, see Mecham, "The Origins of 'Real Patronato de Indias,'" 205–27; Shiels, *King and Church*. On the regalist policies of Ferdinand VI's first government and the Concordat of 1753, see Olaechea, "La Politíca eclesiástica," 142–81.

24. Lynch, *Bourbon Spain*, 187. For an overview of regalism in eighteenth-century Spain, see Noel, "Clerics and Crown," 119–53; see also Egido, "El Regalismo," 123–249.

25. Díaz, "El reconocimiento," 132.

26. Alcaraz Gómez, *Jesuitas y Reformismo*, 574–81.

27. Burriel described his successful strategy in some detail in his correspondence with Gregorio Mayans y Siscar; see Echánove Tuero, *La preparación intelectual*, 60–63.

28. Letter of Burriel to Gregorio Mayans y Siscar, October 6, 1747, in *Gregorio Mayans y Siscar, Epistolario II*, 353, 355. See also Echánove Tuero, *La preparación intelectual*, 62.

29. Rainer Kleinertz, "La zarzuela del siglo XVIII entre ópera y comedia: Dos aspectos de un género musical (1730–1750)," in Kleinertz, *Teatro y Música*, 107–23.

30. He presented his ideas in the "Apuntamientos de algunas ideas para fomentar las letras" (Notes on some ideas for the promotion of the liberal arts), discussed in chapter 1.

31. The *Noticia* appears in the first three volumes of *Obras Californianas del Padre Miguel Venegas, S.J.* On Burriel's work, see Fita Colomé, "Noticia de la California," 396–438.

32. The letter is summarized in Toledo, AC, vol. 68, fols. 180v–181r.

33. A letter of August 1750 mentions in passing that Burriel was told to gather materials on the Mozarabic rite; see Mestre, *Mayans y Burriel*, 477–78.

34. Toledo, AC, vol. 68, fols. 818v–819v.

35. On Palomares's biography and broader historical significance, see the introduction to Seniff, *Francisco Javier de Santiago y Palomares* and the more extended discussion of Palomares's accomplishments in chapter 5.

36. Letter of June 12, 1745, to Gregorio Mayans, in Mestre, *Mayans y Burriel*, 150.

37. Flórez thanks Palomares for his help in the second and fourth volumes of the *España Sagrada*, published in 1747 and 1749, respectively. These references seem to be to

the father, who was customarily called don Francisco Santiago y Palomares, whereas the son's name was usually rendered as Francisco Xavier (or Javier) Santiago (y) Palomares.

38. Palomares, *Polygraphia Gothico-Española*, Madrid, RAH 9/4752, plate 63, parts 4–5.

39. These copies of musical notation are discussed in chapters 2, 3, and 4.

40. For a fascinating example of Iberian "early music" revived by historically informed performers abroad, see Rees, "Adventures," 42–73.

41. The royal request for the Toledo choir books is reported in the *Actas capitulares* for Monday, January 11, 1751: Toledo, AC, vol. 68, fol. 222r–v.

42. For an image of an illuminated page from one of these choir books, see Sancho, *The Royal Palace of Madrid*, 169.

43. See, for example, Ellis, *Interpreting the Musical Past*, 164–70 on French nationalist interpretations of the thirteenth-century *Jeu de Robin et Marion* by Adam de la Halle.

ABBREVIATIONS

AC	Archivo Capitular, Actas Capitulares (Toledo)
BAV	Biblioteca Apostolica Vaticana (Vatican City)
BC	Biblioteca Capitular (Toledo)
BL	British Library (London)
BN	Biblioteca Nacional de España (Madrid)
BNF	Bibliothèque Nationale de France (Paris)
HSA	Hispanic Society of America (New York)
RAH	Real Academia de la Historia (Madrid)

NOTES ON ORTHOGRAPHY AND TERMINOLOGY

In this book I have adopted Anglicized forms of Spanish given names (Ferdinand for Fernando, Barbara for Bárbara, Philip for Felipe). For the second given name of Francisco Xavier de Palomares y Santiago, I have chosen the form Xavier over Javier; both forms were used interchangeably in the eighteenth century, but Palomares himself used the first of these.

I present the orthography of Spanish texts as they appear in publications and manuscripts of the eighteenth century. I have not added diacritical marks or normalized their spellings. Unless otherwise indicated, all transcriptions and translations are my own; many of the translations have been corrected by Liam Moore.

To avoid confusion with modern uses of the word "Gothic," I have translated the Spanish adjective *godo* as "Visigothic" rather than more literally as "Gothic." Likewise I render the substantive *Godos* as "Visigoths" rather than "Goths" because the eighteenth-century texts that I cite make it clear that they use this word to refer to the Visigothic kingdom (as distinguished from the Goths in other parts of Europe).

I employ the term "copy" to designate a drawing made with the intention of reproducing the appearance of the medieval manuscript. In many cases "copy" refers to a hybrid form of transcription that illustrates only certain elements of the original manuscript (such as script or musical notation). To prevent confusion I avoid using the word "reproduction" except when referring to images that were actually reproduced in multiple copies, as in engravings or prints.

Silent Music

Introduction

Until the last decades of the eleventh century, Christians in León-Castile maintained the local Latin liturgical tradition that had originated in the Visigothic period. These usages constituted a rite collectively known by various names: Visigothic, Mozarabic, Old Spanish, or Hispanic. Strictly speaking, the term "Visigothic" applies only to the period before the Arab conquest of the peninsula in 711.[1] In the context of paleography, however, it is used with a broader chronological valence to describe both a style of script and a style of neumatic musical notation used in liturgical manuscripts over several centuries. In this study, the word "Mozarabic" designates the liturgical traditions originally associated with Arabizing Christians who lived under Muslim rule. The term "Mozarab" apparently derives from the Arabic *must'arib*, referring to those who have assimilated Arab customs, such as the Toledan Christians, who adopted Arab styles of dress, took Arabic names, spoke Arabic, and used Arabic in their official documents.[2]

For the purposes of describing the liturgical traditions of the period before 1100, I favor the designations "Old Hispanic" and "Hispanic" over "Old Spanish" or "Spanish," because the latter two terms suggest a unified national configuration that did not yet exist in the Middle Ages and might also be confused with a linguistic term. Hence I use "Hispanic" or "Old Hispanic" broadly to refer to the Latin rites that existed in the Iberian peninsula before the introduction of the Roman rite. The Old Hispanic liturgy differed from the Roman rite in its textual and musical genres for common liturgical functions, as well as in the characteristic structures of the mass and office.[3] Scholars have interpreted some of the variations among the Old Hispanic liturgical manuscripts as indications that two different traditions, known respectively as A and B, existed in the earliest layer of the rite. Both these textual traditions can be found in manuscripts from the Mozarabic churches of Toledo. Tradition A is transmitted both in Toledan manuscripts and in those from northern Spain. Pinell argued that tradition B originated in Seville, while Janini has suggested it was a local Toledan usage.[4] In this book, I focus on the kingdom of León-Castile, and specifically on Toledo, because it was the main subject of Burriel's research.[5] Imposing the Roman liturgy in León-Castile was originally a papal initiative, promoted especially by Pope Gregory VII, who reigned from 1073 to 1085, in the name of the unity of the Latin Church. Gregory's specific intent, however, was to encourage the submission of the Spanish church to Rome.[6] As Roger Reynolds has shown, liturgical reform in the Iberian peninsula was a long process that unfolded in many complex stages.[7] In the northeastern part of the peninsula, which in the eighth century had become part of the Frankish kingdom (the future Carolingian Empire), a mixture of Roman-rite and local Hispanic liturgical traditions had long prevailed.[8] Liturgical change in the west of the peninsula differed from that in other regions, in accordance with historical developments.

The introduction of the Roman rite in Toledo in 1086 entailed the importation of liturgical books, many from southern France.[9] As in other places affected by the liturgical reform, the Visigothic script gradually gave way to Caroline minuscule.[10] Many imported chant melodies were written in Aquitanian musical notation, which indicates musical intervals with precision by means of diastematy, the regular vertical spacing (known as heighting) of the neumes.[11] Since very little Old Hispanic chant was ever recorded in heighted neumes, the majority of the repertory cannot be transcribed.[12]

Even though manuscripts with Aquitanian notation often lack clefs and lines, one can transcribe melodies from them as long as the first note can be determined by referring to another manuscript containing the same chant with a clef or staff. The remaining pitches can be deduced from the relative heighting of the subsequent neumes. The process of transcription is further facilitated by the fact that certain notational signs indicate the interval of a half-step, enabling one to discern with precision the intervallic content of a melody.[13] Figure 1, which shows an opening from a Riojan manuscript of Old Hispanic chant that was the catalyst for this book, provides an example of the contrast between Visigothic and Aquitanian neumes.[14] In the lower margin of the verso side is the beginning of a Roman-rite Alleluia that was added to the manuscript in the twelfth century in Aquitanian neumes. On the recto side, the first six lines present an Old Hispanic chant notated with adiastematic Visigothic neumes; in the absence of sources with heighted versions of this melody, one can only speculate about its pitch content. Slightly more than halfway through the sixth line the Visigothic neumes end with the word "cum" (a cue indicating the repetition of the phrase beginning with this word three lines above), while Aquitanian neumes continue the Alleluia from the verso side, beginning with the word "pacem." This is one of the many ways the manuscript illustrates the effect of the liturgical reform.[15] Although the transition between the two chants appears to be seamless, in history the traditions existed side by side for some time, until the Old Hispanic rite became a relic of the past.

Alfonso VI of León and Castile (r. 1065–1109) introduced the Roman rite into his kingdom in 1076; it is usually assumed that this change was confirmed by the clergy assembled at the council of Burgos in 1080. However, because the acts of the council do not survive, the precise outlines of its decisions are not known.[16] According to Bernard Reilly, the absence of acts from the council, in combination with other evidence, suggests that the Roman rite was imposed by a more informal and ongoing process consisting of "decisions made in the royal court, by the bishops then present, on one occasion and confirmed on another, both at Burgos."[17] After Alfonso captured Toledo in 1085, the Roman rite was introduced in the new cathedral

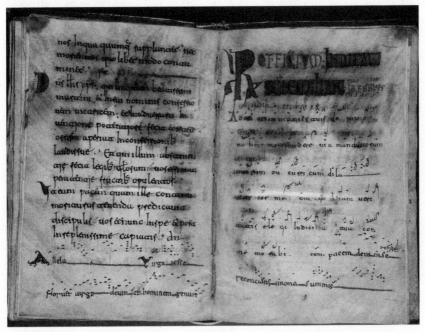

FIGURE 1 New York, HSA, B2916, fols. 51v–52r. Courtesy of the Hispanic Society of America, New York.

by Bernard de Sédirac, a former Cluniac monk who had become abbot of Sahagún and was consecrated archbishop of Toledo in 1086.[18] On the Hispanic feast of the Annunciation (December 18) in 1086, Alfonso reconfirmed the status of Toledo as the primatial see and converted the chief mosque of the city into a Christian cathedral. The Mozarabs' own cathedral had been the church of Santa María de Alficén, in a different part of the city.[19] In the diploma he issued on that occasion, Alfonso claimed to have "restored" to the Christians of Toledo the old Visigothic church dedicated to the Virgin Mary, but in fact he had created an entirely new ecclesiastical center.[20]

Alfonso's appropriation of the mosque for a new cathedral under the foreign archbishop effectively rendered the Mozarabs and their parishes peripheral to the city's structures of power.[21] Apparently with Alfonso's assent, six Mozarabic parishes continued to celebrate the old rite. Thus the production of liturgical books with Visigothic script and neumes continued among the Mozarabs for centuries.[22] Some of the Toledan manuscripts associated with the Mozarabic community were long considered to be products of the ninth and tenth centuries, but the prevailing chronology was revised in 1965 by the paleographer Anscari Mundó, who argued for dates that in some cases were as much as two centuries later than previously thought.[23] The dates assigned to these manuscripts have important implications for the history of the Mozarabic community. An early dating construes them as vestiges of Christians in Toledo at a time when there are few other signs of a Mozarabic community in the city. As historians have pointed out, it is not possible to ascertain the existence of Mozarabs in Toledo during most of the century preceding Alfonso VI's capture of the city in 1085.[24] This observation has led to various versions of the revisionist argument that more Mozarabs came to Toledo in the late eleventh century from elsewhere in the Iberian peninsula than were living there before 1085.[25] Although it is beyond the scope of this book to address the historiography in great detail, it is relevant to point out that Mundó's later dating of the manuscripts situates most of them in the post-1085 period, for which we have far more evidence of the Mozarabic community than before.

In the decades after the Christian conquest of the city, the Toledan Mozarabs achieved an advantageous position, in part because they had been present before 1085 and in part by virtue of their negotiations with Alfonso VI. In response to their complaints about the division of property after 1085, Alfonso established a commission to oversee redistribution of property, and in 1101 granted the Mozarabs their own *fuero*, or privilege.[26] In this way they established what Francisco Hernández has called "the economic foundations of the local patrician class which would dominate the city during the following four centuries."[27] Although the establishment of the Roman rite in the new cathedral excluded the Mozarabic rite by definition, some Mozarabs became members of the cathedral clergy. Over the course of the twelfth century their property and dominant role in the municipal government made them an influential minority group in Toledo.[28]

The lessening of the absolute separation between the cathedral clergy and the Mozarabic parish clergy did not preclude conflict. After some cathedral canons obtained prebends in the Mozarabic parishes, a controversy arose in 1179 that led Pope Alexander III to issue two bulls denouncing the cathedral clergy for violations of the parishes' autonomy.[29] Attitudes toward the Mozarabs were colored by the history of their community in Muslim Toledo. For instance, the thirteenth-century archbishop of Toledo Rodrígo Jiménez de Rada (r. 1209–47) invoked a false etymology in his chronicle *De rebus Hispaniae*, referring to the Mozarabs as *mixtiarabes* (which can be translated loosely as "mixed with Arabs" or possibly even "mixed Arabs") because they had lived in close proximity with Arabs. According to Richard Hitchcock, this passage reflects the archbishop's intention to strengthen the position of the cathedral chapter while diminishing the prominence of the city's Mozarabic community; his purchase of lands from Mozarabs could be interpreted as a more concrete manifestation of this strategy.[30] Lucy Pick suggests, however, that some Mozarabs chose to sell holdings outside Toledo that were difficult to defend from Muslim raiders.[31] In any case, the standing of the Mozarabs in Toledo began to change in this period, along with their culture. In the second half of the thirteenth century Arabic ceded to Romance in their notarial documents, which indicates that they no longer used the language for their official business.[32] The Mozarabic chant tradition seems to have declined in the same period. Susana Zapke has argued that the increasingly symbolic character of the musical notation in the latest Mozarabic manuscripts, which conveys little information beyond the general outline of the melody, might be products of a movement "which championed the old rite then threatened with extinction."[33] Indeed the archbishop of Toledo in 1280–99, Gonzalo Pérez Gudiel, himself a Mozarab, undertook a renewal of the city's Mozarabic parishes, in part with the help of the archdeacon Joffré de Loaysa.[34] This initiative included training clerics to perform the rite and producing new liturgical books.[35]

Finally, the group identity of the Toledan Mozarabs came to be constituted primarily by membership in the Mozarabic parishes.[36] The Old Hispanic liturgy was the single most distinctive characteristic of the group, surviving other aspects of their common heritage, such as the use of the Arabic language.[37] By the fifteenth century the community and its traditions were greatly diminished. Various individuals attempted to save the distinctive liturgy of the Mozarabs from obsolescence. In 1436 Juan Vázquez de Cepeda, bishop of Segovia, founded a chapel for the celebration of the rite, noting that it was not adequately observed in Toledo. In 1480 Isabella of Castile and Ferdinand of Aragón confirmed the privileges of the Mozarabic clergy in Toledo and mandated the appropriate distribution of funds designated for Mozarabic parishes, which were increasingly impoverished. In the same year Alonso Carrillo de Acuña, archbishop of Toledo in 1446–82, forbade the distribution of benefices to clerics who could not perform the rite. In order to secure the future of the rite, Cardinal Pedro González de Mendoza, archbishop of Toledo in 1482–95, sought to consolidate the Mozarabic parishes as autonomous areas by preventing Mozarabs from moving out of them and discouraging others from moving into them. By 1500, however, the rite had become an artifact of a lost culture; there were apparently only six Mozarabs actually residing in Toledo.[38]

Cisneros and the "Neo-Mozarabic" Rite

The most consequential efforts to preserve the Mozarabic liturgy were the initiatives of Francisco Ximénez de Cisneros, archbishop of Toledo from 1495 to 1517. Cisneros energetically promoted the reform of the Toledan liturgy, fostering new publications of the cathedral's Roman rite and of the Mozarabic traditions as well. In 1501 he endowed a new Mozarabic chapel of Corpus Christi in Toledo Cathedral. The chapel was dedicated to the daily celebration of the mass and office according to the Mozarabic rite by thirteen specially appointed chaplains.[39] Cisneros obtained from Julius II a bull in 1508 approving the use of the Mozarabic rite, and another in 1512 confirming the donations for the foundation of the chapel,[40] and under his authority cantorales (choir books) were prepared for the use of singers in the cathedral's Mozarabic Chapel. In the aggregate these manuscripts contain about four hundred chants for all the feasts of the church year. Most of the melodies in the Cisneros cantorales (as they are often called) seem to have been composed specifically for the compilation of the choir books themselves. The majority of the chants bear little resemblance to those with the same texts in the Old Hispanic manuscripts.[41] Even before the production of the cantorales, Cisneros had appointed a commission to publish editions of the Mozarabic liturgy. The director of the commission was Alfonso Ortiz, a canon of Toledo Cathedral. Working with a team that included the rectors of three of the Mozarabic parishes, Ortiz published editions of the Mozarabic missal in 1500 and of the breviary in 1502.[42] While the breviary does not contain any musical notation, the missal includes notated chants in black mensural notation, as in the cantorales.[43]

Rather than being critical editions in the modern sense, the Ortiz editions were a new version of the rite. As stated in the preface, texts in the breviary were "corrected" to suit Renaissance philological standards.[44] The text of the colophon in both the missal and the breviary describes it as "completed and corrected" (*perfectum et emendatum*) by Ortiz.[45] To ensure that the breviary would contain all the requisite texts for the divine office, Ortiz introduced newer elements to complement the contents of the manuscripts containing the Old Hispanic rite.[46] Some of these intentional anachronisms include the formularies for feasts introduced after the suppression of the Old Hispanic rite.[47] Ortiz also altered the ordering of texts in the office manuscripts to bring the services closer to the liturgical organization of the Roman rite. Thus although the Mozarabic cantorales and the Ortiz editions were long thought to transmit the Old Hispanic rite in its medieval state, they are better termed "neo-Mozarabic."[48] The editions in particular reflect a humanist approach to the liturgy as an object of study; they are as much a scholarly project of redaction as a pragmatic effort to encourage performance of the rite. They also served to associate the newly authorized liturgy with the person of Cisneros himself; the title pages of the Mozarabic breviary and missal depict Cisneros being blessed by the Virgin Mary against the background of a shield, evoking a coat of arms. The image is surrounded by elements of Cisneros's heraldry (his cardinal's hat on top and his Franciscan tassels on both sides).[49]

Simply by virtue of having been printed, the Ortiz editions soon became the predominant version of the Mozarabic rite and provided the basis for the new editions that were published in the eighteenth century. The long shadow that the Ortiz editions have cast over the history of Hispanic liturgical scholarship may result in part from the formidable reputation of Cisneros himself, as witnessed by the efforts to canonize him that had already begun in the sixteenth century and lasted well into the eighteenth.[50] In fact because of the prevailing assumption that Ortiz had simply printed the contents of the Old Hispanic liturgical books, the existence of his editions caused scholars to neglect the medieval manuscripts of the rite. Even those who visited Toledo's cathedral library in the eighteenth century may not have consulted the manuscripts at any length. For instance, although the Flemish Bollandist Pinius (Jean Pien, 1671–1749) stayed in Toledo in 1721–22 to carry out research for the *Acta sanctorum*, there is no evidence that he actually studied the early liturgical manuscripts in the cathedral library. Indeed in his treatise on the Mozarabic rite, the summary description of the Hispanic-rite codices in the library is based not on his own consultation of the books, but rather on information supplied by Pedro Camino y Velasco, rector of the Mozarabic parish of San Sebastián and commissioner of the Inquisition in Toledo.[51] Until the Commission on the Archives, Camino y Velasco enjoyed something of a monopoly on Toledo's small collection of liturgical books in Visigothic script.[52] Although his access to the manuscripts extended over at least thirty years, and he owned some liturgical fragments himself, he seems not to have studied the medieval liturgical books closely.[53] Camino's principal interest lay in the history of the Mozarabic families of Toledo; his publication of annotated documents concerning the traditional privileges of the Mozarabs indicates only scant knowledge of the Toledan liturgical manuscripts, which he dated erroneously to the early centuries of the Visigothic church.[54]

Burriel and the Old Hispanic Rite

Burriel was apparently the first person to attempt a thorough description and analysis of the Old Hispanic liturgical codices in the cathedral library. While teaching at the Jesuit College in Toledo from 1742 to 1744, he became aware of the differences between the neo-Mozarabic editions and the manuscripts of the Old Hispanic rite, and this knowledge led him to pursue further comparative study as director of the Commission on the Archives.[55] In a letter to his colleague Pedro de Castro written in 1754, near the end of the Commission's work in Toledo, Burriel outlined the history of the Old Hispanic rite, linking the vicissitudes of the liturgy with the history of the Visigothic script:

> The liturgy is called Mozarabic because when this city of Toledo was conquered by Alfonso VI in 1085, there had remained many Christian families for almost four centuries of captivity since the time of the Visigoths, divided into seven parishes. . . . Not only the Visigothic liturgy but also the Visigothic script were abolished throughout the kingdom by Alfonso VI, but the King who was able to uproot the Visigothic script and liturgy from the cathedrals and monasteries, introducing the Gallican or Roman [liturgy], either failed or refused to deprive Toledo's Mozarabic parishes of it; they preserved it and still preserve it today.[56]

By affirming that the Mozarabic parishes continued to maintain the ancient rite, Burriel here would seem to refer to the oral tradition. He had long been aware of the differences between the manuscripts and early modern editions; indeed in the same letter, while recounting the genesis of the neo-Mozarabic editions, he points out the two principal ways in which they differ from the medieval manuscripts:

> In the beginning of the sixteenth century, when that incomparable man, Cardinal Ximenez de Cisneros, saw that the practice of this rite had diminished in the Mozarabic parishes, he built a magnificent chapel in his primatial church, and founded fourteen chaplaincies so that fourteen Mozarabic curates and beneficed clergy would sing every day their version of the mass and all the canonical hours. For this purpose he gathered the liturgical manuscripts of the parishes and from these, for the use of the chapel and the parishes, he had made the Mozarabic-Isidoran missal and breviary, which he had printed, but mixing in some modern things and omitting other ancient ones.[57]

This account somewhat obfuscates the crucial distinction between the cantorales created for use in the chapel and the neo-Mozarabic editions that were newly confected in the years around 1500. Perhaps Burriel wanted to avoid discrediting the neo-Mozarabic editions, which had been rendered venerable both through long use and by association with Cardinal Cisneros.

Burriel's interest in the manuscripts of the Old Hispanic rite was never purely paleographic or philological; it was inseparable from the conviction (shared by many Spanish historians over the centuries) that these books attested to a uniquely Spanish tradition, centered on Toledo. As he wrote in a letter of 1752 to his patron, Francisco de Rávago, "Spain alone is the nation that can produce its own Bibles, Liturgies, conciliar collection, and the acts of its saints, all under the seal of an authority so respectable in the entire Catholic Church as is that of this church of Toledo, all pure, clean, true, firm, and all ancient, and all conforming completely to what we believe and teach today."[58] This statement seems to have been particularly meaningful for Burriel; in a manuscript copy of the letter that he annotated later, he wrote, "This is like the center and target of all the ideas."[59] With this affirmation Burriel casts the medieval texts of the Hispanic church as prefiguring the religious culture of the modern nation and elides the dramatic changes in the relationship between Rome and Toledo that occurred during and after the liturgical reform of the eleventh century.

Although Burriel in his letter to Rávago presented the entirety of medieval Hispanic ecclesiastical traditions as a unified expression of Spanishness, he was well aware of the diversity of liturgical practice that was the rule both before and after the Council of Trent. Judging from his unpublished notes, he aimed to carry out a survey of all the rites represented in manuscripts and printed books preserved at Toledo Cathedral. He wanted to understand the development of the Old Hispanic rite in the early Middle Ages, the elements that survived after it was supplanted by the Roman rite, and the ramifications of the Roman rite in Spain over the centuries. He described his decision to focus on the Toledan sources in Visigothic script (rather than examining those available elsewhere, as at Silos) as a methodological choice. In order to understand both the history of the Mozarabic rite and the history of the Mozarabic community that preserved it, he sought to consult all the relevant manuscript sources in Toledo.[60]

The Study of the Old Hispanic Rite in the Eighteenth Century

Although the study of medieval manuscripts as a basis for liturgical history was the hallmark of Burriel's method, this approach was not employed by his contemporaries. When the Commission's work in Toledo began, most of the scholarly literature on the Old Hispanic rite was derivative, consisting mainly of reprints of earlier editions and their commentary traditions. The most widely available publication was a two-volume compilation entitled *Liturgia antiqua Hispanica Gothica Isidoriana, Mozarabica Toletana Mixta illustrata* (1746), which includes commentaries by the Italian cardinal Giuseppe Maria Tomasi (1649–1713) and the priests Gaetano Cenni (1698–1762) and Giuseppe Bianchini (1704–64), along with Pinius's 1729 treatise. Burriel referred to this compilation extensively during his work in Toledo Cathedral.[61] Another well-known source that Burriel cited was the 1755 reprint of the Ortiz edition of the neo-Mozarabic missal with critical notes by the Scottish Jesuit Alexander Lesley (1694–1758).[62] At the end of the eighteenth century Archbishop Lorenzana of Toledo reprinted the Ortiz edition with some revisions.[63]

The early modern studies of the Old Hispanic liturgy reflect a set of interlocking circumstances: access to the codices in Toledo Cathedral Library was limited, few read the Visigothic script fluently enough to study the early manuscripts in any systematic way, and most thought that the Ortiz editions contained the medieval rite. Outside Toledo few scholars realized how little the manuscripts had been studied, and even fewer understood the logistical difficulties that any such research could present. Mayans was one of those few who knew that only what he called *un fiel traslado* (a faithful copy or transcription) would make it possible to study the manuscripts' original contents and annotations. In 1746 Blas Jover y Alcázar, a diplomat who acted as royal counsel in the negotiations with the papal nuncio over the Patronato Real, had written to Mayans for his assistance in fulfilling the unusual request of the Maréchal de Noailles, who was in Spain on a diplomatic mission.[64] The Maréchal had expressed a wish to see Iberian liturgical manuscripts from the period prior to the Ortiz editions. In Mayans's reply he pointed out that this was a matter of the "public good," not merely of satisfying an antiquarian's curiosity. Before providing a brief list of the early Toledan liturgical manuscripts, Mayans recommended that Jover commission copies from Don Francisco de Palomares (probably meaning the father of Francisco Xavier, who at this time was only eighteen). Mayans added that it would be advisable for Burriel to make arrangements through the *canonigo doctoral* Juan Antonio de las Infantas, in order to reassure the cathedral chapter that the manuscripts would not be stolen. In this short letter Mayans insists repeatedly that the Maréchal follow his instructions conscientiously in order to gain access to the manuscripts, as "Spain is seen to be deprived of her best books and the public of knowledge about them, because they are greedily or jealously hidden; and thus one's first care must be to assure the owners of books that they will not be taken away by deception or violence, but that they will be copied by a person entirely satisfactory to them."[65] Even for a powerful representative of the state, perhaps especially for such a person, it was essential to tread very lightly when seeking knowledge about the medieval liturgical manuscripts in Toledo Cathedral.[66]

Meanwhile, in the cultural nationalist historiography of Spain, the neo-Mozarabic editions were presumed to contain the liturgy from the time of the Visigoths. Cisneros had created an enduring myth of ritual coherence and antiquity by reaffirming Toledan Mozarabic identity through a reinvention of a medieval liturgy. By the eighteenth century the neo-Mozarabic rite had acquired a symbolic association with the Spanish nation; commentaries on the rite published in this period refer to the luminaries who had attended mass in Toledo's Mozarabic Chapel. Pinius listed in his treatise the "illustrious persons who honored the Mozarabic mass with their presence up to the year 1723," ending with the visit of Philip V and Isabella Farnese.[67]

The creation of the neo-Mozarabic liturgy and its reception represent a process of the type Eric Hobsbawm has termed "the invention of tradition." In the case of Toledo an early modern liturgical tradition was invented through the establishment of fictive continuity with a prestigious Mozarabic (and by extension, Visigothic) past. The practice of the rite in Toledo Cathedral's Mozarabic Chapel ritualized the contents of the Ortiz edition, which accrued venerability as they were repeated over time. Invented traditions that symbolize membership in communities are components of the cultural apparatus associated with the modern nation.[68] The forms of discourse that emerge around such traditions, including historical writing, exercise a powerful effect on the imagination of group identity.[69] Thus the neo-Mozarabic rite, historicized as a medieval tradition, was nostalgically appropriated as a cultural dimension of modern Spain. For Spaniards the symbolic power of the rite was founded on the assumption that the Mozarabs had kept alive the legacy of the Visigoths, maintaining a rite that went back to the earliest Catholics in Spain. The idea that the Mozarabs were continuously present in Toledo and that their identity prefigured that of the Spanish nation has often informed the study of this group.[70]

When the Commission on the Archives began its work in 1750, the liturgical traditions associated with Toledo Cathedral formed three distinct layers: the Old Hispanic, Roman, and neo-Mozarabic rites. The principal services in the cathedral featured Gregorian chant (in the Toledan variant of the post-Tridentine Roman rite), polyphony, and polychoral compositions with instrumental accompaniment.[71] Choir books containing Gregorian chant continued to be produced throughout the eighteenth century.[72] The liturgy celebrated in the Mozarabic Chapel was something of a hybrid, combining early modern melodies and mostly medieval texts, but also purporting to continue the Visigothic tradition. This version of the Mozarabic rite is still celebrated today in a modified form.[73] The earliest layer, represented by the manuscripts of the Old Hispanic rite, silently awaited rediscovery.

Against this background it is all the more remarkable that Burriel anticipated twentieth-century research on Old Hispanic liturgy and chant, particularly by establishing a comparative method for studying liturgical texts that brought out the differences between the early Toledan liturgical manuscripts and the neo-Mozarabic editions published by Ortiz. Decades earlier Pinius had pointed out that many elements in the neo-Mozarabic missal must have originated in liturgical books brought across the Pyrenees to León-Castile after the liturgical reform of the eleventh century.[74] Burriel approached this aspect of the neo-Mozarabic editions through the comparison of manuscripts. In his "Apuntamientos de algunas ideas para fomentar las letras," written before the Commission on the Archives began its work in Toledo, Burriel anticipated that collating the manuscripts with the Cisneros editions would reveal the chronological stratification of the rite, enabling him to discern which texts the Visigothic liturgy comprised during the life of Isidore of Seville and to distinguish them from additions to the rite made in later centuries. Burriel planned to compare the Visigothic rite to Eastern liturgies as well as the Gallican and Roman rites once he had identified the extraneous elements introduced by Ortiz into the neo-Mozarabic editions.[75]

The End of the Commission

Burriel was prevented from carrying out most of these plans by a series of events that inexorably brought the Commission to an end. First, the Concordat of 1753 gave the Spanish crown the long-sought *patronato universal,* the right to present nearly all candidates for clerical appointments.[76] This agreement, which represented the culmination of thirteen years of negotiation between the Spanish government and the Vatican, brought to an end the government's need for the Commission on the Archives. With the most immediate political purpose of the Commission fulfilled by the terms of the Concordat, the work in Toledo Cathedral, from the perspective of the government, soon lost its urgency. Burriel's position was further weakened in 1754 by the death of José de Carvajal, the secretary of state who had appointed him director of the Commission on the Archives in 1749. Yet another event that ultimately diminished support for Burriel was the removal from office in 1754 of the Marques de la Ensenada. Ensenada's efforts to reform taxation, to develop commerce and the navy, and to promote the professional interests of the middle classes had met with opposition from some factions at court. His traditionalist foes forced him from the government in 1754.

The fall of Ensenada inevitably led to the dismissal in 1755 of Burriel's one remaining patron, the royal confessor and Jesuit Francisco de Rávago.[77] Already in 1754 Ricardo Wall, the new, anti-Jesuit secretary of state, had ordered Burriel to finish his work in Toledo immediately and submit his results to the crown. Burriel had been able to defer his departure through the intervention of Rávago, but in 1756 Rávago's position was filled by the inquisitor general Manuel Quintano y Bonifaz, who demanded that Burriel relinquish his materials as previously requested. In a poignant letter to the new inquisitor, Burriel lamented that his incomplete notes and drafts would be incomprehensible and useless to anyone but himself, and he somehow managed to keep his papers until his death in 1762, when the Jesuits gave them to the government.[78]

Burriel remained active as a professor of theology in Toledo until 1760, and then in Madrid until his death. He never published the results of his liturgical research, which went essentially unnoticed until the twentieth century. Even though most of his papers on liturgy are catalogued, they have remained largely unexplored.[79] Likewise the extent of Burriel's collaboration with Palomares is little known, and thus few today are aware of the two men's engagement with the silent music they found in the medieval manuscripts of Toledo Cathedral.

Historians of eighteenth-century Spain tend to see the fate of Burriel as a cautionary tale demonstrating the restrictions faced by intellectuals in the political environment of the early Enlightenment.[80] It is instructive, however, to take a broader view of the Jesuit's endeavors. The Commission on the Archives was just one of several such initiatives that continued until the end of the century, including surveys of civil as well as royal and ecclesiastical archives. As Agustín Millares Carlo first pointed out, it was through these projects, owing to the research of scholars such as Burriel, that a modern concept of history became established in Spain.[81] The process from which the new paradigm emerged was typical of the Enlightenment in Spain in that it depended on the relationship of intellectuals to those in power, which Ruth Hill has described as "the courtship between the literati and kings, and the resulting systematization of monarchical absolutism."[82]

As I argue in this book, studying Burriel's methods yields new insight into the practice of history in the eighteenth century and shows the importance of liturgy and music in the construction of national identity. In particular Burriel's fascination with the Old Hispanic rite shows an Enlightenment historian coming to terms with the rich symbolic capital of the invented neo-Mozarabic tradition, anchored as it was in a particular set of sociopolitical concerns. As we will see in chapter 1, Burriel's account of the past, like that of many of his contemporaries, reveals significant tensions between the ongoing search for a systematic historical method and the form of history as nostalgia that had become axiomatic in the cultural nationalist milieu of Bourbon Spain.

Notes

1. Hillgarth, *The Visigoths*, 79–80, points out that the liturgy and law codes (canon and civil) are the only aspects of Visigothic culture to have survived the Muslim conquest of 711, but that they are Hispano-Roman rather than distinctively Gothic or Germanic.

2. An early Latin term for the Toledan Mozarabs was used in the 1101 *fuero* accorded by Alfonso VI. The original document does not survive, but the later copies contain spellings such as *mostarabes*, *maztarabes*, and *muzaraves*. See Gambra, *Alfonso VI*, 164. For recent discussions of the terminology see Aillet, *Les mozarabes*, 2–5; Hitchcock, *Mozarabs*, ix–xx; Olstein, *La era mozárabe*, 23–25.

3. For introductions to the Old Hispanic rite and its chant, see Brockett, *Antiphons*; Férotin, *Le Liber Mozarabicus Sacramentorum*; Randel and Nadeau, "Mozarabic Chant"; Rojo and Prado, *El canto mozárabe*.

4. See Janini, *Liber missarum*, 2:lx–lxii; Janini, *Liber misticus*, xxvi–xxix; Janini, *Liber misticus de cuaresma y Pascua*, xxiv–xxvi; Pinell, "El problema"; Pinell, "Los textos," 209–64; see also González Barrionuevo, "La música litúrgica," 161–67.

5. The most recent account of liturgical change in northwestern Iberia in this period is Manuel Pedro Ferreira, "Cluny at Fynystere: One Use, Three Fragments," in *Studies*

in Medieval Chant and Liturgy in Honour of David Hiley, ed. Terence Bailey and László Dobszay (Budapest: Institute for Musicology and Ottawa: Institute of Mediaeval Music, 2007), 179–228.

6. See Vones, "The Substitution," 43–59.

7. Reynolds, "Baptismal Rite," 257–72; Reynolds, "The Ordination Rite," 131–55.

8. On the integration of Catalonia into Frankish ecclesiastical structures during the eighth and ninth centuries, see Vones-Liebenstein, "Katalonien zwischen Maurenherrschaft und Frankenreich," 1:453–505. For manuscripts in the Carolingian Empire containing Visigothic-rite texts, see Reynolds, "The Visigothic Liturgy," 2:919–45.

9. For a recent account of a Toledan liturgical manuscript that was apparently copied for the use of Toledo Cathedral from Aquitanian sources (Toledo, BC, MS 44.2), see Collamore, "Aquitanian Collections." On the phenomenon in general, see Huglo, "La pénétration des manuscrits aquitains en Espagne," 249–56.

10. For discussions of this process in other places, see particularly Shailor, "The Scriptorium," 41–61; Walker, *Views of Transition*.

11. On the origins of precise heighting in Aquitanian notation see Grier, *The Musical World*, especially 22–25.

12. Among the few exceptions are twenty chants for the funeral rite in a manuscript from the Riojan abbey of San Millán de la Cogolla; the melodies of these chants were rewritten in Aquitanian-style neumes in Madrid, RAH, Cod. 56. For transcriptions of the chants see Rojo and Prado, *El canto mozárabe*, 66–82. On the manuscript, see Zapke, "Liber ordinum," 260–61.

13. Colette, "La notation," 297–311.

14. This manuscript (New York, HSA, B2916) is discussed in chapter 2.

15. See Boynton, "A Lost Mozarabic Liturgical Manuscript Rediscovered," 189–219.

16. Gonzálvez Ruiz, "The Persistence of the Mozarabic Liturgy," 163.

17. Reilly, *The Kingdom of León-Castilla*, 101. I am grateful to Liam Moore for this reference.

18. Hitchcock, "El rito hispánico," 19–41; O'Callaghan, "The Integration of Christian Spain into Europe," 101–20.

19. On the history of this church see Porres Martín-Cleto, "La iglesia mozárabe."

20. Gambra, *Alfonso VI*, 227.

21. Linehan, *History*, 216–19.

22. Gonzálvez, "Persistence."

23. Mundó, "La datación," 1–25. The datings accepted previously were those proposed by Agustín Millares Carlo in *Los codices visigóticos de la Catedral Toledana*.

24. This point has been made most recently by Aillet, *Les mozarabes*, 47–48.

25. On the revisionist current in the historiography of the Mozarabs see Olstein, *La era mozárabe*, 34–37.

26. Gonzálvez, "The Persistence," 171–74.

27. Hernández, "Language and Cultural Identity," 31.

28. Hernández, "Los mozárabes," 57–124; Burman, *Religious Polemic*, 13–31; Hitchcock, *Mozarabs*, 75–97. Olstein, *La era mozárabe*, 121–23, 141, calculates that the Mozarabs represented approximately 25 percent of the population of Toledo in the years 1085–1180 and grew to approximately 28 percent in 1180–1260.

29. Hernández, "Los mozárabes," 90–92.

30. Hitchcock, *Mozarabs*, 95–96.

31. Pick, *Conflict and Coexistence*, 33–34.

32. On the change of language among the Mozarabs see Hernández, "Language and Cultural Identity"; Olstein, *La era mozárabe*, 133–40.

33. Zapke, "Notation systems," 209.

34. Gómez-Ruiz, *Mozarabs*, 33–34.

35. Gonzálvez, "The Persistence," 178–79; Hernández and Linehan, *The Mozarabic Cardinal*.

36. See Michael, "From the Belles," 277–92.

37. Hernández, "Language and Cultural Identity," 29–48. I am grateful to Peter Linehan for giving me a copy of this publication.

38. Bosch, *Art*, 61–64, citing Meseguer Fernández, "El Cardenal Jiménez de Cisneros," 150–58; Gómez-Ruiz, *Mozarabs*, 33–34.

39. For a history of the chapel see Arellano Garcia, *La Capilla Mozárabe*.

40. Cisneros was not the only proponent of the Old Hispanic liturgy in this period; according to Enrique Flórez, Juan de Tordesillas, bishop of Segovia, founded a college of regular clergy who celebrated the rite in 1436–41, and in 1517 the bishop of Salamanca, Rodrigo Aries Maldonado de Talavera, endowed a chapel in his cathedral where the Mozarabic mass would be celebrated once a month and on some feast days. See Flórez, *España Sagrada*, 3: 336–37.

41. See Fernández Collado, "Los cantorales mozárabes," 145–68; Peñas García, "De los cantorales de Cisneros," 413–34; Peñas García and Casas Gras, "Los cantorales de Cisneros," 261–402; Imbasciani, "Cisneros." The cantorales are now available in facsimile editions: see *Los Cantorales Mozárabes*, ed. Férnandez Collado, Rodríguez González, and Castañeda Tordera.

42. *Missale mixtum* (1500); *Breviarium secundum regulam Beati Isidori*.

43. The *Missale Mixtum* contains notated chants and prayers within the order of mass (fols. 220v–32v), the Eastertide *ad confractionem panis* chant *Vicit leo de tribu iuda* (fol. 233r), and a notated preface (fol. 301r).

44. See Imbasciani, "Cisneros," 10.

45. *Breviarium secundum regulam Beati Isidori*, fol. 432r; *Missale Mixtum*, fol. 472r. The copies I have consulted are in the Library of the Hispanic Society of America.

46. Janini, "Misas mozárabes," 153–63; Janini, *Liber misticus*, xxxi–xliii.

47. Bernadó, "The Hymns," 1: 367–96; Brou, "Etudes," 349–98; Martín Patino, "El Breviarium Mozárabe de Ortiz," 207–97.

48. Imbasciani ("Cisneros," 17), uses the term "neo-Mozarabic" to refer only to the cantorales or their music; I apply it instead to the entire enterprise represented by the Ortiz editions and the Cisneros "restoration" of the rite.

49. These elements also appear in the frontispieces reproduced in color in *Los Cantorales Mozárabes* 1: iv, v, and on unnumbered pages facing the table of contents in both vols. 1 and 2.

50. Rodríguez-Moñino Soriano, *El Cardenal Cisneros*, 116–17.

51. Pinius, *Liturgia Mozarabica*, 109. Burriel, "Apuntamientos," in Echánove Tuero, *La preparación intelectual*, 270, points out that Pinius obtained his manuscript descriptions from Camino y Velasco.

52. Camino y Velasco was commissioner of the Inquisition at Toledo and the chaplain of the Mozarabic parish of San Sebastián in 1731–53. He then became presider of the

Mozarabic congregation in 1754 and remained active until his death in 1761. See Arellano Garcia, *La Capilla Mozárabe*, 81; Mundó, "Datación," 5.

53. On Camino's fragments and his attempts to copy the Visigothic script, see chapters 2 and 5.

54. Camino y Velasco, *Noticia*, [3–4] of unpaginated dedication. For the historical context of this volume, see chapter 3.

55. On Burriel's initial years in Toledo, see Echánove Tuero, *La preparación intelectual*, in *Hispania Sacra* 23 (1970): 102–5.

56. Letter from Toledo, December 30, 1754, to Don Pedro de Castro, in Burriel, *Cartas eruditas y criticas*, 266: "Llamase esta Liturgia Muzarabe, porque quando se conquistó esta Ciudad de Toledo por Don Alonso el VI año de 1085, se hallaron en ella muchas familias christianas conservadas por casi quatro siglos de cautiviedad desde el tiempo de los Godos, divididas en siete Parroquias. . . . Abrogóse en todo el reyno no solo el rito ó Liturgica Goda, sino tambien el cáracter y letra Gótica, por el mismo Rey Don Alonso el VI. Pero el Rey que pudo arrancar letra y Liturgia Goda á las Catedrales y Monasterios, introduciendo la Galicana ó Romana, ó no pudo ó no quiso privar de ella á las Parroquias de los Muzarabes de Toledo, que la conservaron y conservan hasta el dia de hoy." In this passage I translate "Gótica" as "Visigothic" to avoid confusion with the later script known as "Gothic." Throughout this book I translate "Godo" (feminine form "Goda") as "Visigothic."

57. Burriel, *Cartas eruditas*, 267–68: "Aquel incomparable varon el Cardenal Ximenez de Cisneros, viendo caido el uso de este oficio en las Parroquias Muzarabes, á principios del siglo XVI, erigió una magnifica Capilla en esta su Iglesia primada, y fundó catorce capellanías para que los catorce Curas y Beneficiados Muzarabes, cantasen todos los dias en su propio tono la Misa, y todas las horas conónicas. A este fin recogió los libros manuscritos de las Parroquias, y de ellos hizo formar para uso de la Capilla y Parroquias el Misal y Breviario Muzarabe Isidoriano, que mandó imprimir; pero mezclando algunas cosas modernas, y omitiendo otras antiguas."

58. Burriel, *Cartas eruditas*, 253–54: "Sola España es la nación que puede producir como propias Biblias, Liturgias, colleción de Concilios, y obras de Santos suyas; así todo baxo el sello de una autoridad tan respetable en toda la Iglesia Católica, como es la de esta Iglesia de Toledo; puro todo, limpio, verdadero, firme, y antiguo todo, y todo conformísimo con lo mismo que creemos, y enseñamos el dia de hoy."

59. Madrid, RAH MS 9/5921, fol. 111v: "Este es como el centro y blanco de todos las ideas." The annotations must have been made by 1756 because he mentions them in his letter of that year to Quintano y Bonifaz; see Burriel, *Cartas eruditas*, 227.

60. Burriel, *Cartas eruditas*, 245.

61. Copies from and references to Bianchini's text are preserved in Madrid, BN MS 13053 and 13058.

62. *Missale mixtum* (1755).

63. *Breviarium Gothicum*. For a recent discussion of this publication and its context, see Colomina Torner, "El cardenal Lorenzana," 125–39; Vadillo Romero and Fernández Collado, "El breviario mozárabe," 141–52; Fernández Collado, "Razones," 429–38. Lorenzana's introduction to the *Breviarium Gothicum* constitutes a brief treatise on the liturgy that follows in the tradition of Cisneros's philological treatment of the texts rather than Burriel's historical approach. Lorenzana seems to have ignored Burriel's research (see the epilogue).

64. The Maréchal de Noailles (Duke Adrien-Maurice de Noailles, 1678–1766) is known to have owned the trouvère "chansonnier de Noailles" (Paris, BNF fr. 12615) in the early eighteenth century, before it entered the Bibliothèque du Roy in 1733. See Stanley Boorman et al., "Sources, MS," in *Grove Music Online, Oxford Music Online*, www.oxfordmusiconline.com/subscriber/article/grove/music/50158pg3 (accessed March 30, 2010).

65. Mayans y Siscar, *Gregorio Mayans y Siscar, Epistolario*, 325–27. On the role of de las Infantas in the Royal Commission on the Archives, see chapter 2.

66. On Blas Jover de Alcázar see Didier Ozanam, *Les diplomats espagnols du XVIIIème siècle* (Madrid: Casa de Velázquez and Maison des Pays Ibériques, 1998), 305–6.

67. Pinius, *Liturgia Mozarabica*, lxix–lxx.

68. Hobsbawm, "Introduction," 1–14.

69. For the effect of discourse on the construction of the national community see Benedict Anderson, *Imagined Communities: Reflections on the Origin and Spread of Nationalism*, revised edition (London: Verso, 2006).

70. Olstein, *La era mozárabe*, 28–29.

71. On the performing forces for sacred music at Toledo Cathedral in this period, see Martínez Gil, *La Capilla*.

72. For choir books of the Roman rite copied during Burriel's years at the cathedral see Noone and Skinner, "Toledo Cathedral's Collection," 309–11.

73. The Hispanic rite as currently practiced is the result of a commission established in 1982. The rite was approved by the Holy See in 1994. For accounts of the modern rite that situate it historically see Gómez-Ruiz, *Mozarabs, Hispanics, and the Cross*; Pinell, *Liturgia Hispánica*.

74. Pinius, *Liturgia Mozarabica*, cii.

75. Burriel, "Apuntamientos," in Echánove Tuero, *La preparación intelectual*, 269. For fuller discussion of the "Apuntamientos," see chapter 1.

76. For an English translation of the text of the Concordat, see Shiels, *King and Church*, 229–42.

77. Lynch, *Bourbon Spain*, 182–89.

78. Burriel, *Cartas Eruditas* (Madrid: Blas Roman, 1788), 228–29.

79. Descriptions of the papers related to liturgy appear in Janini and Serrano, *Manuscritos litúrgicos*.

80. See, for instance, Mestre Sanchís, *Humanistas*, 114–15.

81. Millares Carlo, "El siglo XVIII español," 515–30.

82. Hill, *Sceptres and Sciences*, 5. See also Mestre Sanchís, *Humanistas*, 114; Mestre, *Despotismo*; Stiffoni, "Alcune tematiche," 20.

1 | Burriel and the Practice of History
in the Spanish Enlightenment

It is evident and certain that today, without great danger, one cannot openly state
the truth—this is what justifies Flórez{'s actions}.

—Burriel to Gregorio Mayans y Siscar, April 11, 1750

The collection of all these venerable monuments of our antiquity would be without
doubt very glorious for our nation: it would constitute an invincible proof of the
tradition of faith in Spain in every aspect of dogma, since the first centuries of
the Church, and would be at the same time a chronological demonstration of the
supreme authority of the Roman Church, and the Apostolic see, acknowledged
without interruption in Spain from the first shining of the Gospel until today.

—Burriel to Pedro de Castro, December 30, 1754

As an intellectual in Bourbon Spain, Andrés Marcos Burriel worked in an
atmosphere of contradiction aptly reflected in the contrast between these
two statements. The first, from a private letter to a scholar who sought but
ultimately did not receive support for his work from the government, attests
to a lack of intellectual freedom that hampered historians in their efforts to
write a new kind of Spanish history, one that would be based on documents,

not on long-standing tradition. The second passage is taken from a more public missive directed to one of Burriel's colleagues; it reflects the nationalist basis of most history writing at the time. As we will see in this chapter, Burriel's letters, like his other writings, reflect a conflict between progress and tradition that can be described (in terms borrowed from Richard Kagan) as the tension between critical history and official history.[1] The differences between these two approaches had to be reconciled at various moments in Burriel's own career. In 1750, for example, he was commissioned by Ferdinand VI to write a biography of Ferdinand III of Castile (1199–1252), who had been canonized in the seventeenth century under the Habsburgs.[2] Although the substance was to be based on archival documents, the assignment was clearly to write an official, even hagiographic history that would pay homage to the reigning Ferdinand, albeit indirectly, through praise of his predecessor.[3]

Although he was in the vanguard of modern methods and projects of historical research, Burriel knew the power of the pious and unsubstantiated fictions that dominated the writing of history in Bourbon Spain. The long-standing belief in the apostolic origins of peninsular Christianity was based on the tradition that the Apostle Paul had visited the Iberian peninsula and that Saint James the Greater (Santiago) had preached there, as attested by the imputed presence of his remains in Compostela. Legends known collectively as the *tradiciones jacobeas*, which related James's coming to the Iberian Peninsula and the Virgin Mary's appearance to him on a pillar, were considered crucial to the image of Spain as a Christian nation.[4] Nonetheless with the increased emphasis on the use of original documents in the eighteenth century, it was inevitable that critical thinkers would begin to question and ultimately to reject such traditions. The debates that resulted were sometimes lively but more commonly were muted by the fear of censorship; Gregorio Mayans y Siscar, for instance, one of the foremost intellectuals in Spain, refuted the tradiciones jacobeas in a personal letter to the papal nuncio in Madrid but declined to have his words on this subject published. In his own letter to Mayans, quoted above, Burriel implied that the danger of challenging the tradiciones jacobeas was significant enough to justify those who upheld them out of fear rather than out of conviction.[5]

That the subject of church history could be contentious, and even risky, signals its crucial importance to the Spanish monarchy as an instrument of church-state politics. In effect the creation of the Royal Commission on the Archives lent state sponsorship to the construction of a new ecclesiastical history that would validate church-state cooperation in the present by documenting its history in the Middle Ages. Ironically, however, this endeavor, which would be unprecedented in its use of original documents instead of traditions, was mandated by a government for which the tradiciones jacobeas remained fundamental to modern discourses of national unity.

More vulnerable to critical attack were the so-called *falsos cronicones*, or "false chronicles," a collective term used for various fictional accounts of the early history of Spain that were written in the fifteenth and six-teenth centuries.[6] Challenges to the veracity of the tradiciones jacobeas and the falsos cronicones formed one component of the increasingly critical approaches to historical texts that characterized the early Enlightenment in Spain.[7] The catalysts of the Spanish Enlightenment were the so-called *novatores* of the late seventeenth century and early eighteenth, "innovators" from a broad cross-section of Spanish society who explored new scientific and philosophical ideas from abroad.[8] The novatores were shaped as much by English empiricist thought as by Continental influences.[9] Cartesian phil-osophical principles were not foremost in their syncretic blend of ideas, owing perhaps to the fact that ecclesiastical and government censorship in Spain banned many of the central texts of the French Enlightenment, such as the *Encyclopédie* and the works of Rousseau and Voltaire.[10] Consequently it can be misleading even to use the same term for the French Enlighten-ment and the Spanish Enlightenment, so fundamentally do they differ in inspiration, cast of characters, and historical context.[11] Richard Kagan traces the "rebirth of national history" to the undermining of the false chronicles beginning in the seventeenth century by novatores such as Nicolás Anto-nio (1617–84).[12] However, it was a sign of the times that the tradiciones jacobeas were once again reaffirmed by what was perhaps the most influ-ential work of the early Enlightenment in Spain, the first volume of the *Teatro crítico universal*, published in 1726 by the Benedictine monk Benito Jerónimo Feijoo y Montenegro (1676–1764).[13]

The *Teatro crítico* is a sprawling work of eighteenth-century encyclope-dism, a veritable cornucopia of erudition that, according to the fashion of the time, purported to present a summation of all available knowledge. One finds the most representative example of Feijoo's approach to historiography in the fourth volume; the first part of the *Glorias de España*, which com-prises discourse 13, is an apologetic for the prestige of the "Spanish nation" that begins with a focus on the view from afar. Feijoo first rebuts the crit-icisms of Spain by a crowd of unspecified "foreigners," then cites praise for Spain by other foreigners. The text is interrupted for a brief apostrophe to the dedicatee, the Infante (the future King Charles III), and continues with encomia to Spanish personages, monuments, and achievements beginning in antiquity (including the Roman emperors Trajan, Hadrian, and Theodosius).

Among these early "glories" Feijoo includes the purported coming of Saint James the Greater, the foundation of the fictional tradiciones jacobeas. By way of commentary on its authenticity, he notes only that "one cannot reasonably doubt it after so many erudite writings have proven it."[14] The same paragraph includes a reference to the Virgin of the Pillar, supported by a similarly tautological statement: "If the testimony of tradition is not sufficient to give prudent agreement to a miracle, one must condemn as fictions almost everything written in ecclesiastical histories."[15] (Later, in response to accusations by French historians that Spaniards lent credence to fictions such as the falsos cronicones, Feijoo devotes most of a paragraph to rebutting French ecclesiastical traditions of similarly dubious verisimilitude.)[16]

Although Feijoo became the most acclaimed intellectual of the day, the fortunes of the new critical approach to history are better illustrated by the careers of some of his contemporaries: Mayans, the Benedictine Martín Sarmiento, the Augustinian Enrique Flórez, and the Jesuit Burriel. In this period, most prominent scholars in Spain were members of religious orders. Whereas the clergy was central to the history of ideas in early Enlightenment France as well, and not only in its opposition to the philosophes,[17] in Spain the mainstream of intellectual life was thoroughly clerical and remained largely subject to control by the state and religious orders until the late eighteenth century. Mayans, the only layman in the group, was at once the most brilliant and the least successful in obtaining patronage for his endeavors. Some of the obstacles he faced can perhaps be attributed to the fact that his father had been a partisan of the Habsburgs during the war of Spanish succession; with the accession of the Bourbons to the throne, the social stigma associated with this past adhered to the son.[18] For the most part, however, Mayans encountered opposition because his approach to history ran against the apologist currents of the time.

Mayans had studied law, then served as royal librarian from 1733 to 1739, and in 1742 published an edition of the Censura de historias fabulosas by Nicolás Antonio, whose Bibliotheca hispana nova had already demonstrated the illegitimacy of the falsos cronicones. The Censura further discredited the falsos cronicones and also rejected the authenticity of the plomos de Granada, a set of lead books allegedly discovered in that city in 1595;[19] these contained inscriptions recounting the supposed conversion of the city in the first century by its first bishop, who, according to the tradiciones jacobeas, was a disciple of Santiago. The inscriptions were taken to be proof of Santiago's voyage to the peninsula, but they were apparently fabricated by the Morisco scholars who translated them, Miguel de Luna and Alonso del Castillo.[20] Although the plomos were condemned by the pope as forgeries in 1682, they remained important to the city's self-image.[21] The canons of the basilica of Sacromonte (which had been built to house the tablets) took offense at the publication of Antonio's *Censura*, and the Council of Castile ordered the seizure of all of Mayans's papers. In the end, with the help of powerful connections, he was able to get the judgment reversed, but the episode demonstrates the resistance Mayans faced in his attempt to apply critical scholarly methods to Spanish history.

Mayans's other projects fared no better. He founded the Valencian Academy to promote the critical editing of texts, but by 1751 it had disappeared for lack of government support. In his preface to the *Obras cronológicas* of Mondéjar (1746) he proposed an ambitious project of publishing diverse texts for the history of Spain: synods and councils, antiphonaries, laws and legal codes, bulls and royal decrees, and registers of the archives of the nobility.[22] Although he never won government funding for the individual scholarly projects he proposed, Mayans exercised considerable influence on Enrique Flórez, and later on Burriel's own plans as well.[23] Nonetheless Mayans saw all too clearly the shortcomings of contemporaries like Flórez, whom he denounced (in a private letter to Burriel) as a sophist whose works were not in the true interest of Spain (the *nación*), but rather against it. At the conclusion of the letter, however, he begged Burriel not to tell anyone what he had said about Flórez, whom he did not wish to have as an enemy.[24]

Church History as National History

The experience of Mayans illustrates the challenges independent thinkers faced in Spain, where reformist intellectuals were shaped by patronage to an even greater extent than elsewhere in eighteenth-century Europe.[25] Above all, scholarship in Bourbon Spain was expected to serve the aims of the absolutist state and to enhance the idea of the *nación*, a term frequently invoked in the writings of eighteenth-century intellectuals. Thus the Spanish Enlightenment emphasized new methods for the writing of national history, inspired by the example of foreign historians such as the Italian priest Ludovico Antonio Muratori (1672–1750), the Maurists in France, and the Bollandists of Antwerp.[26] The most important influence was the French Maurist Benedictine Jean Mabillon (1632–1707), best represented in his foundational *De re diplomatica libri sex*, first published in 1681.[27] Mabillon pioneered the discipline known today as diplomatics (which concerns the analysis, dating, and authentication of medieval charters) and also advanced paleography and codicology.[28] Spanish historians may have seen themselves as working in Mabillon's shadow when they promoted the use of original documents, but eighteenth-century historiography in Spain was still based largely on previously published sources.[29] In any case the *De re diplomatica* did not provide an obvious model for the study of historical documents in Spain; it does not present any examples in Visigothic script and includes only one charter of a Spanish king (Alfonso IX).[30] The coincidence of the early Enlightenment with the ascent of the Bourbon monarchy influenced the atmosphere for scholarship, inevitably compromising the vaunted critical rigor of the new historiography. Under the Bourbons the king's confessor was also in charge of making appointments to the Royal Library.[31] This position gave the confessor absolute power over a major center of intellectual life, with the effect that scholarly innovation remained under government control.[32] In the middle decades of the eighteenth century the royal confessors opposed the new practice of historical criticism by suppressing texts that refuted the authenticity of the tradiciones jacobeas and the Virgin of the Pillar.[33] Writers who were associated with or officially commended by the court were thus understandably hesitant to debunk the tradiciones jacobeas and other pious legends.

These unresolved tensions between methodological ideals and political reality caused some scholars to be rewarded for conformism—that is, upholding the authenticity of the tradiciones jacobeas—while others were punished for questioning tradition.[34] Special favor, for example, was accorded to Feijoo, who synthesized recent work in the natural sciences and philosophy. Feijoo's authority had been established by his *Teatro crítico* and then cemented by government fiat in 1750, when Ferdinand VI issued an edict prohibiting criticism of Feijoo's works and of all other writings expressing similar ideas. This official gesture of state support discouraged critics of traditional historiography, such as Mayans, from attempting to modernize the writing of history.[35]

The resurgence of interest in Spanish ecclesiastical history had begun in the late seventeenth century, with the publication of two monumental editions, the *Bibliotheca Hispana nova* of Nicolás Antonio (published in 1672–96) and the *Collectio maxima conciliorum Hispaniae et Novi Orbis* (1693–94) of Sáenz de Aguirre. As Antonio Mestre Sanchís has pointed out, the Spanish regalists of the eighteenth century took Sáenz de Aguirre's edition of the decisions of councils in Spain as "an arsenal of ideas for emphasizing the idea of a national Church."[36] In particular the councils of the Visigothic church held in Toledo gave Spanish historians of the eighteenth century a model for a reinvigorated national church in their own time.[37] The political implications of renewed interest in the Visigothic church suffused Spanish Enlightenment historical writing; the Visigothic kingdom became a symbol of the reign of Ferdinand VI (as it had been for the medieval Castilian kings Alfonso III and Alfonso VI), and the authority of the Visigothic church was viewed as a precedent for the *patronato real* sought so tenaciously by Ferdinand's ministers.[38] In the central decades of the eighteenth century the writing of national history was manifestly shaped by the coexistence of these two layers of meaning.

Bourbons and Visigoths: Sarmiento's Sistema

Self-consciously drawn parallels between the Spanish Bourbons and the Visigothic kings were depicted most vividly in the program of decoration devised by the Benedictine monk Martín Sarmiento (1695–1772) for the new royal palace in Madrid.[39] After the royal palace of the Habsburgs (the old Alcázar of Madrid) burned to the ground on Christmas Eve in 1734, the reigning monarch, Philip V, initiated construction of a new palace on the same site in 1738. It is fitting testimony to the Bourbons' patronage of historians that Ferdinand VI called on the erudite Sarmiento to create a design for this palace, conceived as a monumental symbol of Bourbon rule in Spain. Sarmiento, a historian and philologist from Galicia, was initially consulted in 1743, but it was only in 1747 that he was invited to submit a proposal for a program of decorations. Upon approval of his proposal by Ferdinand VI, Sarmiento began to write the program, and in 1754 he finished the text known as the *Sistema de adornos del Palacio Real de Madrid*. In it he envisaged a series of statues on the exterior of the palace, enabling a viewer to follow the succession of the Spanish monarchy from its origins to the present day.[40] This decorative program would have been a striking visual affirmation of the Spanish Bourbons' legitimacy, but its iconography went mostly unrealized. When Charles III acceded to the throne in 1759, he brought with him the architect Francisco Sabatini (1721–97), who revised the previous plans for the palace.[41] Although the construction of the building was complete in 1754, the palace was not inhabited until 1764, when the interior decoration was finished.

Sarmiento's *Sistema* nevertheless is an important historical source for understanding the mode of apologetic history fostered by Bourbon patronage;[42] it was also the first systematic representation of the monarchy in Spain. Sarmiento's glorification of the Bourbon monarchs drew upon a variety of frameworks, including the paradigm of biblical kingship (likening Philip V and Ferdinand VI to kings David and Solomon) and the sovereignty of the Roman emperors (noting that Ferdinand VI's birthday was the same as that of the emperor Augustus). Sarmiento placed the Visigothic saints and kings in a symbolic system that aligned them implicitly, and sometimes explicitly, with the members of the Bourbon dynasty. For instance, in his introductory discourse he discusses the Gothic etymology of the name Ferdinand, which signifies "peacemaker" (from *frede*, meaning "peace," and *senand*, meaning "conciliator"), and in comparison cites similar etymologies of Solomon's name.[43] The idea that Ferdinand's reign augured an exceptional period of peace and cultivation of the arts and letters was frequently reiterated in discourse associated with the court.[44] As Irene Cioffi has pointed out, Sarmiento barely acknowledged the role of the Habsburgs in Spanish history, his purpose being to glorify the Bourbons. Likewise the *Sistema* juxtaposes the Visigothic king Hermengild with the medieval saint Mary de la Cabeza, who was in some sense a saint of the Bourbon monarchy, as she was canonized in 1752 (during the reign of Ferdinand VI).[45]

Implicit connections between the Visigoths and the Bourbons, suggested by the association of Ferdinand with the Visigothic kings, also appear in a letter of January 1759 that constitutes a postscript to the *Sistema*. Here Sarmiento proposes that the sainted kings Hermengild (d. 585) and Ferdinand III, as representatives of the Spanish monarchy, should flank the medallion over the central door of the royal chapel. Hermengild would represent the Visigothic crown, and Ferdinand the Castilian. Among the Christian attributes of these figures, Sarmiento specified that Hermengild should carry a banderole with the first phrase of the Nicene Creed (because, Sarmiento stated, Hermengild died to defend Catholic doctrine against Arianism), and Ferdinand should hold a globe topped by a cross.[46] Sarmiento thus obliquely reaffirms the link between Ferdinand VI, Ferdinand III, and the Visigothic saint Hermengild by reiterating that Saint Ferdinand belonged in the decorative program because he and the Visigoth formed a pair of sainted Spanish kings. In conclusion Sarmiento notes the felicitous coincidence of Ferdinand's name with that of the reigning monarch.[47] (Parallels between Ferdinand VI and his predecessors of the same name—Ferdinand I, III, and V—were thematized in other works associated with the court as well, such as José Antonio Porcel y Salablanca's "Canción heroica," which was written for the king's accession to the throne in 1746.)[48]

Sarmiento's *Sistema* was part of the gradual "nationalization" of Spanish culture, which can already be observed in historical scholarship of the 1730s and 1740s, but which became increasingly prominent in the 1750s.[49] In the area of philology the nationalizing tendency encouraged investigations into the history of "the Spanish language" that began with the founding of the

Real Academia de la Lengua Española, which was inspired by the example of the Académie Française, under Philip V. For cultural nationalists of the eighteenth century "the Spanish language" meant Castilian as a Spanish lingua franca, even though they acknowledged that it was only one of many languages spoken in the modern nation.[50] Some of the most noteworthy examples of this Castilianism are Mayans's *Orígenes de la lengua española* (1737) and Sarmiento's own *Memorias para la historia de la poesía y de los poetas españoles* (written in 1741 but published posthumously in 1775). In the introduction to the *Memorias* Sarmiento prefaces his call for national histories of poetry with criticism of historians who emphasize military campaigns at the expense of other human endeavors.[51] By framing the history of a language within the history of the nation, Sarmiento takes the same approach we will observe in Burriel's treatise on "Spanish" paleography, in which narratives of regional and national history underlie the history of language and handwriting.

The España Sagrada

In the writing of ecclesiastical history the model that came to prevail in eighteenth-century Spain was the fifty-two-volume *España Sagrada*, initiated by the Augustinian Enrique Flórez (1701–73). This encyclopedia was based on earlier examples from abroad, such as the *Italia Sacra* of Ferdinando Ughelli (ten volumes published in Venice in 1717–22) and the *Gallia Christiana* of Denis de Sainte-Marthe (thirteen volumes published in Paris in 1715–85).[52] Planning for the *España Sagrada* began in 1744, and publication began in 1747, the year after Ferdinand VI took the throne.[53] The ecclesiastical politics of Ferdinand's government seem to have influenced the contents of the *España Sagrada*; in the dedicatory epistle of the fourth volume, for instance, dedicated to the king, Flórez dwells on the close connection between the Spanish church and crown since the conversion of the Visigoths to Catholicism.[54] It is no coincidence that this volume, on the origins and development of the episcopate in Spain, was published in 1749, the same year the government inaugurated the Royal Commission on the Archives to obtain crucial evidence for negotiations with the Holy See.

Like Sarmiento, Flórez emphasizes the name linking the reigning monarch to his sainted predecessor, enumerating Ferdinand III's contributions to the church in a closing encomium that invokes the promise of church history in the reign of Ferdinand VI.[55] The *España Sagrada* came under royal patronage with the publication in 1750 of the fifth volume, which contains a lengthy treatise on the "antiquity and excellences of Toledo" (including a discourse on the episcopal seat and a catalogue of bishops). The appendixes serve to illustrate the history of the see; they include Isidore of Seville's accounts of the early bishops of Toledo (from his *De viris illustribus*), unedited sermons of Ildefonsus of Toledo (a bishop of Toledo who died in 657), and some *vitae* of Ildefonsus. Once again the *España Sagrada* was working in parallel with the Royal Commission on the Archives, which arrived in Toledo in the same year to undertake research for a new ecclesiastical history of Spain.[56]

Once the *España Sagrada* was under the patronage of Ferdinand VI, its agenda directly mirrored his ministers' aspirations for the national church, and its success reflected the government's preference for history in the form of nationalist apologetic.[57] The sixth volume, published in 1751, was devoted entirely to the church of Toledo and was dedicated to the secretary of state and royal confessor Francisco de Rávago, who initiated the Royal Commission on the Archives. Among the prefatory texts to this volume was a systematic rebuttal, point by point, of the twenty-third chapter in the second volume of Tommaso Maria Mamachi's *Origines et Antiquitates Christianae*, published in Rome in 1750.[58] Mamachi (1713–92), a Dominican theologian and historian, had challenged the presentation of the tradiciones jacobeas in the third volume of the *España Sagrada*. His refutation of the tradiciones jacobeas was probably as much a political as a historical statement; he was known for supporting the prerogatives of the papacy in response to regalist assertions of independence from Rome.[59] Flórez's response to Mamachi also must be understood in the context of Spanish regalism. It was fitting, and perhaps more than a felicitous coincidence, that the rebuttal of Mamachi appeared in the volume on the primatial see of Spain; as a royal and ecclesiastical capital Toledo was crucial to the arguments of the regalists in the Spanish government.

Against this background of historiography in early Enlightenment Spain, Burriel clearly shared his contemporaries' nationalist view of Hispanic ecclesiastical traditions. His discussion of canon law in the "Apuntamientos" alludes obliquely to Spanish relations with Rome, citing the sixth canon of the twelfth council of Toledo (681). This canon gives the clergy of Toledo the right to choose for all of Spain and for Visigothic Gaul the bishops who could be elected, approved, or presented to the king. Burriel adds that the canon allowed for this process to be carried out "without the remotest memory of recourse to Rome" ("sin la más remota memoria de recurso a Roma").[60] As a historical statement his comment seems redundant; it is a given that the Visigothic church was juridically independent from Rome in the seventh century. His aim here, however, was not to clarify the historical circumstances of the canon; on the contrary, his remark addresses the concerns of the ministers of Ferdinand VI (the intended readers of the "Apuntamientos"), whose doctrine of regalism was promoted by the government's establishment of the Royal Commission on the Archives.

Burriel's preface (*aprobación*) to the third volume of the *España Sagrada* (published in 1748) represents his official position on the state of church history in Spain during the time he taught philosophy at the Colegio Maximo at the University of Alcalá.[61] One of the first sentences appears to affirm the tradiciones jacobeas by referring to the "seed of the Gospel planted by the Apostles themselves in [Spain] before almost all nations."[62] Elsewhere in the text he laments the lack of a general church history of Spain, a lacuna that would not be filled by the *España Sagrada* (because it was not a critical history), but that the work of Flórez would ultimately help to remedy. After citing the words of Aróstegui to this effect (an exhortation to an assembly of Spanish ecclesiastics in Rome in 1747, around the time the Spanish Academy of Church History was founded), Burriel describes texts such as the falsos cronicones, the plomos of Granada, and others that were considered more reliable but that were nonetheless equally apocryphal. He points out that many of the most important texts necessary for a general church history of Spain were still unpublished, suggesting a need for further research on manuscript sources. This is the direction in which Burriel would take the Commission on the Archives. Before the Commission came into being, however, Burriel had begun to pursue a more expansive project: he sought to improve the state of humanistic knowledge in Spain.

The "Apuntamientos"

While awaiting specific directives from the government in 1749–50 Burriel designed his own mandate. The first version of his plans appears in the "Apuntamientos de algunas ideas para fomentar las letras" (Notes on some ideas for the promotion of the liberal arts), which set forth his proposal for the cultural renewal of Spain in an exhaustive study of the humanities by a committee composed entirely of Jesuits.[63] The numerous projects described in the text were for the most part never brought to fruition; the committee, or *junta*—essentially a scholarly academy—was not created. Instead the Commission was formed to undertake a survey of Spanish archives. However, the "Apuntamientos" are instructive because they reveal Burriel's ideals and aspirations in 1749.

Several of the initiatives described in the "Apuntamientos" closely resemble those conceived earlier by Gregorio Mayans y Siscar, who discussed his ideas with Burriel in their correspondence during the 1740s.[64] About ten years before Burriel's "Apuntamientos" Mayans had formulated an ambitious program of cultural renewal in his "Pensamientos literarios," but Mayans himself was never able to realize the projects it described. The "Pensamientos" exercised an indirect influence, however, on Burriel's own plans.[65] Burriel's "Apuntamientos" were addressed to his patron, Francisco de Rávago, the Jesuit who served as the king's confessor. At the center of power in this period, Rávago was a major force in the reforms of the 1740s and had appointed Burriel to his post. The scope of Burriel's costly all-Jesuit project, and the manner in which he presented his plans to a fellow Jesuit (and a close associate of the king), attest to the enormous power of the Society in the reign of Fernando VI until the middle of the 1750s, when anti-Jesuit sentiment began to permeate the court, ultimately leading to the expulsion of the order in 1767.[66] In the "Apuntamientos" Burriel envisioned a well-funded academy of Jesuit scholars working together in the order's Imperial College, located in the center of Madrid.[67] The treatise presents a detailed program of research and publication for which Burriel saw two principal purposes: the first was to "honor the nation among foreigners with great works of profound and abstruse erudition, such as a new and excellent collection of the Councils of Spain, an Arabic-Latin edition of all the Arabic codices, or of the most singular ones of the Escorial"; the second was to create "a *Corpus Diplomaticum* of all the royal privileges extant in Spain."[68] These distinctively Spanish cultural products were the main focus of Burriel's plans. The "great works of profound and abstruse erudition" included a new edition of the Latin translation of the Bible preserved in Visigothic manuscripts, as well as a thorough treatment of the Old Hispanic rite. Burriel described the current state of scholarship on the rite in a passage that reveals his dissatisfaction with Italian domination of this field. He stated the need for

> a thoughtful exposition of the ancient Spanish liturgy, called Mozarabic, Toledan, Isidoran, etc., on which Pisa, Robles, Villegas, Aguirre have written, and [concerning which] recently Father Pinius wrote a folio volume which he inserted in volume 6 of July. Cayetano Cenni, Roman cleric, cruel enemy (albeit disguised) of the Spanish nation, which gave him the income on which he lives [has also written on this subject]. Don Alfonso Clemente made a short while ago in Rome a collection of all the authors in two folio volumes, in which he printed that which Tomasi, Bianchini, etc. [had already] published from a certain codex of Verona; and finally, Father Flórez in his third volume wrote a treatise that contains many good things. All this can help the

commission, but the work I have in mind is much more illustrious and grand. One must examine the manuscripts in Toledo of the Mozarabic breviary and missal, which Cardinal Ximénez printed, and which are used in the chapel of the cathedral and the six Mozarabic parishes of Toledo. One must read carefully that which Bianchini, Tomasi, and other Italians have written on the Verona codex, concerning our most venerable traditions such as the coming of Santiago, the finding of his body, the antiquity of the hymns, and other things about the liturgy, on which they have written with considerable roguishness.[69]

Burriel here proposes a two-part strategy for advancing the state of research on the Hispanic liturgy. Consultation of the manuscripts and comparisons with the neo-Mozarabic editions must be combined with close reading of the published scholarship. He suggests furthermore that the accounts of the Old Hispanic liturgy written by Italians were not entirely trustworthy, the implicit reasoning being that the Italians' rejection of the tradiciones jacobeas rendered them adversaries of Spain and its most revered religious traditions. Thus Gaetano Cenni, who maintained that the Roman rite predated the Visigothic rite in the Iberian peninsula, is cast in this passage as an "enemy" of the Spanish nation.[70]

In Spain the most widely available treatise on the Old Hispanic liturgy was that of Flórez in the third volume of his *España Sagrada*, which consists of responses to existing treatments of the subject. It is based on published texts, especially Visigothic church councils, rather than on manuscripts. Like other historians in Spain, Flórez devoted extensive space to challenging foreign scholars' accounts of the Visigothic liturgy, particularly those by Pinius, Cenni, and Bianchini, framing the debate implicitly or explicitly in terms of the political tensions between papal Rome and the Spanish crown.[71] In a similar vein Burriel described the Hispanic liturgical books of Toledo and the Mozarabic liturgical tradition as a national treasure that was the envy of Rome:

> The glory of having kept this treasure redounds to Spain, and the utility that it will offer in its demonstration is well worth knowing. This was well known to the great intellect of Cardinal Ximénez, who put so much effort into preserving it: and in this can be seen the misfortune preceding our century, that in Toledo, where I lived for seven years, a thousand attempts were made to do away with the foundations of Ximénez and to invalidate the concessions given to the Mozarabs, when they only needed to correct the abuses that there were; and moreover all should agree to maintain that which I judge to be the

greatest and most solid glory of the nation, which Rome lacks, and maybe for this reason finds fault with it and envies it.[72]

Burriel's allusion to the efforts to suppress "concessions given to the Mozarabs" refers to the tax exemptions of the Toledan Mozarabs that were challenged in court in the early 1740s. In his mind, the special status of the Mozarabs in the eighteenth century was directly associated with the foundation of the Mozarabic chapel by Cisneros at the beginning of the sixteenth. As we will see in chapter 3, Burriel took an interest in the status of the living Mozarabic community, its history, and neo-Mozarabic rite as he studied the medieval manuscripts in the cathedral library.

In addition to a study of the medieval codices in the cathedral library of Toledo, Burriel proposed the publication of two new editions of the Mozarabic missal and breviary. One edition would be for parish use in Toledo and in the chapels of Salamanca, Palencia, and other places where the Mozarabic rite was still practiced—and "another chapel of this rite that the King, if only for the curiosity of natives and foreigners who come here, should establish in the Court."[73] This last statement clearly casts the neo-Mozarabic rite as a feature of Spanish national identity. Another edition, with an introduction and notes, would be intended principally for a scholarly audience.[74] Burriel was aware not only of the need to publish the Hispanic rite, but also of the great variety in the Roman rite as practiced in Spain. He pointed out that each church, military order, religious order, and monastery had its own particular liturgy, and that Toledo Cathedral's library had twenty-six different printed breviaries reflecting the uses of various churches, which he had begun to compare in the 1740s.[75]

Throughout the "Apuntamientos" Burriel underlined the need to revise the historiography of Spain, starting with new editions of primary sources. He proposed a collection of historical texts that would be organized by subject:

1. References to Spain in biblical and other ancient texts
2. Early historians of Spain
3. Royal annals (from the Middle Ages)
4. Arabic texts pertinent to Spain and unpublished Castilian manuscripts of Spanish history
5. Historical texts from the Habsburg period, starting with the reign of Charles V
6. Lives of famous Spaniards
7. Royal chronicles written in modern times
8. Histories of individual kingdoms, provinces, and cities[76]

In addition to the publication of chronicles and the like, he called for a new diplomatic corpus of royal charters.[77] Turning to literary sources he stated the need for a collected edition of works written by rulers of Spain, revisions of existing text collections, reprints of the works of various authors, and a *bibliotheca universal española*.[78]

Burriel's discussion of the state of history writing in Spain returns frequently to the field of church history; France provides a ready model for imitation, as well as an object of competition. He proposed a *Hispania Christiana* collection, which would include the history of every church in Spain, along the lines of the *Gallia Christiana*.[79] He also pointed out that, despite royal patronage for the project, the French had not yet finished writing their ecclesiastical history. Nevertheless Burriel cited the four-volume *Doctrina et disciplina ecclesiae* of Louis Dumesnil (1667–1727) as a model of the kind of ecclesiastical history that could be written for Spain, noting also the need to expand on the representation of Spanish antiquities in the fifteen-volume compilation *L'antiquité expliquée et représentée en figures* by the French Maurist Bernard de Montfaucon (1655–1741).[80] Montfaucon's works represent an increasing interest among his contemporaries in the use of images as historical sources.[81] The new importance that French historians accorded an accurate rendering of the visual record influenced the work of Burriel and other Spanish scholars, such as Flórez.

While enumerating the improvements to be made in scholarly publishing, Burriel also proposed the publication of new and revised tools for research and teaching, such as improved dictionaries, textbooks for Latin and Greek, and critical editions of the authors of Spain's Golden Age, as well as of Latin authors.[82] His plan for the *junta*'s work included compendia of history and geography for pedagogical use.[83] Burriel compared the renewal of learning that would be accomplished through these projects to the contributions of the early sixteenth century under the Catholic monarchs Ferdinand and Isabella; he saw in the reign of Ferdinand VI the same promise for scholarly achievement.[84]

Many of Burriel's goals as expressed in the "Apuntamientos" resemble those put forth a quarter-century earlier by French medievalists in the Académie Royale des Inscriptions et Belles-Lettres, such as Camille Falconnet (1671–1762). Moreover Falconnet's younger contemporary La Curne de Sainte-Palaye (1697–1781), the foremost eighteenth-century French scholar of the Middle Ages, wrote a plan for the Académie, hoping, like Burriel, to promote study of the national past.[85] Thus the program described in the "Apuntamientos" represents an approach that was common to French academicians and some Spanish scholars alike; its central aim was a survey of the textual patrimony of the absolutist state.[86] In the end, however, the "Apuntamientos" was a provisional outline for collaborative work that remained mostly unrealized, and as such it reveals more about Burriel's interests than his actual accomplishments.

The Commission on the Archives enabled Burriel to formulate more concrete projects based on the documents and manuscripts in the archives and library of Toledo Cathedral. Consequently his correspondence from his years in Toledo illuminate his extraordinary knowledge of Hispanic canon and civil law, church councils, the Visigothic Bible, the liturgy, and hagiography, and a concomitant abundance of ideas for new scholarly endeavors, including planned critical editions (see chapter 2).[87] Although most of these efforts did not result in publication, the unparalleled knowledge of manuscripts that Burriel acquired in Toledo was the foundation for his treatise on the history of handwriting in the Iberian peninsula, the *Paleografía Española*, which illustrates the central place of manuscripts in his historiography. For him the history of script was coterminous with the history of Spain.

The Paleografía Española

In his "Apuntamientos" Burriel observed that the foremost existing work on Spanish paleography, the *Bibliotheca Universal de la Polygraphia Española* of Cristóbal Rodríguez (published by the royal librarian Blas Nassarre in 1738), was too unwieldy, expensive, and specialized for most readers.[88] He proposed the publication of a smaller volume that would extend the coverage to include not only manuscripts, but also documents such as charters, diplomas, and bulls, as well as drawings of seals, numerals, and so on:

> The *Poligrafía española* [sic] of Don Cristóbal Rodríguez, which Don Blas Nasarre published with a most erudite preface, is a very costly volume, and [intended] for the few. One could write a smaller, handier, and less expensive book that would employ a better method and more coverage of Spanish subjects, in which there would be specimens of the script of old books and privileges, the characteristics of diplomas and bulls with their alphabets, interlinear glosses, drawings of seals, lead seals, codes, numbers, etc., in order to facilitate for all those who are curious the understanding of ancient writing, which inspires remarkable terror at first.[89]

The "smaller, handier, and less expensive book" appeared in 1755 as Burriel's *Paleografía Española*, published within a Spanish translation of the French encyclopedia *Le spectacle de la Nature* by Nöel-Antoine Pluche (1688–1761).[90] The translation, by a Jesuit professor of mathematics, Esteban Terreros y Pando, substituted a treatise on Spanish paleography for the treatment of French paleography that had formed part of the original encyclopedia.[91] *Paleografía Española* was also printed as a separate volume in 1758.[92] According to Michel Dubuis, both the earlier treatise by Rodríguez and Burriel's *Paleografía* may have been influenced by the prestige of Mabillon in Spain, although Burriel referred to Mabillon only to criticize his interpretation of the charter of Alfonso IX.[93] Certainly the *De re diplomatica* offered a model for a paleography treatise with engraved plates; a major difference between Mabillon's work and those of the Spanish paleographers was that the Maurist wrote in Latin, presumably for an audience composed principally of academicians, whereas Rodríguez and Burriel wrote in the vernacular for a broader readership of *curiosos*, and also included far fewer illustrations.

Although the *Paleografía Española* appeared under the name of Terreros y Pando, the consensus since the eighteenth century has been that Burriel was its author.[94] Indeed Burriel identified himself as the author in handwritten notes he added to the copies of the book that are still in Toledo Cathedral's library today. A note on the reverse of the first flyleaf in the 1755 edition identifies him as the author, despite the appearance of Terreros's name on the title page, stating that Burriel wrote the book at the request of Terreros and corrected the proofs himself.[95] A similarly placed annotation, also in Burriel's hand, appears in Toledo Cathedral's copy of the 1758 edition of the *Paleografía Española*.[96]

The text of the treatise itself is somewhat equivocal in this regard, but the conclusion, written in the voice of Terreros, acknowledges Burriel's help, stating that the Jesuit provided the treatise's eighteen plates, drawn by Palomares:

> To avoid in this example of *Paleographía Castellana* [*sic*] the failings that can be observed in others' works created along the same lines, I asked Father Andrés Marcos Burriel of the Company of Jesus, professor of Theology in the College of Toledo, at the time when, on the king's orders, he was preparing the inventory of the very ample archives and library of manuscripts in the holy Primatial Church of that city, to send me precise drawings of the letters used in Spain throughout the centuries, adapted to the method employed by M. Pluche in his treatise on French paleography. The said Father, generously condescending to my request, gave me drawings of the eighteen plates published in this treatise, executed by Don Francisco Xavier de Santiago y Palomares. . . . There can

be no doubt as to the faithfulness of the drawings, because Don Francisco Xavier's skill in this area is unequaled, and Father Burriel compared them extensively to the originals.[97]

No accurate reproductions of a text in Visigothic script had ever been printed before.[98] In Spain at this time most engravers reproduced paintings of the great masters. French engraving techniques had been introduced in the early eighteenth century, but there was no systematic method in Spain for teaching engraving until the founding of the Royal Academy of Fine Arts. Thereafter some engravers (along with other artists) received funding from the crown to study abroad so that they could return to Spain to apply their skills.[99] Because prints of documents and antiquities were rare in Spain, the quality of the reproductions in the *Paleografía* was unprecedented and unparalleled; as Palomares himself remarked in his own, later treatise on Visigothic paleography, "Even though they have some defects, they are the most accurate that have been engraved until now."[100]

Moreover, although its title suggests otherwise, the *Paleografía Española* is as much a history of language as of handwriting, as reflected in the title page of the 1758 edition: "*Paleografía Española*, which contains all the known ways of writing that have existed in Spain, since its origins and foundation to the present, in order to facilitate the inventory of Archives and the reading of manuscripts, and the possessions of each individual; along with a brief history of the common language of Castile, and further languages or dialects that are recognized as proper to these kingdoms."[101] Although the description of the book's contents in this title cast the linguistic material as accessory to the main subject of the treatise, Burriel's approach is in fact thoroughly philological, and it is so to a greater degree than in most studies of paleography published before or since. In this regard the *Paleografía Española* seems to conform to the emerging cultural nationalism that shaped discourse on language in Bourbon Spain, and yet Burriel's work blends antiquarianism and patriotism with historical linguistics in a spirit that is quite distinct from the publications of the Real Academia de la Lengua. Neither the *Diccionario de autoridades* (the dictionary of the Spanish language published by the Real Academia de la Lengua in 1726–39), for example, nor the *Ortografía de la lengua española* (as it was called in its first edition of 1741) addresses the history of the language; both are concerned with regulating contemporary usage.[102]

In spite of its uniqueness in these respects, Burriel's treatise was not the first to approach paleography through the lens of philology. Sarmiento had already used this methodology in his *Memorias para la historia de la poesía y poetas españoles* (written in 1741 but published only in 1775), and in a letter of January 1755 addressed to Terreros. The twentieth-century paleographer Agustín Millares Carlo argued that these two texts, which Sarmiento wrote before Burriel's treatise appeared, were the earliest attempts to account systematically for the history of Spanish handwriting. Nonetheless Sarmiento's work on this subject was probably unknown to Burriel.[103]

The first thirty-two pages of Burriel's *Paleografía* are devoted to the history of the various languages spoken in the Iberian peninsula from antiquity, beginning with the period before the arrival of the Romans and ending in the eighteenth century. Burriel presents his remarks on the Latin, Basque, Galician, Portuguese, Catalan, Valencian, and Arabic languages as a frame for the history of Castilian (which, as he notes, is called Spanish "by antonomasia"). Only after this survey does he turn to the presentation of the plates. His commentary on the illustrations is divided chronologically into sections, beginning with the fifteenth century and the reign of the Catholic monarchs Ferdinand and Isabella. It progresses in reverse chronological order, to conclude with Roman inscriptions and finally some examples of Kufic script. In the main text the description and transcription of each plate is prefaced by the heading "script and language" (*escritura y lenguage*) for each period.

In Burriel's account the "Spanish" (meaning Castilian) language and its handwriting form part of an imagined premodern nation that was more or less coterminous with the medieval kingdom of Castile. It is no coincidence that the first reference to the history of script in the *Paleografía Española* occurs in Burriel's account of the aftermath of the Christian capture of Toledo, when the Old Hispanic rite was suppressed and the liturgical books in Visigothic script were thereby rendered irrelevant. As this part of the *Paleografía* demonstrates the essence of Burriel's approach to history, it is worth quoting at length:

> The reconquest of Toledo, accomplished by Alfonso VI, son of Don Ferdinand the Great at the end of the eleventh century and in the year 1085, gave new and greater extension to the Castilian language, whose earliest youth, so to say, lasted almost two centuries, until reaching the age of discretion in the happy reign of Saint Ferdinand III and in that of his son Don Alfonso el Sabio. Toledo, then a most strongly fortified town, situated in the middle of our peninsula, has held in both secular and ecclesiastical senses the place of the heart in the body of the Spanish monarchy. Once Toledo was lost, Spain was lost, even though some provinces maintained their freedom. Once Toledo was recovered, Spain returned to its ancient liberty, although the Moors remained in control

of some of the principal provinces. This city, and the principal places in its kingdom, were populated by five classes of people: Mozarabs, Castilians, Franks, *moros de paz* [Muslims who lived in Christian territories under specific agreements or pacts], and Jews. Mozarabs were the Christians descended from the Visigoths of the Court, and the crown province, who almost four centuries earlier, the king and the army being lost, surrendered themselves to the Moors with agreements, and for all this time preserved the Christian religion, the ecclesiastical hierarchy, and their ancient Visigothic laws in the midst of Mahometan oppression. They considered themselves very noble, with reason, because those who at that time were Christians, apart from the excellence of their origins and the prerogative of the religion maintained despite everything, could not have a drop of Moorish blood, since according to the Koran, the children of a man or woman who married a Moor had to follow the Mahometan religion and thus lost their line of descent in the Christian population. The conqueror king honored these Mozarabs above all others, giving them the offices of mayor and bailiff, or the supreme government of the city and province, and ordering that the economy and criminal justice should be in the hands of the Mozarabic mayor and bailiff alone, according to the *Forum iudicum* or the Visigothic Laws. In their most ancient parishes he permitted them the use of the Visigothic ecclesiastical rite, which he had removed from all the cathedrals, monasteries, and parishes of his kingdom, introducing the Roman or Gallican rite, leaving them [the Mozarabs] (not without a pact to preserve their distinction and nobility) parishioners by blood, and not by territory, which was divided into the newly established parishes.[104]

Burriel's use of the term "reconquista" at the beginning of this passage is extremely unusual, if not unparalleled, in the eighteenth century. Early modern writers in Spain tended to characterize the Christian conquests of Muslim-ruled Iberia in the Middle Ages as part of a coherent centuries-long "restoration," implying continuity between the Visigothic kingdom and the Christian kingdoms after 711.[105] It is in this vein that Burriel describes the Mozarabs as descendents of the Visigoths. The term "reconquista," which casts the Christian conquests as a broader, coordinated campaign of reconquest, was coined by nineteenth-century nationalist historians of Spain.[106]

Toledo's unique position as the ecclesiastical and political center of Castile featured prominently in the complex negotiations for regional power that went on for centuries, continuing long after the city had come under Christian rule in 1085.[107] The city's history as a seat of cultural, religious, and political power dated back to the seventh century, when King Wamba (r. 672–80) decreed it the capital of the Visigothic kingdom.[108] The Twelfth Council of Toledo (681) made the city the primatial see, giving its bishops the authority to consecrate bishops in the other ecclesiastical provinces of the kingdom; the bishops also claimed the right to consecrate the Visigothic kings by anointing them.[109] For Burriel, evoking the status of Toledo as the capital of the Visigothic kingdom and church, the history of that city represented the history of the Spanish nation itself: "Once Toledo was lost, Spain was lost, even though some provinces maintained their freedom." The history of script and language in Toledo, as Burriel described it, fused with the vicissitudes of its liturgy.

Like most early modern accounts of the liturgical reform at the end of the eleventh century, Burriel's narrative redounds with a sense of foreign encroachment upon national traditions.[110] Always considering language change concurrently with changes in handwriting, Burriel goes on to recount the linguistic developments that emerged from the new social organization of Toledo, which he links to the abolition of the Visigothic script. The devastating results of Alfonso VI's decision to render Visigothic script obsolete are evoked in the concluding passage: the "Spaniards" (by which Burriel means natives of Castile) are left without access to Latin book culture, over which the Franks are given exclusive control. By "Franks" Burriel means "all the foreigners who came in great numbers for the holy war, or to settle, and then to do business."[111]

Of this mixture of nations in the city and kingdom of Toledo, which also passed to other provinces to some extent, resulted the extension of the Castilian language. The King, his courtiers, and the new inhabitants spoke the language of Old Castile, already quite separate from the Latin in which were still composed royal communiqués and most of the written communications among vassals. The Franks brought with them the language of their countries. The Mozarabs, Moors, and Jews spoke Arabic as their native language, although the Jews also maintained the use of Hebrew. The conqueror king, under the influence of the Franks, ordered, against all good policy, that the ancient Visigothic script should no longer be used, and that instead everything should be written in Gallican or French script.[112] Only the Mozarabic clerics of Toledo, strongly devoted to their ancient customs, and even to their clothing, preserved in their liturgical books the use of the Visigothic script, which perhaps for this reason was called Mozarabic in later writings, just as their Visigothic rite and law code were also called Mozarabic. With this edict of change they rendered useless all the books and Latin codices written in Visigothic script that existed in the kingdom, because in order to read them one needed, as is the case now, study and a particular taste. For Spaniards, the door to learning Latin and any ecclesiastical erudition in their Visigothic books was almost closed, and the Franks were left practically the sole proprietors of the Latin language, and consequently of the sciences and ecclesiastical positions, notaries and chanceries of the kings, and of the people, exercising the primary influence on the ecclesiastical and secular government of the kingdom. The only books to read in this French script were those few that the Franks either brought with them or copied here.[113]

Burriel argues that the profound cultural change wrought by the eradication of the Visigothic script led to the exclusion of the Mozarabs from power. Modern national affiliations shape this account, of course; the Mozarabs are the "Spaniards" who lose access to Latin letters, while the Franks take control with their "French" script. Not only books, but also language use distinguishes communities from one another, as the use of the emerging Castilian vernacular in parallel with Arabic and Latin signals the differing fortunes of the corresponding segments of the local population. In delineating the confluence of national identity, manuscript production, and ritual tradition, Burriel's cultural history of handwriting fuses social history with book production.

Although Burriel does not refer explicitly to music in his account of Toledo after 1085, elsewhere in the *Paleografía* he discusses musical notation. The Old Hispanic chant is the subject of a telling allusion in an annotation to his commentary on an illustration of a manuscript containing the *Septenario* of Alfonso X: "The music of the Visigoths, which we read about in the works of Saint Isidore, still remains in the books of the Mozarabic liturgy; however, the value of its notes is unknown to us."[114] The term "valor" could be interpreted as "value" in the modern sense of the length of a note, but in this context it seems to extend to the general meaning of the sign constituted by a neume. Burriel then describes the style of "Gallican" notation that appears in the chant books of the Roman liturgy that were introduced into Spain at the end of the eleventh century. Once again he distinguishes between the scripts used by the Mozarabs and those used by the Franks in Toledo, and extends the comparison to their musical notations. He notes that the contrast between the Frankish and Toledan notational styles accounted for the loss of the Mozarabic chant melodies; they still survive in the Toledan liturgical manuscripts, but only as silent music. This is a conclusion shared by most musicologists today, but it was not common knowledge in the eighteenth century because the Old Hispanic chant manuscripts preserved in the library of Toledo Cathedral went largely ignored; their graphic features, including their script and notation, were essentially unknown.

Burriel's decision to reproduce a tiny sample of Toledan notation in the *Paleografía* made the graphic appearance of this distinctive tradition accessible to a wide readership. It was the first time an Old Hispanic chant melody with its notation appeared in print.[115] The fourth part of plate 15 comprises two notated lines of chant, "Liberabo eum dicit dominus alleluia alleluia," a *psallendo* (psalm antiphon) for Vespers of Saint Stephen. Palomares copied the chant from the late eleventh-century manuscript Toledo, BC 35.7.[116] Not only did Burriel consider Toledo 35.7 the earliest of the Old Hispanic liturgical books in Toledo Cathedral, but he also attributed the music of its services to Ildefonsus of Toledo himself, which served to link the contents of the book to the Visigothic period.[117]

Because of the manuscript's great age, symbolic value, and curious appearance, already in 1752 Burriel had commissioned from Palomares a full-color parchment facsimile that was presented to Ferdinand VI in 1755, near the conclusion of the Commission on the Archives.[118] The facsimile is the most spectacular manifestation of a sustained fascination with musical notation on the part of both Burriel and Palomares.[119] Both men took the unusual step of discussing and illustrating musical notation in their respective treatises on paleography.[120] At the time it was unconventional to include early forms of music writing as a category of paleography because music was rarely taken into consideration in the study of historical documents. As the next chapter will show, the work of Burriel and Palomares in Toledo was remarkably innovative, exemplifying the best of the new historical method while standing out for its close attention to the music in the manuscripts.

Notes

The first epigraph is from a letter of Burriel to Gregorio Mayans y Siscar, April 11, 1750, in Mayans y Siscar, *Gregorio Mayans y Siscar, Epistolario II*, 462: "Es evidente y cierto que hoi sin mucho peligro no puede decirse desnudamente la verdad y vea Vmd. aquí lo que justifica a Flórez." The second epigraph is from a letter of Burriel from Toledo, December 30, 1754, to Don Pedro de Castro, in Burriel, *Cartas eruditas y críticas*, 272: "El conjunto de todas estas venerables memorias de nuestra antiguedad, sería sin duda muy glorioso a nuestra nacion: formaria una prueba invencible de esta tradicion de la fé en España en todos los puntos del dogma, desde los primeros siglos de la Iglesia, y sería al mismo tiempo un convencimiento cronologico de la suprema autoridad de la Iglesia Romana, y silla Apostólica, reconocida sin interrupcion en España desde las primeras luces Evangelicas, hasta el dia de hoy."

1. Kagan, *Clio and the Crown*, 251–89. I am grateful to Simon Doubleday for bringing this book to my attention.

2. On the canonization of Ferdinand III see Wunder, "The Search."

3. Burriel undertook the compilation of relevant texts but did not finish the biography, which was completed later by the editor. See Burriel, *Memorias para la vida del santo rey Don Fernando III*.

4. For a useful, brief summary of the Pauline and Jacobine traditions in historiography, see Maldonado, "*Angelorum Participes*," at 151–53.

5. Mestre Sanchís, "Nueva dinastía," 555–56.

6. See Kagan, *Clio and the Crown*, 265–62; Olds, "'The False Chronicles.'" The foundational study of the false chronicles is Godoy Alcántara, *Historia crítica*.

7. Although the Spanish Enlightenment is often identified with the reign of Charles III (1759–88), historians increasingly locate the beginnings of later eighteenth-century trends in the reigns of the first two Spanish Bourbons. See Sánchez Blanco, *El absolutismo*; Sánchez Blanco, *La mentalidad ilustrada*, 331–33.

8. See the review article by Philip Deacon, "Early Enlightenment and the Spanish World," 129–40; Hill, *Sceptres and Sciences*; Pérez Magallón, *Construyendo la modernidad*.

9. Israel, *Radical Enlightenment*, 528–32.

10. For a recent overview of the intellectual history of the French Enlightenment, see Israel, *Enlightenment Contested*, 699–862.

11. To be sure the Enlightenment was nowhere a unified or homogeneous movement. As Jeffrey Burson has recently pointed out, the notion of a consistent dichotomy opposing *philosophes* to representatives of the Counter-Enlightenment is a scholarly construct; it does not adequately reflect the fragmentation and diversity that characterized the French "republic of letters" in the first half of the eighteenth century ("Towards a New Comparative History," 173–87).

12. Kagan, *Clio and the Crown*, 262–65.

13. The *Teatro crítico universal* was published in nine volumes in 1726–40.

14. Feijoo, *Teatro crítico universal*, book 4 (1730), texto tomado de la edición de Madrid 1775, 4:368: "No se puede dudar razonablemente después de tantos y tan doctos escritos como la han comprobado."

15. Feijoo, *Teatro crítico universal*, 4:369: "Si para dar prudente asenso a un milagro no basta el testimonio de la tradición, será preciso condenar como fabulosos casi todos cuantos se hallan escritos en las Historias Eclesiásticas."

16. Feijoo, *Teatro crítico universal*, 4:380–83.

17. On the involvement of clergy in the French Enlightenment see Burson, "The Crystallization," 955–1002.

18. Mestre Sanchís, *La ilustración española*, 32.

19. Antonio, *Censura de historias fabulosas*.

20. Hitchcock, "Mozarabs and Moriscos," 175–79, argues that one of the false chronicles was concocted by Jerónimo Román de la Higuera y Lupián to enhance the status of the Toledan Mozarabs, whose numbers diminished greatly in the sixteenth century. See, most recently, García-Arenal and Rodríguez Mediano, "Jerónimo Román de la Higuera"; Grieve, *The Eve of Spain*, 161–63. I am grateful to Patricia Grieve for kindly giving me a copy of her book.

21. For the history of the tablets, see Harris, *From Muslim to Christian Granada*.

22. Mestre Sanchís, *La ilustración española*, 34.

23. On Mayans, among the many studies by Mestre, see in particular *Historia, fueros y actitudes políticas*.

24. Letter of Mayans to Burriel, 7 February 1750, in *Mayans y Burriel*, 456–57.

25. Nevertheless the vaunted independence of Enlightenment philosophers in northern Europe may have been a convenient fiction invented to veil their actual reliance on patronage; see in particular Andrew, *Patrons of Enlightenment*.

26. Cañizares-Esguerra, *How to Write the History of the New World*, 142.

27. Mabillon, *De re diplomatica*.

28. For a recent account of Mabillon's life and works, see Lenain, *Histoire Littéraire*, 480–544.

29. Mestre Sanchís, "Historia crítica," 111–32; Dubuis, "Erudition et piété," especially 136–42; Dubuis, "Mabillon," 185–202.

30. Mabillon, *De re diplomatica*, 432 and table 45.

31. Cuesta Gutierrez, "Jesuitas confesores de reyes," 129–75.

32. Álvarez Barrientos, *Los hombres de letras*, 255–61.

33. Mestre Sanchís, "Clausura," 349–53.

34. Valero, "Razón y nación."

35. Mestre Sanchís, *La ilustración española*, 25–33; Stiffoni, "Alcune tematiche del Settecento," 19–23.

36. Mestre Sanchís, "Nueva dinastía," 550.

37. Mestre Sanchís, "Nueva dinastía," 554.

38. Mestre Sanchís, "Nueva dinastía," 557.

39. On Sarmiento's life and works, see the introduction to Sarmiento, *Sistema de adornos*, 15–30.

40. Cioffi, "Corrado Giaquinto at the Spanish Court," xli.

41. Sancho, "Francisco Sabatini," 146. I am grateful to Robin Thomas for referring me to this publication.

42. Sarmiento, *Sistema de adornos*, 38. On Sarmiento as a historian, see in particular Muniain Ederra, *El programa escultórico*, 209–26, 245–64.

43. Sarmiento, *Sistema de adornos*, 159–61; see also Cioffi, "Corrado Giaquinto at the Spanish Court," 95.

44. On this theme, see Bonet Correa, "Introducción," 1–8.

45. Cioffi, "Corrado Giaquinto at the Spanish Court," 281.

46. Hermengild converted from Arianism to Catholicism in about 582 and was killed in 585; although the circumstances of his death remain unclear, he was later venerated as a saint because Gregory the Great described him as a martyr. See Collins, *Visigothic Spain*, 57–59.

47. Sarmiento, *Sistema de adornos*, 427–29.

48. Porcel, "Canción Heroica," lines 37–50, in Polt, *Poesía*, 106.

49. Álvarez Barrientos, "Monarquía y 'Nación Española,'" 191–213.

50. For a discussion that frames the nationalist discourse on the Castilian language in a wider context of myth making, see Kamen, *Imagining Spain*, 150–71 ("The Myth of a Universal Language").

51. Sarmiento, *Obras posthumas*, 7–8.

52. These were the works that Burriel cited in his "Apuntamentios" of 1749 as fitting models for future publications on church history in Spain.

53. Flórez himself wrote the first twenty-nine volumes. For an introduction to the work of Flórez, see Campos y Fernández de Sevilla, "Estudio preliminar," 1:ix–lx.

54. Flórez, *España Sagrada*, 4:v–vi.

55. Flórez, *España Sagrada*, 4:ix–xii.

56. Flórez, *España Sagrada*, 5:417–506.

57. Mestre Sanchís, "Clausura," 355.

58. Flórez, "Respondese a la nueva obra del Maestro Mamachi," in *España Sagrada*, 6: unpaginated prefatory matter.

59. Van Kley, "Piety and Politics," 124.

60. Van Kley, "Piety and Politics," 274.

61. For an analysis of this preface, see Echánove Tuero, *La preparación intelectual*, 102–8.

62. Flórez, *España Sagrada*, 3: unpaginated prefatory matter: "Plantada en ella, con anticipacion a casi todas las Naciones, la semilla del Evangelio por los Apostoles mismos."

63. The "Apuntamientos" were edited by Alfonso Echánove Tuero, originally as "Apuntamientos de algunas ideas para fomentar las letras del P. Andrés Burriel," *Hispania Sacra* (20) 1967: 363– 37, reprinted as *La preparación intelectual*, 254–327. On the practical organization of the committee (*junta*), its membership, and the financing of its research and publications see especially 254–67.

64. Mestre Sanchís, *Despotismo*, 102–3.

65. Mestre Sanchís, *La ilustración española*, 32.

66. Mestre Sanchís, in *Humanistas*, 127–29, states that by this time close collaboration between the government and the Jesuits had already created considerable anti-Jesuit sentiment, and that the fate of Burriel and the Royal Commission on the Archives was symptomatic of the embattled intellectual climate that permeated Spain beginning in 1754.

67. On Burriel's "Apuntamientos" in the context of other projects for cultural renewal during this period, see Àlvarez Barrientos, *Los hombres de letras*, 268–71.

68. Burriel, "Apuntamientos," in Echánove Tuero, *La preparación intelectual*, 267.

69. Burriel, "Apuntamientos," in Echánove Tuero, *La preparación intelectual*, 269: "Una ilustración cumplida del oficio antiquísimo español, llamado mozárabe, toledano, isidoriano, etc. sobre el cual escribieron Pisa, Robles, Villegas, Aguirre, y modernamente un tomo en fol. el P. Pinio (que lo insertó en el tomo 6.º de julio), Cayetano Cenni, clérigo romano, cruel enemigo, aunque disimulado, de la nación espanōla que le ha dado sus rentas con que vive: Don Alfonso Clemente hizo poco ha en Roma una colleción de todos los autores en dos tomos fol., donde se imprimió lo que de cierto código de Verona imprimió Tomassi, Blanchini, etc.; y en fin, el P. Flórez en su tomo 3º hizo una disertación que tiene muchas cosas buenas. De todo esto se ha de ayudar la Junta; pero es mucho más ilustre y grande el trabajo de mi idea. Deben, pues, reconocerse los mismos breviarios y misales muzárabes manuscritos de Toledo, que imprimió el card. Ximénez, y que se usan en la capilla de la catedral y seis parroquias muzárabes de Toledo. Debe mirarse bien lo que Blanchini, Tomassi, y otros italianos han escrito sobre el códice de Verona en lo que se interesan nuestras más venerables antigüedades como la venida de Santiago, la invención de su cuerpo, antigüedad de los himnos, y otras cosas del oficio sobre los que ellos han escrito con gran bellaquería."

70. Cenni, *De antiquitate ecclesiae Hispaniae*, 2:354.

71. Flórez, *España Sagrada*, 3:345–46.

72. Burriel, "Apuntamientos," in Echánove Tuero, *La preparación intelectual*, 270: "La gloria que de haber guardado este sagrado depósito resulta a España, y la utilidad que tendrá en su ilustración bien se da a conocer. Bien conoció esto la gran cabeza del cardenal Ximénez, que tanto esfuerzo puso en conservarle: y por aquél se verá la infelicidad antecedente de nro. siglo, que en Toledo, donde he vivido siete años se han hecho mil esfuerzos para acabar, si se pudiera, con las fundaciones de Ximénez, y hacer vanas la concesiones hechas a los mozárabes, cuando sólo se debiera tratar de corregir los abusos que haya; y en lo demás concurrir todos a mantener ésta que juzgo ser la mayor y más sólida gloria de la nación, que Roma no tiene, y quizá por eso la muerde y la envidia."

73. Burriel, "Apuntamientos," in Echánove Tuero, *La preparación intelectual*, 270–71.

74. Burriel, "Apuntamientos," in Echánove Tuero, *La preparación intelectual*, 271.

75. Burriel, "Apuntamientos," in Echánove Tuero, *La preparación intelectual*, 272.

76. Burriel, "Apuntamientos," in Echánove Tuero, *La preparación intelectual*, 276–83.

77. Burriel, "Apuntamientos," in Echánove Tuero, *La preparación intelectual*, 283–84.

78. Burriel, "Apuntamientos," in Echánove Tuero, *La preparación intelectual*, 287–97.

79. Burriel, "Apuntamientos," in Echánove Tuero, *La preparación intelectual*, 303.

80. Burriel, "Apuntamientos," in Echánove Tuero, *La preparación intelectual*, 307. The first volume was published in 1719; a five-volume supplement followed the initial ten-volume publication. For a recent description of this work, see Lenain, *Histoire Littéraire*, 2:501–3.

81. Haskell, *History and Its Images*, 131–32. I am grateful to Catherine Whistler for referring me to this book.

82. Haskell, *History and Its Images*, 316–27.

83. Haskell, *History and Its Images*, 267. On the historical context for the *Corpus Diplomaticum*, see Millares Carlo, "El siglo XVIII español."

84. Burriel, "Apuntamientos," in Echánove Tuero, *La preparación intelectual*, 268.

85. See Gossman, *Medievalism*, 163–69. I am grateful to Frederic Clark for referring me to Gossman's study of Sainte-Palaye.

86. For an introduction to the history of the Maurist and the Académie des Inscriptions, see Barret-Kriegel, *Les Académies de l'histoire*.

87. Alcaraz Gómez, *Jesuitas y Reformismo*, 585.

88. On this treatise, see, most recently, García Cuadrado and Montalbán Jiménez, "Bibliotheca Universal," 113–43.

89. Burriel, "Apuntamientos," in Echánove Tuero, *La preparación intelectual*, 321–22: "La Poligrafía española de D. Cristóbal Rodríguez, que sacó a luz D. Blas Nasarre con una eruditísima prefacción, es tomo costosísimo y para pocos. Podrá hacerse otro tomo más pequeño y manual, y menos costoso, con mejor método y más extensión de cosas de España, en donde se den las muestras de las letras de los libros y Privilegios antiguos, los caracteres de Diplomas y Bulas con sus alfabetos, glosas interlineales, dibujos de sellos, plomos, cifras, números, etc., para que se facilite a todos los curiosos la inteligencia de las letras antiguas que al principio infunde notable horror."

90. *Le spectacle de la nature* was first published in eight volumes in Paris in 1732–50. On its many editions and translations, see Trinkle, "Noël-Antoine Pluche's *Le Spectacle de la nature*," 93–134. Jonathan Israel calls it "one of the greatest literary sensations of the age" and describes it as the high point of "a French physico-theological trend" (*Enlightenment Contested*, 743).

91. *Espectáculo de la Naturaleza*, 201–360.

92. Burriel, *Paleografía Española*. On Burriel's treatise in the context of other eighteenth-century works on Spanish paleography, see Millares Carlo, *Tratado de Paleografía Española*, 1:311–14.

93. Dubuis, "La réflexion historiographique," 201; Dubuis, "Erudition et piété," 129.

94. Already in the list of Burriel's books and papers prepared for the court after his death by Juan de Santander, "Memoria de los libros y papeles manuscritos que se hallaban en el aposento del padre Andrés Marcos Burriel de la Compañia de Jesús, además de los correpondientes a la comisión que tuvo en Toledo de Real Orden" (Madrid, August 1, 1762), are included thirty-four copies of plates from the "*Paleografía* que publicó el Padre Burriel," implying that he was already known to be the author of the treatise. See Galende Díaz, "Repertorio bibliográfico del Padre Burriel," 263, number 30.

95. Toledo, BC 82-21: "I wrote this treatise in 1755 at the request of Padre Esteban de Terreros y Pando, who wished to insert it in Tome 13 of his translation of the Spectacle de la Nature. . . . In this first printing, although I wrote in the name of another, it was all mine, and I even corrected the proofs, so that I am responsible for all the errors of form and substance that the work might contain." ("Este discurso escribí en 1755, â ruego del P. Esteban de Terreros, y Pando, que quiso insertarle en el Tomo XIII de su traducción del *Espectáculo de la Natureleza* en lugar de otro tal, que tiene el original sobre la *Paleographia Francesa*. . . . En esta impresion primera, aunque hablé en nombre ageno, todo fuè mio, porque cuidè tambien de la coreccion de las pruebas de Imprenta. Así soi responsable de los yerros formales, y materiales, que se hallaren. Andres Marcos Burriel. [signature].") See also Octavio de Toledo, *Catálogo*, 93–94. An unpublished letter from Burriel to Terreros y Pando confirms that Burriel corrected proofs and worked with Terreros to distribute the single-volume publication (Madrid, RAH 9-3535/4).

96. Toledo, BC, 82-22: "In this second printing, a few things were changed without my knowledge, and many separate copies were produced." ("En esta segunda impresión se mudaron algunas pocas cosas sin noticia mia, y se tiraron muchos exemplares sueltos. [Burriel's signature]").

97. Burriel, *Paleografía Española*, 159–60: "Para evitar en este especimen de *Paleographía Castellana* [*sic*] las faltas, que se advierten en las Obras de otros, nacidas de estos principios, rogué al P. Andrés Marcos Burriel, de la Compañia de Jesus, Maestro de Prima de Theología en el Colegio de Toledo, à tiempo que de orden del Rey nuestro Señor estaba reconociendo los copiosisimos Archivos, y Librería de manuscritos de la santa Iglesia Primada de aquella Ciudad, que me embiáse dibujos puntuales de las letras usadas en España en todos tiempos, acomodados al método, empleado por M. Pluche en su discurso sobre la Paleographía Francesa. Dicho Padre, condescendiendo francamente á mi ruego, me remitió los diseños de las diez y ocho làminas, colocadas en este Discurso, formados por Don Francisco Xavier de Santiago y Palomares. . . . De la fidelidad de los dibujos no se puede dudar: porque la destreza de dicho Don Francisco Xaviér en esta materia es sin igual, y dicho P. Burriel los cotejó prolijamente con los originales."

98. One plate showing the script appeared in the 1606 edition of Aldrete, *Del origen y principio de la lengua castellana ò romance que oi se usa en España* (facsimile ed., 1:252). Mabillon did not include the Visigothic script in his *De re diplomatica* (1681).

99. Carrete Parrondo, "El grabado en el siglo XVIII," 395–96, 439; Zanardi, "Preservation and Promotion," 305. Another sign of the increased interest in engraving

techniques around midcentury was the publication of the first Spanish-language manual on engraving: De Rueda, *Instrucción para grabar en cobre*.

100. Palomares, *Polygraphia Gothico-Española* in Madrid, RAH 9/4752, 42: "Y aunque tienen algunos defectos son las mas exactas que se han gravado hasta nuestro tiempo."

101. *Paleografía Española, que contiene todos los modos conocidos, que ha habido de escribir en España, desde su principio y fundacion, haste el presente, á fin de facilitar el registro de los Archivos, y lectura de los manuscritos, y pertenencias de cada particular; juntamente con una historia sucinta del idioma comun de Castilla, y demás lenguas, ó dialectos, que se conocen como proprios en estos Reynos. Paleografía Española* (Madrid: Joachin Ibarra, 1758), title page.

102. I am grateful to Michael Agnew for pointing this out to me.

103. Millares Carlo, *Tratado de Paleografía Española*, 1:313–14.

104. Burriel, *Paleografía Española*, 16–18: "Pero la reconquista de Toledo, hecha por Don Alonso VI, hijo de Don Fernando Magno a fines del Siglo XI y año 1085 diò nueva y mayor extension à la Lengua Castellana, cuya primera juventud, por decirlo asi, durò casi dos Siglos, hasta entrar en edad de discrecion en el feliz Reynado de San Fernando III. Y en el de su hijo Don Alonso el Sabio. Toledo, Plaza entonces fortissima, situada en medio de nuestra Peninsula, ha tenido en ambas lineas Secular, y Eclesiastica las veces de corazon en el cuerpo de la Monarquia Española. Perdida Toledo, se perdiò España, aunque se conservase la libertad en algunas Provincias. Recobrada Toledo, bolvió España à su antigua libertad, aunque quedasen dueños de algunas Provincias principales los Moros. Esta Ciudad, y los Lugares mayores de su Reynado, quedaron poblados de cinco clases de gentes: Muzarabes, Castellanos, Francos, Moros de paz, y Judios. *Muzarabes* eran los Christianos descendientes de los Godos de la Corte, y Provincia Principe, que quasi quatro siglos antes, perdido el Rey, y el Exercito se entragaron à los Moros por pactos, y por todo este tiempo conservaron la Religion Christiana, la Gerarquía Eclesiastica, y sus antiguas Leyes Godas en medio de la opression Mahometana. Tenianse con razon por muy nobles, por que los que entonces eran Christianos, fuera de la excelencia de su origen, y prerogativa de la Religion, conservada à toda prueba, no podían tener una gota de sangre Mora, pues segun el Alcorán, los hijos del que, ò la que casaba con Moro, ò Mora, debía seguir la Religion Mahometana; y asi su descendencia perecia para el Pueblo de los Christianos. A estos Muzarabes honrò el Rey Conquistador sobre todos los demás, confiandoles la Alcaldia, y Alguacilato, ò supremo Gobierno de la Ciudad, y Provincia, mandando, que la economía, y justicia criminal estuviesse en manos de solo el Alcalde, y Alguacil Muzarabes, segun el *Forum Judicum*, ò Leyes Godas. Permitioles en sus antiquissimas Parroquias el uso del rito Eclesiastico Godo, que havia abrogado en todas las Cathedrales, Monasterios, y Parroquias de su Reyno, introduciendo el Romano, ò Galico, quedando ellos no sin acuerdo, para conservar su distincion, y nobleza, Feligreses por razon de sangre, y no por territorio, que se repartiò à las Parroquias nuevamente eregidas."

105. On the framing of this idea in the central Middle Ages, see Deswarte, *De la destruction à la restauration*.

106. Ríos Saloma, "De la Restauración a la Reconquista," 379–414; Ríos Saloma, *La Reconquista*. I am grateful to the author for sharing his doctoral dissertation with me before its publication as a book.

107. Linehan, "El concepto de capital," 21–27; Linehan, "The Toledo Forgeries," 642–74.

108. Stocking, *Bishops*, 176. On the development of Toledo as a capital in the Visigothic period, see Martin, *La géographie*, 205–74.

109. Collins, *Early Medieval Spain*, 70–71.

110. Palomares took up this idea later on in the *Polygraphia Gothico-Española* (see chapter 5), in which he quoted extensively from this section of Burriel's *Paleografía* (pp. 16–20).

111. Burriel, *Paleografía*, 18: "En el nombre de *Francos* se comprehendían todos los Estrangeros, que vinieron en gran numero a la guerra santa, o a poblar, y comerciar, despues de ella."

112. I translate Burriel's *galicano* as "Gallican," but he might have meant something closer in meaning to the modern term "Gallic."

113. Burriel, *Paleografía*, 19–20: "De esta mezcla de gentes en la Ciudad, y Reyno de Toledo, que tambien alcanzaba en parte à las demas Provincias, resultó la extension de la lengua Castellana. El Rey, sus Cortesanos, y los nuevos Pobladores hablaban la lengua de Castilla la vieja, muy separada ya de la Latina, en que todavia se formaban los despachos Reales, y gran parte de la Escrituras entre los Vasallos. Los Francos trageron consigo la lengua de sus Paises. Los Muzarabes, Moros, y Judios hablaban el Arabe como lengua nativa, aunque los Judios tambien conservaban el uso de la Hebréa. El Rey Conquistador, à influjo de los Francos, mandó, contra toda buena politica, que no se usase mas de la antiqua letra Gothica, y que en su lugar se escribiesse todo en letra Galicana, ò Francesca. Solo los Clerigos Muzarabes de Toledo, fuertemente asidos [*sic*] à sus antiguas costumbres, y aun al modo de vestir conservaron en sus Libros Liturgicos el uso de la letra Gothico, que acaso por esta razon se appelidó Muzarabe en escrituras posteriores, como tambien se llamò Muzarabe su Rito, y su Fuero Godos. Con este Decreto de mudanza quedaron in-utiles todos los Libros, y Codigos Latinos escritos en letra Gothica, que havia en el Reyno; por que para leerlos era, como ahora es, necesario estudio y gusto particular. A los Espa-ñoles quedò casi cerrada la puerta para aprender el latin, y alguna erudicion Eclesiastica en sus libros Gothicos, y los Francos quedaron casi unicos dueños de la Lengua Latina, y por consiguiente de las ciencias y empleos Eclesiasticos, de las Notarias y Escribanias de los Reyes, y de los Pueblos, y con el primer influxo en el Gobierno Eclesiastico, y secular del Reyno. En esta letra francesa solo havia que leer aquellos pocos libros, que o trageron, o copiaron acà los Francos."

114. Burriel, *Paleografía*, 81: "La Musica de los Godos, cuya noticia leemos en San Isidoro, dura aún en los Libros del Oficio Muzárabe; pero todavia nos es desconocido el valor de sus notas."

115. There are no Iberian examples among the many engravings of chant notation in Gerbert, *De Cantu et Musica Sacra*. I am grateful to Joseph Dyer for referring me to the facsimile reprint.

116. Toledo, BC 35.7, fol. 73r.

117. Burriel, *Paleografía Española*, 117.

118. This facsimile is the subject of chapter 3.

119. The only other example of musical notation to appear in the *Paleografía Española* was the beginning of the prologue to the *Cantigas de Santa María*, on which see chapter 4.

120. On the treatment of neumes in Palomares's treatise, see chapter 5.

2 | The Commission on the Archives in Toledo Cathedral

Because the Commission on the Archives was formed to serve two intertwined and overarching purposes—the enhancement of Bourbon sovereignty and the strengthening of the national church—Burriel's work in Toledo was, at least in theory, subject to the wishes of his patrons in the government. In practice, however, he expanded the scope of the project to embrace a far wider range of sources than archival documents alone. A royal order of September 17, 1750 instructed the Commission to carry out a "reconnaissance" (*reconocimiento*), or survey, of the archives of Toledo. The letter of introduction from Carvajal to the cathedral chapter asked the canons to facilitate the Commission's work in the archives and, ideally, to appoint one of the canons to assist in the consultation and transcription of the documents most pertinent to a new ecclesiastical history of Spain.[1] On October 5 the canons agreed to give full access to the collection, on the condition that a member of the chapter would supervise them at all times.[2] The decision to grant access was not a formality; few outside the cathedral chapter were admitted.[3] The canons decided that Juan Antonio de las Infantas, the *canónigo doctoral*, should assist the Commission.[4] He had been a friend of Burriel's since Burriel taught at the Jesuit College in Toledo, and he became an ally to the Jesuit in his dealings with the chapter.[5] De las Infantas had already contributed to another important project of Spanish church history, the *España Sagrada*, by supplying Flórez with transcriptions of documents in Toledo Cathedral's archives.[6]

In October 1750 Burriel began his work in collaboration with Francisco Pérez Bayer (1699–1781), an eminent philologist and jurist at the University of Salamanca. Their team reported directly to Francisco de Rávago. The commissioners in Barcelona, Cordoba, Madrid, Cuenca, Valencia, Oviedo, Zaragoza, and Girona were under the authority of the secretary of state, José de Carvajal y Lancaster, although they were expected to submit their findings to Burriel.[7] Presumably the pragmatic ministers of Ferdinand VI considered this centralized system more useful than the broader initiative proposed in 1743 by Martín Sarmiento, who had simply suggested (in an open letter to the royal librarian, Juan de Iriarte) that the government order the cathedrals, monasteries, city governments, and aristocracy to print the documents in their archives.[8]

The Commission began by transcribing and copying the texts of the Visigothic church councils. Less than a year later Burriel and Pérez Bayer had already copied the requisite archival documents and had moved on to the manuscripts in the cathedral library, according to the report presented by de las Infantas to the chapter on September 1, 1751. As a precaution the chapter asked Burriel and Pérez Bayer to compile and sign an inventory of every charter and document they had copied. The two canons who assisted them, de las Infantas and the *penitenciario* Joseph Salcedo, also had to sign the inventory. The conclusion of the record for that meeting in September 1751 seems to indicate uncertainty about the nature of the copies being made: "For this reason we once again emphasized that it was important for everything copied from the archive—and whatever else seems advisable—to be copied in ordinary modern script, taking into account the facility with which it can now be done for the copies that [Burriel and Pérez Bayer] have made with great care and accuracy."[9] Thus the chapter expressed its preference for transcriptions of documents over copies that might imitate the appearance of the originals. The canons may well have thought that the appearance of the documents was as important a part of their juridical authority and historical importance as their texts. Subsequent events suggest that the chapter also took this view of the medieval manuscripts in the cathedral library, fearing that exact copies circulating outside the Cathedral would lessen the validity of the originals preserved in the library. Nevertheless, regardless of any instructions the canons may have given to Burriel, the Commission continued to produce not only transcriptions and copies using modern script, but also imitations of medieval scripts and various combinations of the two. De las Infantas helped them with this work. In 1752, for instance, he corrected one of the transcriptions as Burriel read aloud from the original manuscript.[10]

By late March 1754 the canons had become seriously concerned: they thought that Burriel and his collaborators were transcribing and copying the entire contents of the library. The capitular acts note that those canons who were supposed to have been supervising the Commission's work had stopped going to the archives in the cold weather, leaving the members of the Commission alone. The canons apparently feared that the precision of the copies would lead to confusion between copies and originals, potentially facilitating forgery and theft and generally lessening the chapter's sense of control over its holdings. As we have seen, the canons had already expressed such reservations among themselves in 1751. If Burriel was aware of their anxiety, he seems not to have anticipated its consequences. On March 23, 1754, the chapter voted unanimously to take away his key to the archive so that he could not work there unsupervised.[11]

This decision signals the inherent tension between the canons' conservative pragmatism and the antiquarian fervor that fueled the work of Burriel and Palomares. Years earlier, in his "Apuntamientos de algunas ideas para fomentar las letras" of 1749, Burriel had ridiculed the notion that familiarity with the appearance of historical scripts could encourage forgeries and falsifications of medieval documents, referring to the fears unleashed by the publication of the *Bibliotheca Universal de la Polygraphia Española* of Cristóbal Rodríguez by the royal librarian Blas Nassarre.[12] The canons of Toledo, however, saw the copies as diminishing their authority over the documents and manuscripts in their care. Their view of the situation seems to have been justified; the pursuit of evidence that had led to the founding of the Commission could generate pressure on the chapter and even threats of lawsuits. In March and April 1754 the canons dealt with a petition from the Jesuit Pedro Ignacio Altamirano, Procurator General of the Indies, for historical documents needed in court cases on royal privileges and rights to tithes in the province of Chile. In the meeting of March 23 this request was mentioned immediately before the decision to limit Burriel's access; the canons noted that Burriel, a member of the same order as Altamirano, must already have copied the relevant privileges.[13] A month after the canons received the petition Altamirano wrote again, maintaining that there was no reason to withhold the copies of the pertinent papal bulls and royal privileges, and adding that the government could demand the documents in court.[14] Burriel's work in Toledo became increasingly hampered by his dependence on the members of the cathedral chapter for access to the cathedral archives and library. In his correspondence from the winter of 1754–55 he lamented the canons' reluctance to open the archives for him and to remain there to supervise him in cold weather. Finally, with the advent of warmer weather, Burriel managed to explain his project to the canons in terms that promised to glorify the role of the primatial see in the history of Spain. In their meeting of June 10, 1754, the canons resolved to allow him to resume his work unhindered, establishing a regular rotation of their members to monitor him.[15] Burriel's labors in Toledo Cathedral continued for another two years.[16]

The work of the Commission under Burriel was groundbreaking in several ways. Routine processes of transcription and description were combined with more unusual modes of copying and analysis. For the first time in the modern history of Toledo's medieval manuscripts (and perhaps for the first time in Spain), medieval chant notation was carefully studied and copied. In this chapter I reconstruct the methods of study that the members of the Commission used in Toledo, based on Burriel's unpublished papers now in Madrid's National Library. Although much of this material was catalogued by José Janini in the 1970s, until now the whole corpus has never been analyzed in parallel with Palomares's career, nor situated in its historical context. As Janini and Ramón Gonzálvez have pointed out, if Burriel's unpublished observations had made available, they would have advanced the discipline of liturgical studies considerably.

Burriel and the Roman Rite

In August 1752 Pérez Bayer obtained a canonry in Barcelona, leaving Burriel to direct the Commission alone in Toledo.[17] Up to that time Burriel had been working primarily on manuscripts of liturgy, canon law, and patristics, but he came to focus increasingly on medieval liturgy. In his letter of December 1752 to Rávago he described the numerous categories of books he had copied or planned to have copied. These included not only the eleven manuscripts in Visigothic script, but also books of the Roman rite: martyrologies, office lectionaries, passionaries, breviaries, antiphoners, and missals. He intended to use the broad scope of source materials described in the letter as a basis for comparison with the manuscripts of the Old Hispanic rite. Because the manuscripts had never been studied in detail, most scholars relied on early-modern editions for the texts of the Mozarabic liturgy.[18] Burriel was the first to study the Toledan traditions on the basis of the manuscripts and to differentiate between the stages represented by the early medieval rite, the Roman rite as adapted for use in Spain, and the diocesan uses of the Iberian peninsula in the late Middle Ages.

The letter to Rávago outlines Burriel's periodization of the Roman liturgy in the Iberian kingdoms, a trajectory he divided into two stages. The first stage corresponded to the period from the introduction of the Roman rite in the late eleventh century to the time of the Catholic kings; the second stage ended with the Council of Trent. Burriel does not specify a date range, but presumably he considered the time of the Catholic kings to begin in 1474, when Ferdinand V and Isabella of Castile began their joint reign of Castile and León. Liturgical reform was enacted after the Council of Trent, which met in twenty-five sessions from 1545 to 1563, by a scholarly commission established under Pope Pius V. The commission prepared new editions of the Roman breviary (1568) and missal (1570) that were to be used in place of local diocesan liturgies and liturgies of religious orders that could not claim a tradition of at least two hundred years. These editions, however, usually called "Tridentine" because they originated after the council, did not immediately replace diocesan usages. For most of the sixteenth century variety reigned in the printed liturgical books of Spanish dioceses.

Burriel acknowledged the importance of the Roman rite manuscripts in his first stage of liturgical history but admitted that he did not have sufficient time to do justice to them because his research in Toledo was focused on the Old Hispanic rite. He wrote at length, however, on the later history of the Roman rite in Spain, emphasizing particularly the diversity of uses he found in the printed diocesan breviaries of the sixteenth century. He associated the composition of these books with the "renewal of letters since the happy reign of Lord Ferdinand and Lady Isabella,"[19] a reference to Iberian humanist scholarship in the late fifteenth century and early sixteenth. In his letter he expressed his intention to have the amanuenses copy numerous texts and excerpts of texts from the printed liturgical books in the cathedral library in order to prepare for a projected collected edition of Spanish liturgies.[20]

Burriel's Comparative Method

In the course of surveying the liturgical books in Toledo, Burriel developed methods that were unusual at the time but that anticipated more recent approaches to medieval liturgical traditions. One of the more innovative aspects of his research on the liturgical books in Toledo Cathedral was the comparison of various manuscripts and printed editions representing the Old Hispanic rite. He also compared the medieval Hispanic manuscripts with witnesses to the Roman rite. In this regard Burriel's method is related to the modern discipline of comparative liturgy, which compares diverse liturgical traditions to determine the age of specific texts and rites. Comparative liturgy first developed in the nineteenth century and early twentieth in imitation of the scientific method, particularly of the organicist study of biology, and many historians of liturgy continue to practice a modified form of the comparative method espoused by its early advocates.[21] Burriel's comparisons drew on sources from different chronological strata and various dioceses. By applying the comparative method to all the sources transmitting formularies for several feasts of particular interest, he was able to identify elements of continuity, determine which were the original proper texts, and understand the transformations of formularies as the feast was altered over time.

Burriel's procedure was to examine manuscripts and prepare descriptions, oversee the transcriptions, correct them, and annotate them, often by comparing them to other manuscripts and to the Ortiz editions. Once he had approved a transcription, he dated it and signed his name. Each complete transcription of a manuscript was bound as a volume with its own formal title page, which described (in Latin) the contents of the manuscript, gave the date of completion, and indicated that the transcription was "illustrated with notes and observations" by Burriel.

For the transcriptions Burriel and Pérez Bayer were assisted by amanuenses.[22] Two of these scribes were Francisco Santiago y Palomares (who was twenty-two when the Commission began its work in Toledo) and his brother.[23] It is clear that several other scribes also worked simultaneously on some projects. For instance, in a three-volume copy from 1753 of the passionary Toledo, BC 44.11 (then 35-6), each volume combines the work of several different scribes who apparently worked separately, each transcribing a section equivalent to one saint's life.[24] After copying a section the scribe marked it with the manuscript shelf mark at the beginning in the upper left corner. Burriel himself wrote the description of the manuscript at the beginning of the first volume, with critical notes that referred to his comparisons with manuscripts and printed books.[25]

Altogether Burriel apparently had the help of five scribes who were able to transcribe texts in Visigothic script.[26] This was quite a rare skill in the eighteenth century, as knowledge of the script was uncommon among even the most educated. In his "Apuntamientos" Burriel referred to a widespread misconception that the script of the Cisneros editions was Visigothic, whereas it is a common typeface from around 1500.[27] Despite the apparent skill of the amanuenses, however, it appears that not all of them were equally competent, making it necessary for Burriel himself to check each page of text that was transcribed.[28] Presumably the recondite nature of the material formed part of the difficulty; the genre designators of the Old Hispanic rite were unfamiliar to those accustomed to the Roman rite, and the Latin of the medieval liturgical texts differed somewhat from the more classicizing Latin that would have been studied in the eighteenth century. In addition certain elements of the Visigothic script proved particularly challenging to Burriel's assistants, especially abbreviations for the names of liturgical genres that did not exist in the Roman rite. One such obstacle to correct transcription was the ubiquitous CNPL ligature for a prayer called "conpleturia" (often spelled "completuria" in the eighteenth century). The scribes of the two earliest copies of liturgical books, both from 1752, did not resolve the abbreviation correctly. In the transcription of the liturgical book Madrid, BN 10110, the scribe simply copied the abbreviation without attempting to resolve it at all.[29] Later on either the same scribe or another one went through the entire text to add the word *completuria* in the relevant passages. Likewise throughout the two-volume copy of Toledo, BC 35.4 in Madrid, BN 13048 and 13049 (from 1753), one scribe has written "capitula" (apparently misreading the abbreviation for "completuria"); this error is corrected by two contemporaneous hands, including Burriel's.[30] It is possible that the erroneous interpretation in the Ortiz editions was the cause of this mistake among Burriel's assistants, who may have used the editions as references for deciphering the texts.[31]

While most of Burriel's annotations to the transcription volumes are corrections of scribal errors, in many copies he also added textual variants or emendations of the text.[32] Some annotations are comparative, making reference to other liturgical manuscripts and comparing the textual contents of the transcription to the corresponding section in the Ortiz editions.[33] For instance, in a copy of the mid-thirteenth-century manuscript Toledo, BC 35.5, many of the marginal notes by Burriel are collations with other manuscripts, suggesting that he was preparing an edition of the text.[34] Burriel frequently noted the differences in content between the manuscript and the printed neo-Mozarabic editions. His comments anticipated the conclusions of José Janini, who in several studies pointed out that the Ortiz edition of the Mozarabic breviary was a newly rearranged version of the medieval rite.[35]

The contrast between Toledo 35.5 and the neo-Mozarabic edition seems to have impressed Burriel particularly in the Paschal Triduum, where it is abundantly clear that Ortiz created a strange admixture of the Old Hispanic and Roman rites. On Good Friday, for instance, Burriel pointed out that the printed breviary included the hymn "Pange lingua" instead of the deacon's prayer before the Improperia.[36] Next to the text of the Old Hispanic Preces from the Toledan manuscript, he noted that the Ortiz edition of the missal contained the Roman rubrics and chant for the Adoration of the Cross, which of course were nowhere to be found in the medieval manuscript.[37] Burriel also commented on Ortiz's interpolation of prayers to be said in front of the altar before the lighting of the new fire, as well as his addition of a rubric from the Roman rite for placing grains of incense on the Paschal candle. He noted, however, that the edition did include the Old Hispanic Inlatio (or Illatio, a mass prayer comparable to the Preface prayer in the mass of the Roman rite) for the blessing of the candle itself.[38] Later in the same transcription he pointed out that the antiphons *Ad accedentes*, the Old Hispanic equivalents of the communion antiphons in the Roman rite, have musical notation in Toledo, BC 35.5, and are far more numerous in the manuscript than in the Ortiz missal.[39]

Several miscellany manuscripts now in the Biblioteca Nacional in Madrid reveal Burriel's methods of work and collaboration with his assistants even more clearly than the transcriptions.[40] For a collection of notes on printed breviaries, he gave each assistant a quire of paper on which to transcribe a saint's office or calendar from a particular liturgical book, and then assembled and annotated these excerpts.[41] The material may have been compiled over a period of years; the many discrete parts of the manuscript represent all the different scribes seen in the copies. Burriel himself reviewed each of the independent booklets, as almost every section has either his notes at the beginning or annotations in his hand. He may also have assembled them in the current order, although it is possible that they were collected and bound together later.

The principal aim of the enterprise seems to have been to gather information on the liturgy of Saints Justa and Rufina, two virgin martyrs of Seville who were the titular saints of a Mozarabic parish church in Toledo. Liturgical manuscripts from this church had been the basis of the Ortiz editions, which in Burriel's lifetime were still the best-known sources for the Old Hispanic rite. The texts Burriel gathered, along with his annotations, suggest that he was using the printed breviaries as a control group, a basis for comparison in order to determine the earliest form of the proper texts for the liturgical veneration of these saints.[42] Beginning in 1753 he collated the office and mass of Saints Justa and Rufina with textual variants from the printed Mozarabic Breviary as well as from the Visigothic *orationale* in Verona published by Bianchini; the collation was complete by 1755 or 1756.[43] He also investigated the relationship between liturgical formularies for their feast and those of other virgin martyrs, as well as connections with the common of virgins (a set of liturgical texts that could be used for the feast of any virgin saint). Comparing all the pre-Tridentine manuscripts and printed books that were available to him in Toledo, Burriel observed that in a Roman rite missal of Toledo (Toledo, BC 29.30) several important Spanish saints' feasts were added in the margins, with reference to a supplement; the feast of Justa and Rufina was not among them. The omission of this important feast demonstrated that elements of the early Hispanic calendar were not always reintegrated into the books of the Roman rite produced in the Iberian peninsula, even when the contents were otherwise apparently adapted for use in Spanish dioceses. Burriel's interest in the cult of these two virgin martyrs of Seville informed his projected history of the Mozarabic parish of Saints Justa and Rufina in Toledo. This work, which was never brought to completion, was going to include chapters on the liturgy of the saints; although unfinished, it was published in the early nineteenth century.[44]

Paleographic analysis was an important part of Burriel's research on medieval liturgy. Many of his annotations in the transcriptions of Toledan manuscripts date the hands of additions to the text. For instance, in a copy of the liturgical book Toledo, BC 35.4 (which has been dated to around 1200), he assigned certain passages and annotations to the thirteenth or fourteenth century and others to the early modern period.[45] In several cases, he copied an annotation in Arabic script.[46] Although for most of the two centuries following Burriel's tenure in Toledo much earlier dates were assigned to these liturgical books, some of the dates he proposed (but never published) are close to those now widely accepted. As we will see in chapter 3, for example, Burriel estimated a date of around 1085 for the manuscript Toledo, BC 35.7, which has recently been dated to the late eleventh century or around 1100. Concerning Toledo, BC 35.6, Burriel pointed out, "Nowhere in the entire manuscript is it indicated when it was written or by whom," adding, "but I believe that the manuscript was written before the restoration of Toledo by Alfonso VI: elsewhere, I shall attempt to demonstrate that everything it contains was in use before the invasion of the Moors."[47] In this assessment he anticipated the conclusions published by Anscari Mundó and José Janini over two hundred years later, which hold that the manuscript should be dated to the end of the tenth century or the beginning of the eleventh; it is now considered to be the earliest of the Toledan liturgical manuscripts in Visigothic script.[48]

Burriel critically examined the latest Toledan liturgical manuscript in Visigothic script (now Madrid, BN 10110, and formerly Toledo, BC 35.2). According to Mundó and Janini, this book was produced between about 1250 and 1300.[49] It was one of the first liturgical manuscripts to be transcribed for the Commission, in 1752.[50] The colophon, which had been published by Pinius, indicated that the scribe had worked "during the reign of Lord Alfonso" (*regnante domno adefonso*), which Burriel took to refer to Alfonso VI or VII, implying that the manuscript dated to the early or mid-twelfth century. However, when in 1756 Burriel and de las Infantas (formerly the *canónigo doctoral* and now the dean of the cathedral) compared the published version of the colophon to that in the original manuscript, they concluded that the reference to Alfonso was not original, and that Camino y Velasco had added it himself in order to support his own dating of the manuscript.[51] In any case, Burriel argued that Madrid 10110 was produced after conquest of Toledo, which (as Mundó pointed out) was for centuries the hypothesis closest to the dating of the manuscript that is accepted today.[52]

Palomares's Copies

Like Burriel, Palomares had an unusual eye for detail and took a particular interest in musical notation. He copied neumes not only while working with Burriel in Toledo, but also in the course of later projects, and he wrote about neumes at various times throughout his career (see chapter 5). Palomares's punctilious copying of medieval musical notation suggests that he thought that the very inscrutability of the signs demanded faithful imitation. To this end, because he knew that copying was the only way to convey them and to make them both available and comprehensible to future generations, he assimilated and reproduced the contours of the neumes with great care. He mastered both the style of Hispanic neumatic notation generally associated with the north of the peninsula, often referred to as "vertical," and Toledan notation, which is characterized by diagonally oriented neumes that are slightly inclined to the right.[53]

Many of the transcriptions of entire manuscripts include a copy drawn by Palomares of a single page from the original, usually one or two per manuscript. Inserted in the transcription volumes, these copies attest to the care with which the appearance of the manuscript page was recorded for the Commission on the Archives. As we will see in the descriptions that follow, Palomares's extremely accurate rendering of the musical notation was part of Burriel's systematic approach to the study of the Old Hispanic liturgical codices.

The transcription of Toledo, BC 35.4 in Madrid, BN 13048 contains an oversize foldout single-page copy of fol. 169r signed by Palomares in 1754 (Figure 2.1). This page is one of Palomares's more modest efforts; the initial letters of the original are rendered impressionistically, and the only colored inks employed are red for rubrics and for some of the initial letters (whereas the medieval original features initials in green, red, and bright yellow). The main focus of the copy was calligraphic. In the third line of text in the right column, he rendered the inserted word "fuciem" in thinner strokes to communicate the effect of the lighter, very faded brown ink. He also used cross-hatching to represent the erasure of two letters at the end of the word "filii" (which was originally "filium"). As always Palomares sought to reproduce the Toledan neumatic notation accurately, but the parchment was evidently already quite rubbed, preventing him from seeing (or at least from copying) the neumes on the first syllable of the first chant ("Te decet ymnus in syon"), the first syllable of the penultimate chant ("Emendunt"), and the second syllable of the final chant ("Tu domine conuertere").

A more detailed single-page copy was made in 1753 for inclusion in Madrid, BN 13052 (the transcription of Toledo, BC 35.5). The large fold-out copy of fol. 15r by Palomares (Figure 2.2) provides an impression of the page that is generally accurate, including the structure of the decorated letter. However, Palomares made some changes that may have been intended to improve or clean up the appearance of the manuscript page. Part of the parchment was already missing from the lower left margin before the

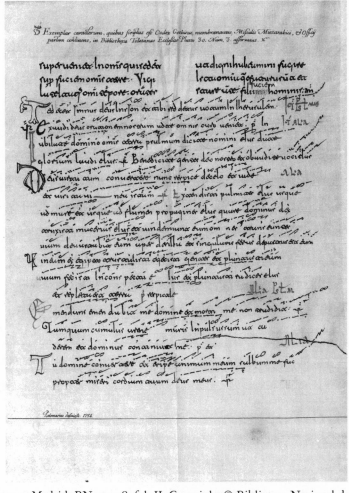

FIGURE 2.1 Madrid, BN 13048, fol. II. Copyright © Biblioteca Nacional de España.

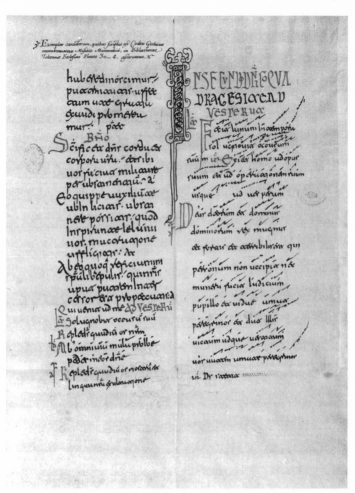

FIGURE 2.2 Madrid, BN 13052, fol. V. Copyright © Biblioteca Nacional de España.

manuscript was written, so the scribe of Toledo 35.5 had placed the text somewhat asymmetrically to accommodate for the lack of space; in the copy, however, Palomares wrote the text in the entire column as if the parchment of the left column were intact. He omitted the later annotation that had been written perpendicular to the text between the columns. Finally, he (apparently inadvertently) left out one line of the Toledan notation in the middle of the right column (for the text "et fortis et terribilis est qui"). Despite these adjustments the copy is more accurate than any that were available in print at the time. Although those accustomed to photographic reproduction may find fault with the details, Palomares was capable of producing very close likenesses.

Another single-page copy made in the same year (1753) for inclusion in the transcription of Toledo, BC 35.6, shows Palomares's efforts to imitate the original with absolute precision (Figure 2.3: Madrid, BN 13053, p. 483). Both the drawing itself and the accompanying text show greater attention to detail than other copies. Here a loss of parchment from the lower-left corner (a damage that occurred after the manuscript was finished) is carefully indicated with cross-hatching; the initial letters are copied almost perfectly, and the northern notation is accurately rendered. Palomares's signature includes not only the calligrapher's name but also the additional specification that he "copied exactly from the autograph original" ("ad vivum ex Autographo originali exscripsit"). Presumably the consummate accuracy of the copy reflects the initiative of Burriel, who characterized it as an exact copy in his commentary on the manuscript at the end of the transcription: "To illustrate for the reader the form both of the Visigothic letters and of the musical signs, I had the page with the beginning of the office of Saint John the Baptist accurately copied or depicted exactly, on the following folio, with the autograph."[54] Burriel's close scrutiny of script and musical notation can be seen in his commission of the copy from Palomares, as well as in his annotations to the transcription. Describing the incomplete notation of this manuscript Burriel wrote, "The antiphons, responsories, *laudes*, etc. are written leaving space for musical notation between the syllables, but neumes are lacking almost throughout the manuscript, and the music is notated only over some antiphons, the hymn of St. John the Baptist, and other small elements of the offices."[55] This commentary suggests that he chose the page for Palomares to copy (the office of John the Baptist) based on the presence of musical notation. Burriel's observations also demonstrate that he considered musical notation an integral element in the composition of the page, noting that the format of the manuscript allowed for neumes that were absent.

A Focus on Neumes

Besides the single-page copies drawn by Palomares, the transcriptions of liturgical manuscripts made for the Commission did not usually include any representations of the original appearance of the medieval originals. In a few cases, however, Palomares copied more extensive passages of Visigothic script and musical notation, going so far as to copy the musical notation of an entire book for the first time in 1752. The medieval original, a manuscript produced in the second quarter or middle of the eleventh century at the abbey of San Millán de la Cogolla in the Rioja, became part of Toledo Cathedral's

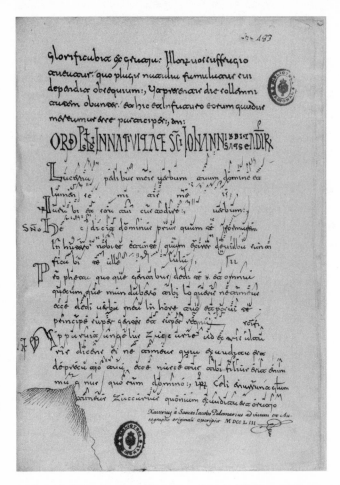

FIGURE 2.3 Madrid, BN 13053, p. 483. Copyright © Biblioteca Nacional de España.

library in the Middle Ages and is now in New York at the Hispanic Society of America (New York, HSA B2916, formerly Toledo, BC 33.2).[56] In the 1752 copy (which combines procedures of transcription and copying) the diversity of approaches to musical notation and to the Visigothic script suggests experimentation in format. In many cases both the appearance of the script and the neumes (in the style of the north of the peninsula) were preserved. The textual content was the highest priority, so texts are transcribed into modern script. For most chants, a copy of the original script and neumes is followed by a transcription. Figure 2.4 shows a typical example. The first text is a prayer, transcribed in modern script. The next item on the page is a copy of the alleluiaticus *In Sion firmata sum* for the office of the Assumption of the

Virgin Mary.[57] The incipit of this alleluiatic antiphon appears as a heading above the copy. Below the copy is the transcription of the chant text. The verse *Manus enim mea* is written on a separate line to show that it is a separate element. In the medieval original the text of the verse follows immediately upon the conclusion of the chant, but is distinguished from it by the verse's lack of notation and smaller text. Comparing Palomares's copy to the original manuscript confirms that the copy is extremely accurate, although two neumes were omitted (one note of a three-note melisma on the second syllable of two words, "Sion" and "firmata"). The placement of these notes immediately above the other neumes might have caused Palomares to interpret them

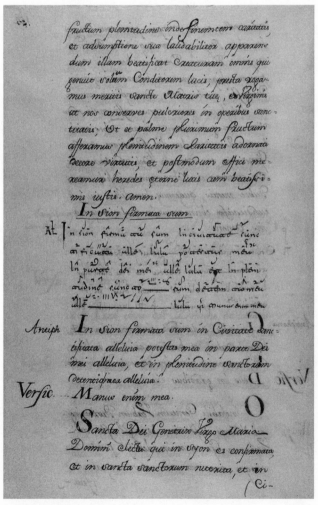

FIGURE 2.4 Madrid, BN 13060, fol. 182v. Copyright © Biblioteca Nacional de España.

as parts of a letter in the line above rather than as musical signs. Another subtle difference between the original and the copy results from the slight inclination to the right with which Palomares drew the neumes, which are more upright in the original manuscript. Whereas the predominant method in the copy of New York, HSA 2916, is to juxtapose transcriptions of chant texts with faithful copies of the notated chants, a different approach earlier in the copy resulted in a hybrid. In Figure 2.5 the neumes are written above the text transcribed in a modern hand. Below, the text is transcribed separately, with the genre of the chant identified in the margin.

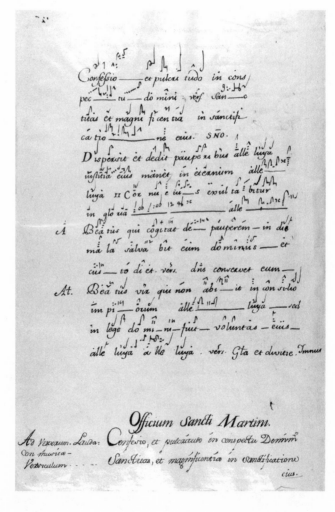

FIGURE 2.5 Madrid, BN 13060, fol. 122v. Copyright © Biblioteca Nacional de España.

Several scribes appear to have participated in the creation of this volume, and it is possible that Palomares copied the chants in space left for him by scribes who had transcribed the texts. This order of work would explain two distinctive features of the copy. First, the phrase "antiphona con musica" was written in the margin next to many of the chant texts, which would be redundant unless it were meant to indicate which texts were to be accompanied by notated copies. Second, some of the chants were transcribed without notation, but the notated copies of these chants appear in an appendix keyed to the textual transcriptions with capital letters or other signs that were evidently added later. The separation of transcriptions from copies in these cases suggests an inadvertent omission on the part of certain scribes.

Another layer of the transcription and copy consists of Burriel's annotations and corrections. His treatment of the Roman rite Alleluia *Virga iesse floruit*, added to the Hispanic Society manuscript in the twelfth century, attests to his attention to detail and to the chronology of hands in the manuscript.[58] The addition of an Alleluia is striking not only because it is a new composition of the twelfth century in the Franco-Roman chant tradition, but also because it is a proper chant for the mass, whereas the manuscript is a collection of three offices for saints. The Alleluia concludes, incongruously, in the space that had been left blank below the end of the first responsory in the office of San Millan. (Compare Figure 2.6 to Figure 1.) Burriel crossed out the text and separated the Alleluia from the rest of the page with a dividing line, noting in the left margin that it was added later ("esto ultimo es parte de la antiphona añadida posteriormente"). This intriguing later addition is the only one that Palomares included in his copy of the manuscript; he ignored several other pieces added to the margins in Caroline minuscule and Aquitanian notation in the twelfth and thirteenth centuries, perhaps because he found them less interesting, or because of their position in the margins.[59] As we will see in chapter 3, his facsimile of a Toledan manuscript in Visigothic script omits an added chant with Aquitanian notation.

Another example that illustrates different methods employed by the Commission is the two-volume transcription made in 1754 of a breviary of the late twelfth or early thirteenth century (now Madrid, BN 10001; previously Toledo, BC 35.1).[60] The decision to place the transcriptions in two separate volumes is justified by the fact that the psalter and hymnary form distinct codicological sections of the original manuscript. The copy of the psalter portion (Madrid, BN 13050) represents a compromise between simple transcription and copying. The scribe (presumably Palomares) conveyed the appearance of the original script and musical notation by including copies of each antiphon and notated psalm incipit. The title page of the volume signals

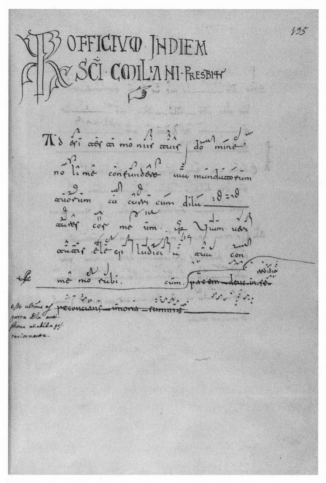

FIGURE 2.6 Madrid, BN 13060, fol. 195r. Copyright © Biblioteca Nacional de España.

the presence of musical notation and also attributes the version of the Psalms in the manuscript to Isidore of Seville: "A Mozarabic codex containing the entire Psalter divided into five books, with antiphons, and with the musical notation of each psalm, according to the new (we believe) edition prepared by Isidore of Seville."[61] (In the eighteenth century, on the basis of medieval texts referring to Isidore's use of the Bible, it was common to credit him with a revision of the Vulgate, including the Psalter.)[62]

Whereas in the original manuscript the texts follow one another without interruption, in the copy each psalm begins on a new page. Generally Palomares fit each psalm incipit into a single line, whereas in the original manuscript they start on one line and continue on the next. He made no attempt to reproduce the decorated initials.[63] As seen in Figure 2.7, a copy of each antiphon with its Toledan notation is followed by just the incipit of the psalm in Visigothic script. Then the entire psalm is transcribed in eighteenth-century italic script. The copy was apparently intended as the basis for an edition Burriel hoped to print of the Latin psalter in the version employed by the Old Hispanic rite. The paper is folded down the center of the page to create two columns, one for the psalm text and the other for variants and notes.[64] Palomares drew nearly all the neumes in the manuscript, enabling us to recover some notation that is now difficult to see.[65] Throughout Madrid, BN 10001, the surface of the parchment is faded and decayed.

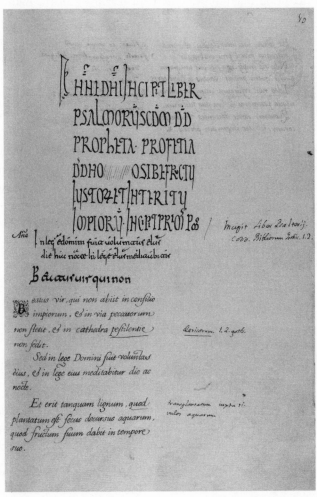

FIGURE 2.7 Madrid, BN 13050, fol. 10r. Copyright © Biblioteca Nacional de España.

The neumes are frequently almost illegible, or even nearly invisible. The original must have been easier to read in 1754, but the copy, which is much clearer, now functions as much as a restitution or restoration as it does as a copy. The painstaking drawing of the neumes in this manuscript reflects the same attention to detail that led Palomares to copy the prefatory title of the psalter in Visigothic script, as seen in Figure 2.7 ("In nomine domini incipit liber psalmorum secundum dauid propheta. . .").

A very different approach was taken in Madrid, BN 13056, a copy of the 184 hymns in Madrid, BN 10001.[66] The result is a hybrid of copy and transcription. The text of each hymn is transcribed in an eighteenth-century cursive. For the notated hymns, Toledan neumes are drawn between the lines of the transcription in a different ink than that used for the main text. The copy contains transcription errors corrected by various hands (sometimes by the main hand), but not all the errors are corrected. Some pages were left blank after every hymn, presumably for the purpose of writing critical notes.

In the two-volume copy of Toledo, BC 35.4 (Madrid, BN 13048 and 13049), a prefatory note states that Burriel collated the text with the Visigothic *orationale* of Verona.[67] This copy, made in 1753,[68] is written entirely in eighteenth-century cursive. Only occasionally does the scribe gesture toward the original hierarchy of scripts to show a decorated letter at the beginning of a text.[69] The copy contains no musical notation, but lines are skipped between the chant texts, as if to leave space for neumes that were never added. Burriel did make reference to the missing music, however, noting in one place, "Here and below, the musical notes vary," and in another indicating the presence of notation in the original with the word "music."[70]

Liturgical Texts as Witnesses to the History of the Mozarabic Community

Burriel was also interested in the historical context of the manuscripts and the texts they contained. Understanding that the Mozarabs of Toledo were a community whose collective identity was defined most of all by liturgical tradition, he studied the history of the Mozarabic parishes alongside the medieval manuscripts of the Old Hispanic liturgy that were used in these parishes. Although Burriel's account of the cult of the virgin martyrs Justa and Rufina was primarily a history of the Toledan parish that bears their name, his unpublished papers on the subject indicate that he intended it to be a history of their liturgical commemoration as well. For him the offices and masses for these saints illustrated the culture of the Mozarabic community. In fact the implications of his treatise on the Mozarabic parish of Saints Justa and Rufina went far beyond the confines of Seville or Toledo as religious communities. His ultimate purpose in writing this history was "to increase devotion to these saints and trust in their patronage, confirmation of our holy faith, lustre of Seville and sacred honor of our entire Nation."[71] Thus Burriel extended cultural meanings associated with the Sevillan patron saints of a Mozarabic parish in Toledo to the religious identity of Spain as a whole. The conflation of the traditions of local religious communities with ideas of national identity had long been an important theme in the historiography of the Iberian peninsula;[72] Burriel continued this practice by defining the liturgy of the Mozarabs as a characteristic of the contemporary Spanish nation.

Thus Burriel's approach to the Latin texts of the liturgy was grounded not only in philology and comparative liturgy, but also in the historical context and meaning of chants and prayers as cultural artifacts of the religious communities that used them. He frequently combined philological arguments with historical ones; for example, he argued that the office of the Assumption of the Virgin in Toledo, BC 35.7, must have been composed after the Visigothic period, even though it was commonly attributed to Ildefonsus of Toledo.[73] Among the reasons for his dating of these texts is his assessment of their Latinity, which he described as distinctively Visigothic, albeit barbaric and decadent:

> Although the golden purity of the Augustan age is lacking in all the texts of the Visigoths, in them we find a Visigothic-sounding Latinity. Nevertheless, even that age had its writers and the ecclesiastical offices have a certain charm and beauty, and even in that decadent Latinity there are certain observable traces of a more correct style. But neither Isidore, Ildefonsus, nor Julian can be believed to be the authors of this barbarous office, nor would they ever have approved of an office composed by someone else being sung in their churches. Moreover, the *Postnomina* prayer mentions captives. All these things seem to me to suggest that the service was composed after the domination of the Moors was established, and I do not believe that it belongs to the Ildefonsian corpus of *missae*.[74]

With style criticism of this kind Burriel sought to differentiate chronological layers of the texts contained in Toledan manuscripts, distinguishing the date of a manuscript's production from the age of its contents.

Likewise in his commentary on the latest Mozarabic manuscript (now Madrid, BN 10110, formerly Toledo, BC 35.2) Burriel took note of certain passages that might shed light on the experience of the Mozarabs under Muslim rule. For instance, with regard to the phrase "eripiat ab hoste captivos" in the prayer "Emitte lucem tuam" he wrote, "From these [words] one might suspect, not without reason, that this office was composed at the time when the Spaniards were captives in the power of the Moors."[75] His interpretation of this prayer is supported by José Janini, who argues that the prototype for Madrid 10110 goes back to the early ninth century, or even to the late eighth, even though the manuscript itself is centuries later in date.[76] Likewise in the prayer "Ecce Domine posui in perturbatione mundana quietem solitudinis eligentes . . ." Burriel saw a possible reference to Islam:

> This phrase, "Therefore, we who do not expect the prepared rest of places," appears thus in the codex. I suspect that in it there is an allusion to the Mahometans' impure dogma regarding Paradise, from which, the text states, the Christians praying are far removed. If this [reading] is unacceptable, the "non" should be deleted, so the prayer may render its sound and catholic sense; it is fitting that the strength of the opposing meaning be rendered void. Perhaps also one may think that the contrast is being made in this prayer not between Moors and Christians, but between [Christians] and Jews who are going to the places prepared for them by God in the Promised Land. As if it said: "We who do not expect (as the Jews in the desert expected) the earthly places prepared for us and the promised repose, we beseech, etc." This meaning is intelligent and sound, and fits with the preceding antiphon, which is about the desert.[77]

Burriel's reading combines an interpretation attentive to historical context with one that considers conventional biblical typology. At the same time, he considered the relationship between the prayer and the Sacrificium chant immediately preceding it. His attempt to understand the meaning of the text's language is informed by textual criticism; the crux is in the presence of the Latin word "non" because it makes the text seem to be a paradox. Burriel's understanding of this prayer as a reflection of Muslim or Jewish traditions, or rather of one of these traditions in dialogue with Christian beliefs, shows that he was aware of the contact of faiths in the medieval Toledan milieu in which the manuscript was produced. His commentary appears to acknowledge that there was important theological interaction in Toledo between the three "religions of the book," and that Muslim theology could have been a source of influence for a conception of Paradise in a Christian liturgical text.

Burriel's approach to this text can be linked to the modern scholarly thesis that the theology of the Toledan Mozarabs was influenced by ideas from Islam. He may have been aware of preexisting Christian anti-Islamic polemics associated with Toledo in the second half of the thirteenth century, precisely the period in which the manuscript containing the prayer was produced (according to the dating by Mundó).[78] His interpretation thus has some foundation in the historical context of the manuscript, but at the same time reflects the scholarly transmission of ideas about Islam in early modern Spain.

Burriel and Adoptionism

Another subject of theological polemic that attracted Burriel's attention was the christological controversy of the late eighth century, which brought to the fore significant differences between Frankish theological traditions and those Visigothic ones that were the cultural inheritance of Iberian Christians. In his annotations on the transcriptions of certain Toledan liturgical books, Burriel pointed out the presence of adoptionist ideas in the liturgical texts cited in the writings of Elipandus of Toledo (archbishop of Toledo from 754 to 808). Elipandus stated that Christ, in his humanity, was an adoptive son of God by action of grace. This theology of adoptionism was denounced as a heresy in 785 by Beatus of Liebana. At the request of Elipandus another bishop, Felix of Urgell, issued his own statements in support of Elipandus's ideas. Since Urgell had just been integrated into the Frankish kingdom, the controversy reached the court of Charlemagne, and the king's advisor Alcuin of York (c. 734–804) became involved. Felix recanted after the Council of Regensburg condemned adoptionism in 792. In response Elipandus wrote a defense of his theology addressed to the Frankish bishops. The Council of Frankfurt called by Charlemagne in 794 then condemned Elipandus along with Felix.[79]

Elipandus's epistles to Alcuin and to the Frankish bishops include several Latin terms derived from the word "adoptio" as they were found in prayers of the Visigothic rite.[80] In both letters Elipandus attributed the texts to his predecessors in the see of Toledo. The epistle to Alcuin casts the Visigothic rite as a continuation of the patristic corpus, following the treatment of adoptionist language in the fathers of the church by introducing the liturgical texts as "the testimonies of the holy, venerable fathers serving Toledo, related in the prophecies of the *missae*" ("testimonia sanctorum patrum uenerabilium Toleto deseruientium in missarum oraculis edita").[81] In the Old Hispanic mass a *missa* is a lengthy prayer addressed to the congregation by the priest after the singing of the sacrificium (which corresponds to the offertory chant in the Roman rite).[82] Such prayers, and other texts of the Old Hispanic rite, were traditionally ascribed to one of the Visigothic bishops of Toledo or to Isidore of Seville. Burriel was one of the first to question such attributions of liturgical texts, all of which are anonymous in the medieval manuscript sources.[83]

For Elipandus the authorship of the prayers guaranteed their orthodoxy; the language of adoptionism in liturgical texts was thus integral to the theology of the Hispanic church. However, the outcome of the adoptionist controversy had the effect of attaching the suspicion, and sometimes even an outright accusation, of heresy to the Old Hispanic rite, which was one of the factors that led Gregory VII to advocate its suppression in the eleventh century.[84] The result was a long-standing misperception of Spanish adoptionist doctrine as heterodox that remained influential through the twentieth century. As John Cavadini has shown, the history of Hispanic adoptionism has been written almost exclusively from the perspective of those who perceived it as a variant of Arianism or Nestorianism. Cavadini, in contrast, describes Hispanic adoptionism as an orthodox doctrine emanating from a distinctively Iberian intellectual milieu that was grounded in the Latin patristic tradition, rather than strongly influenced by the late-antique Eastern theological disputes that shaped most Carolingian theology.[85] However, the prevailing view of adoptionism since the eighth century has been that of Alcuin, who, according to Cavadini, fundamentally misunderstood the premises and arguments of the Iberian writers.[86] Essentially reinscribing Alcuin's view in the twentieth century, Juan Francisco Rivera Recio sees the proponents of adoptionism as influenced by Nestorianism, while also hypothesizing that the doctrine reflected the Mozarabs' efforts to reach some kind of compromise or middle ground with Islamic theology.[87] This dual explanation echoes earlier accounts of adoptionism, the most widely read being those in the *Historia general de España* of Juan de Mariana (1526–1624) and in the fifth volume of Flórez's *España Sagrada* (1750). Here the entry on Elipandus in the catalogue of Toledan bishops describes adoptionism as one of the inevitable consequences of contact between Christians and Muslims, including intermarriage.[88] Both Juan de Mariana and Flórez portray the rise of adoptionism as a threat to Catholicism in Spain, a menace that was inseparable from Muslim rule.[89]

In its original context of the late eighth century, the theological debate around adoptionism carried a political meaning as well: it was framed by the tension between the autonomy of the Hispanic church and the expansion of the Frankish kingdom in cooperation with the papacy. The defeat of Hispanic adoptionism was therefore as much a victory for Carolingian control over the western church as it was an ideological triumph.[90] Perhaps the underlying politics of the controversy (pitting Romano-Frankish primacy against the autonomy of the Hispanic church, and particularly the Toledan primate) were never really forgotten. One can imagine that Burriel perceived parallels between the political context of the adoptionist controversy and the concerns of his own time, when the aspirations of the Spanish national church conflicted with the prerogatives claimed by Rome.

Above all, Burriel's interest in adoptionism is yet another facet of his antiquarianism. The letters of Elipandus and the rest of the adoptionist theological corpus formed a part of the Iberian heritage that he sought to bring to the attention of his contemporaries.[91] For Burriel adoptionist ideas constituted an artifact of Spanish ecclesiastical history, as well as a vestige of the past. While annotating the transcriptions of liturgical manuscripts he pointed out instances of adoptionist language, which he recognized from reading the letters of Elipandus. Thus whereas Elipandus had cited the liturgy as evidence for his christology, Burriel reversed the process, reading the letters of Elipandus as evidence for adoptionism in the liturgy.[92] In short Burriel read the prayers in the Toledan manuscripts through the lens of the eighth-century adoptionist controversy. As Cavadini argues, the use of liturgical texts by Elipandus amounts to a new and particularly Hispanic interpretation of their original theological language, independent of the meaning of those texts at the time they were composed in the seventh or early eighth century.[93]

In the transcriptions of Toledan Mozarabic liturgical manuscripts, Burriel annotated phrases that had been cited by Elipandus in his epistle of the Spanish bishops to the Frankish bishops assembled at the Council of Frankfurt in 794. One of these was a phrase from an Inlatio for Maundy Thursday, as found in Toledo, BC 35.3: "who, while through the adoption of his birth he does not indulge in the body, nevertheless he did not spare it for us" ("qui per adoptionem natiuitatis sue dum suo non indulget corpori, nostro demum, non pepercit").[94] According to Burriel, Elipandus attributed these words to Eugenius of Toledo, but altered them somewhat in his own rendition of the phrase.[95] Indeed the epistle to the Frankish bishops reads not "through the adoption of his birth" but rather "through the passion of the adoptive man," a formulation Elipandus associates with three of his august predecessors in the see of Toledo, Bishops Eugenius, Ildefonsus, and Julian.[96] The version of the sentence quoted by Elipandus was not an invention, but can be found in the Old Hispanic rite; the phrase "passion of the adoptive man" occurs, among other places, in a mass prayer for the Friday of Easter week in Toledo, BC 35.6.[97] In a transcription of this prayer from Toledo, BC

35.6, Burriel recognized the phrase "the adoptive man" and wrote next to it, "Note that these words were adduced by Elipandus in the Epistle to the fathers at Frankfurt."[98] Clearly, Burriel understood that Elipandus's substitution of the phrase "passion of the adoptive man" for "through the adoption of his birth" in the Inlatio for Maundy Thursday was a quotation from another prayer of the Old Hispanic rite.[99] Elipandus, whether consciously or not, had rewritten the text, or at the very least conflated two different prayers. Indeed his words are representative of the language of adoption that was so troubling to those at the Carolingian court, like Alcuin, whose christology was formed by the ongoing debate between East and West. It is noteworthy that Burriel, a professor of theology, associated this phrase with a liturgical text rather than identifying it as an expression of Nestorianism; in fact the "passion of the adoptive man" is a key concept in the debate through which adoptionism came to be perceived as a heresy. Burriel also pointed out both appearances of the sentence "Hodie saluator noster post adoptionem carnis sedem repetit deitatis" ("Today, after the adoption of the flesh, our savior returns to the seat of the deity") from the *missa* for the feast of the Ascension as transmitted in two Toledan liturgical books.[100] He noted that Elipandus had invoked this text in his epistle of the Spanish bishops, attributing it to Ildefonsus of Toledo.[101] Burriel thus situated the theological language used by Elipandus in its original historical context of the Old Hispanic rite. This contextualization enabled him to understand the christology of Elipandus on its own terms rather than as heretical.

Burriel's approach to adoptionism is typical of his methods of liturgical study: it combines analysis and annotation of the texts as found in medieval manuscripts with close attention to the historical context in which they were written and performed. His interest in the adoptionist controversy stemmed in part from the transmission of the texts in Toledan liturgical books. As we will see in chapter 3, Burriel understood the Toledan manuscripts in Visigothic script not only as objects of historical study, but also as symbolic vessels of a Toledan tradition going back to the Visigothic era and the ritual community of the Mozarabs in Toledo.

Notes

1. For the text of the royal order see Galende Diaz, "Repertorio," 242; RAH, signatura 9/5921, fol. 13r–v.

2. Toledo, AC, vol. 68, fols. 180v–181r.

3. Among the few exceptions was the Benedictine Martín Sarmiento, who had prepared an index of the library's collection in 1727 but did not study the manuscripts in any detail. The index is now preserved in Madrid, BN 13413 (olim Toledo, BC 42-35).

4. The *canónigo doctoral* (a benefice established in Castile and Leon with the permission of Sixtus IV in 1474) was the legal counsel of the chapter and was a bachelor or doctor of law; see Villacorta Rodríguez, *El Cabildo Catedral de León*, 124–27. I am grateful to Liam Moore for this information.

5. Echánove Tuero, *La preparación intelectual*, 106.

6. Flórez, *España Sagrada*, 4: xl–xli. In these acknowledgments Flórez also thanked Burriel, who by then was teaching at Alcalá, for his earlier help with the manuscripts in the library of the Jesuit College in Toledo (presumably when Burriel was teaching there in 1742–44). We do not know whether Flórez needed help from Burriel and de las Infantas because he could not gain access to the archives of Toledo Cathedral, or because he lacked the skill to make the relevant transcriptions himself.

7. Alcaraz Gómez, *Jesuitas y Reformismo*, 582. On the work of the Commission in centers other than Toledo, see 589–90; and especially Díaz, "El reconocimiento," 131–70.

8. Dubuis, "Mabillon," 199.

9. "Con este motivo se bolvio a excitar lo importante que seria copiar de letra usual, y moderna todo lo que seria copiado del archivo, y lo demas que de el parezca conveniente, respecto de la facilidad con que ahora puede hacerse para las copias que estos sugetos han sacado con el major cuidado y exactitud." AC, vol. 68, fols. 818v–819v (Wednesday, September 1, 1751).

10. Madrid, BN 12992, fol. 158v: "Cotejè esta copia con dicho original gothico en compañia de Don Juan Antonio de las Infantas, Canonigo Doctoral de la misma Iglesia, leyendo yo el tomo manuscrito y enmendando Don Juan esta copia de su mano. Acabose el cotejo en 12 de Agosto de 1752. Andres Burriel."

11. AC, vol. 70, fol. 45r–v (Saturday, March 23, 1754).

12. Burriel, "Apuntamientos," in Echánove Tuero, *La preparación intelectual*, 322: "Es muy despreciable el temor de que con esto se facilite el falseamiento de instrumentos, donaciones y privilegios antiguos con cuyo terror pánico se detuvo mucho la edición de Rodríguez." On this treatise, see chapter 5.

13. Toledo, AC, vol. 70, fol. 44v.

14. Toledo, AC, vol. 70, fol. 54v (Tuesday, April 23, 1754).

15. AC, vol. 70, fols. 76r–77v.

16. On the reasons for which the Commission in Toledo came to an end in 1756, see the introduction.

17. Alcaraz Gómez, *Jesuitas y Reformismo*, 584.

18. On the Ortiz editions, see the introduction.

19. Burriel, *Cartas eruditas*, 244–47.

20. Burriel, *Cartas eruditas*, 248–49.

21. On the history of comparative liturgy as a concept and method, see Bradshaw, *The Search*, 9–14. The foundational work for twentieth-century studies in the field is Baumstark, *Comparative Liturgy*; on the legacy of Baumstark see *Comparative Liturgy Fifty Years after Anton Baumstark*, ed. Taft and Winkler.

22. Alcaraz Gómez, *Jesuitas y Reformismo*, 583, notes that Rávago authorized Burriel to hire amanuenses.

23. Díaz, "Un erudito español," 10, states that Burriel was assisted by the two sons of the scholar Santiago y Palomares, the older one (Francisco Javier) already a magnificent calligrapher at the age of twenty-two.

24. Madrid, BN 13015, 13016, and 13017. In the first of these three manuscripts, the work was distributed among five scribes, each copying a complete passion. Three scribes collaborated on the second manuscript, and three others on the third.

25. Madrid, BN 13015, fols. 1–19v. See Janini and Serrano, *Manuscritos litúrgicos*, 155.

26. Burriel, *Cartas eruditas*, 242 (letter of December 1752 to Rávago).

27. Burriel, "Apuntamientos," in Echánove Tuero, *La preparación intelectual*, 271.

28. For instance, in Madrid, BN 13053, which is a transcription of Toledo, BC 35.6, the scribe seems to have made a great many mistakes, which is odd since, of all the early Toledan liturgical books, this one contains the script that seems easiest for the uninitiated to read.

29. The copy is Madrid, BN 13047.

30. For example, on fol. 4r: "fere melius completuria" ("perhaps *completuria* would be better") followed by a drawing of the original abbreviation.

31. On the misreading *capitula* for *completuria* see Brou, "Deux mauvaises lectures," 1:175–202.

32. For instance, Madrid, BN 13048, fol. 42v, where Burriel noted the difference between the version of Exodus 15.1 (the "Canticum Moysi") in the liturgical book and the Vulgate edition ("Maxime uariat a uulgata editione").

33. Usually Toledo, BC 35.3 (then 30-2), Toledo, BC 35.5 (then 30-4), the Verona orationale as published by Bianchini, and the printed Mozarabic breviary.

34. Madrid, BN 13052. On this transcription, made in 1753, see Janini and Serrano, *Manuscritos litúrgicos*, 161–62. On Toledo, BC 35.5 see Janini and Gonzálvez, *Catálogo*, 101–2; Mundó, "Datación," 12–13. The text is edited with an extensive introduction in Janini, ed., *Liber misticus de cuaresma y Pascua.*

35. Janini, "El oficio mozárabe," 14–18; Janini, ed., *Liber misticus de cuaresma*, xxxi–xliii; Janini, ed., *Liber missarum*, 2:lxviii–lxxii; Janini, ed., *Liber misticus de cuaresma y Pascua*, xxxiii–xxxvi; Janini, "Las piezas litúrgicas," 161–77; Janini, "La reforma cisneriana de la liturgia mozárabe," in the introduction to Janini and Gonzálvez, *Catálogo*, 39–49.

36. Madrid, BN 13053, p. 404, where the deacon says, "Incipiente ora nona omnes in eglesia conveniamus," Burriel wrote, "Deest hoc in Breviario excusso, in quo sequitur Hymnus Pange Lingua ad Adorationem crucis" (This is lacking in the printed breviary, in which there follows the hymn "Pange lingua" for the Adoration of the Cross).

37. Madrid, BN 13053, p. 424: "Hic in Missali excusso extant Rubricae, et Cantus ad adorationem crucis, de qua in hoc manuscripto codice nullum est vestigium" (In this place, in the printed missal there are rubrics and chant for the Adoration of the Cross of which there is no trace in this manuscript).

38. Madrid, BN 13053, p. 421, below the prayer "Desideratum lucernae splendorem obtatum" on Holy Saturday: "Hoc loco in excusso extat alia oratio: 'Deus, qui filios Israhel' et cetera dicenda ante altare, loco precedentis. Post eam sequitur rubrica de granis incensi cereo affigendi, et de aliquibus, quae desunt in codice manuscripto. Post id sequitur Benedictio cerei, seu inlatio, quae in manuscripto etiam immediate extat'" (In this place in the printed breviary there is another prayer: "Deus, qui filios Israhel" to be said before the altar, in place of the preceding prayer. There follows the rubric concerning the grains of incense to be affixed to the candle, and other things not in the original

manuscript. Afterwards there follows the blessing of the candle, or the Inlatio, which also follows immediately in the manuscript).

39. Madrid, BN 13053, p. 449.

40. Madrid, BN 13054, 13058, 13059, 13061.

41. For instance, Madrid, BN 13059; see Janini and Serrano, *Manuscritos litúrgicos*, 172–75.

42. Madrid, BN 13049, fols. 417–418v, is a separate bifolium with notes in four different hands on the presence of elements of the mass of Saints Justa and Rufina in various Toledan liturgical manuscripts and printed books.

43. The collation is in Madrid, BN 13053, pp. 355–78; the commentary is in Madrid, BN 13059, fol. 49r–v. Madrid, BN 13054, fols. 125–31 contains three copies of the Acts of Saints Justa and Rufina, the second with marginal annotations indicating the variants from the Passionary Toledo, BC 44.11 (35-6), the third copy with marginal annotations giving variants from the office lectionaries Toledo, BC 48.11 (30-21), and Toledo, BC 48.1 (36-2). The rest of Madrid, BN 13054, contains various notes and transcriptions on the liturgy of the two virgin martyrs; fols. 188r–198r contains Burriel's collation of the mass and office made in 1755.

44. Burriel, "Memorias auténticas," 1:5–52. Madrid, BN 2924, is a fair copy of the "Memorias auténticas" that begins with an introduction listing projected chapters on the liturgy and its books. Madrid, BN 13054, fols. 125–98, gathers some of Burriel's notes on the office and mass of Justa and Rufina. Burriel's working draft of the treatise occupies fols. 1–36v of Madrid, BN 13127.

45. Madrid, BN 13048, fol. 117r, 189r, and Madrid, BN 13049, fol. 397r. In Madrid, BN 13048, fol. 114v, next to "Dicite in nationibus Dominus regnauit a ligno" Burriel wrote, "Todo esto de letra mas moderna capellana de 1300" (All this is written in a more modern hand of 1300); on fol. 150v he underlined "Intende nostris sensibus" and added "Emendatum caracteribus seculi XIV" (Corrected in fourteenth-century script); on fol. 151r he underlined "Psallendum. Exultate Dominum" and added "Notatur id caracteribus seculi XIV" (This is written in fourteenth-century script).

46. Madrid, BN 13048, fol. 123r; Madrid, BN 13054, fol. 2r.

47. Janini and Serrano, *Manuscritos litúrgicos*, 164 (Madrid, BN 13053, p. 481): "Nullibi in toto codice tempus, quo scriptus is fuerit, vel a quo, notatur. . . . Ego vero Codicem ante Toleti per Alfonsum VI. restaurationem scriptum fuisse, credo: omne vero id, quod continet, ante Maurorum invasionem in usu fuisse, in divinis officiis, alibi probare conabor."

48. Janini, ed., *Liber missarum*, 2:xxxv; Janini and Gonzálvez, *Catalogo*, 102–3; *Hispania Vetus*, 300; Mundó, "Datación," 19–20.

49. For a description, paleographical analysis (by Anscari Mundó), and edition of Madrid 10110 see Janini, *Liber misticus de cuaresma*; see also Janini and Serrano, *Manuscritos Litúrgicos*, 133–42; Mundó, "Datación," 2–8. Burriel's description is in Madrid, BN 13054, fols. 62–68.

50. On the copy (Madrid, BN 13047), see Janini and Serrano, *Manuscritos litúrgicos*, 159.

51. Janini and Serrano, *Manuscritos litúrgicos*, 159: "Sed Caminus preconcepta opinione forsan delusus est. Subscriptionem hanc iterato cum Authographo ipso contulimus,

coram V(iro) CL(arissimo) mihi supra modum omnem amando, excolendo D. Joanne Antonio de las Infantas, olim Canonico, ut vocant Doctorali, nunc Decano meritissimo, qui mecum vidit, Caminum de suo addidisse tó Regnante Adefonso: meamque hanc excriptionem ad verbum authographo respondere. 1756."

52. Mundó, in Janini, *Liber misticus de cuaresma*, xxi.

53. For the most recent overview of early chant notation in the Iberian peninsula see Zapke, "Notation Systems," 189–243.

54. Janini and Serrano, *Manuscritos litúrgicos*, 164: "Ut lectori manifestetur tum caracterum gothicorum, tum musicalium notarum forma, pagellam, in qua officii S. Iohannis Baptistae initium est, feci acurate ad vivum excribi, seu depingi folio sequenti, cum authographo."

55. Janini and Serrano, *Manuscritos litúrgicos*, 163–64 (Madrid, BN 13053, p. 480): "Antiphonae, Responsoria, Laudes, etc. interseccione dictionum ad notas musicales accomodandas descriptae sunt: desunt tamen hee musicales notae in toto fere codice, tantumque supra aliquas antiphonas, hymnum S. Iohannis Baptistae, aliasque pauculas aliquorum officiorum particulas musica notata est."

56. See Boynton, "A Lost Mozarabic Liturgical Manuscript," 189–219. The copy is preserved in the second half of Madrid, BN 13060. For a partial editions of the manuscript's contents, based on the copy in Madrid, BN 13060, see Janini, ed. *Liber missarum*, 2:275–99.

57. The page from which this chant was copied is New York, HSA, B2916, fol. 94v.

58. On this chant see Hiley, *Western Plainchant: Alleluia-Melodien II*, 822–29.

59. These other items are edited in Boynton, "A Lost Mozarabic Liturgical Manuscript."

60. Janini and Serrano, *Manuscritos Litúrgicos*, 120–23, date the manuscript to the eleventh century; I follow the date proposed by Mundó, "Datación," 14, 21.

61. "Codex Muzarabicus continens Psalterium Integrum Libris V. distinctum, cum Antiphonis, notisque musicalibus uniuscujusque Psalmi propriis, iuxta novam (ut conjicimus) a D. Isidoro Hispalensi adornatam editionem."

62. Ayuso Marazuela, "Algunos problemas," 143–91.

63. An exception is the copy in Madrid, BN 13050, fols. 32r–34r of Madrid, BN 10001, fol. 5r–v, where Palomares copied the incipit on two lines (as in the original) and drew approximate likenesses of the initial letters for Psalms 11 and 12.

64. However, there are notes only for Psalms 1–4 (fols. 10–16), which are mostly corrections of the transcription.

65. Palomares left out the notation of the canticles and one of the hymns. A few omissions appear to be simple mistakes. For instance, the copies of the antiphons on fols. 12r, 22v, 39r, 46v, 51v, and 53r lack notation. In other cases the neumes were probably nearly invisible already in 1754: fols. 16r (the neumes on "ego sum"), 13v, 25v, 26r, 92v. On fol. 37v Palomares omitted the neumes just on the last word of the antiphon. Palomares did not include the notated fragments that now form the flyleaves of the manuscript, but they might not have been bound with it in 1754. In his *Polygraphia* Palomares included copies from one of these flyleaves (see chapter 5).

66. On this copy see Janini and Serrano, *Manuscritos litúrgicos*, 168.

67. Madrid, BN 13048, unfoliated gathering at beginning: "Este codice con su tomo segundo fue cotejado por el P. Burriel con otro de Verona, sacando del original toledano

y añadiendo muchos trozos que faltan en el Veronense." On the Verona orationale, see chapter 1. Several annotations in the copy refer to comparisons with the Verona manuscript, which Burriel noted lacks the prayers on fols. 10–40 of Toledo, BC 35.4.

68. On this manuscript see Janini and Serrano, *Manuscritos Litúrgicos*, 160.

69. See, for instance, Madrid, BN 13048, fol. 33r.

70. Burriel wrote "Nota. Hic, et infra variantur notae musicales" next to "Emitte lucem tuam Domine" on fol. 37v and he added the word "musica" in the margin next to "In te Domine speraui" and "Parce Domine" on fol. 196r.

71. Madrid, BN 2924, fol. 1r: "aumento de la devocion y confianza en su Patrocinio, confirmacion de nuestra Santa Fé, lustre de Sevilla y honor sagrado de toda nuestra Nación."

72. Linehan, "Religion," 161–99.

73. Toledo, BC 35.7, fols. 45v–55r contains the Assumption office.

74. Madrid, BN 13060, fol. 16v: "Et licet in omnibus Gothorum monumentis aurea Augustei saeculi puritas desideretur, gothice que sonantem latinitatem in ipsis reperiamus; habent tamen ejus aeui scriptores, habent et Ecclesiastica Officia leporem quendam, et venustatem, et ipsa ruente latinitate quaedam accuratioris styli non obscura vestigia. Neque vero Isidorus, Ildefonsus, Julianusve barbari hujus officii credi possunt Auctores, nec ab alio compositum in suis Ecclesiis cani, umquam probassent. Praeterea in oratione, *Post nomina* compellata, *Captivorum* mentis fit. Quae omnia mihi argumento, sunt ut officium post Maurorum dominationem conditum fuisse, persuasum habeam, atque ad Ildefonsianum Missarum Codicem nullatenus pertinere, credam." The word "missa" in this passage probably refers to a genre of prayer.

75. Madrid, BN 13047, fol. 38v: "Suspicetur ex his non incongrue aliquis, haec officia composita eo tempore fuisse, quo in Maurorum potestate captiui erant Hispani."

76. Janini, *Liber misticus de cuaresma*, xxx.

77. Madrid, BN 13047, fols. 154v–155r: "Haec clausula, Qui ergo non locorum praeparatum requiem expectamus, ita reperitur in Codice. Suspicor in ea alludi ad impurum Mahometanorum dogma de Paradyso, a quo longe esse orantes christianos, explicat. Si id non placet, deleri debet to *non*, ut sanum, et catholicum sensum oratio reddat; licet uis aduersatiue sentente paenitus euaquatur. Forte etiam suspicetur quis, contrapositionem fieri in oratione non inter Mauros, et Christianos, sed inter hos et Judeos in Promissionis terram, locosque sibi a Deo praeparatos euntes. Quasi diceret: Nos qui non expectamus, ut Judei in solitudine expectabant, locorum terrenam sibi praeparatam et promissam requiem, quaesumus, ut etc. Sensus hic etiam acutus, et sanus est, antiphonaeque praecedenti, quae de solitudine agit, conformi."

78. For the influence of Muslim theology on the Toledan Mozarabs see Burman, *Religious Polemic*, 326–31.

79. The fundamental study of this controversy is Cavadini, *The Last Christology*. For a recent account of Elipandus in relation to the council, see Cavadini, "Elipandus and His Critics," 2:787–807; see also Hainthaler, "Von Toledo nach Frankfurt," 2:809–60.

80. For the texts cited by Elipandus see Rivera Recio, *El adopcionismo*, 144–45; a detailed analysis is in Rivera Recio, "La controversia adopcionista," 506–36.

81. *Corpus scriptorum muzarabicorum*, 1:102.

82. On the mass in the Mozarabic rite, see Gómez-Ruiz, "Mozarabic Rite," 10:44–47.

83. Rivera Recio, *San Ildefonso*, 222, notes that the attribution of anonymous liturgical texts to Ildefonsus of Toledo has not been supported by research on the Old Hispanic rite.

84. Gómez-Ruiz, *Mozarabs*, 132–36; Orlandis, "Toletanae illusionis superstitio," 197–213.

85. Cavadini, *Last Christology*, 3–6.

86. Cavadini, *Last Christology*, 103–6; Firey, "Carolingian Ecclesiology," 253–316.

87. Rivera Recio, *El adopcionismo*, 77–83.

88. Mariana, *Historia General de España*, 7.8, "Del Elipando Arçobispo de Toledo," 1:267–68; Enrique Flórez, *España Sagrada*, 5:334.

89. For a more nuanced argument that Christian perceptions of Islam influenced adoptionism, see Urvoy, "Les conséquences christologiques," 2:981–92.

90. This theory was first developed by Ramón de Abadal y Vinyals in *La batalla del adopcionismo en la desintegración de la Iglesia visigoda*. A more recent study that places adoptionism in this context is Orlandis, "La circunstancia histórica," 1074–91.

91. Burriel, *Cartas eruditas*, 250 (letter of December 1752 to Francisco de Rávago).

92. Burriel studied these texts in part through a collection of them he had made, now preserved in Madrid, BN 12998. He also analyzed in detail the contents and construction of Toledo, BC 14.23, an eleventh-century manuscript that contains the letters of Elipandus; see Díaz y Díaz, *Manuscritos visigóticos*, 34.

93. Cavadini, *Last Christology*, 37–38.

94. "Dignus et iustum est nos tibi gratias agree . . . qui ab illa super celos" in Toledo BC 35.3, fol. 113r; for a transcription see Férotin, *Liber mozarabicus sacramentorum*, col. 237.

95. Madrid, BN 13046, p. 406 (annotation to the copy of Toledo, BC 35.3): "Haec verba Elipandus in Epistola ad Patres Francofordienses Eugenio Toletano tribuit, licet pauluum immutata, sic: 'Qui per adoptiui hominis passionem, dum suo non indulgit corpori, nostro demum, idest iterum non pepercit.'"

96. *Corpus scriptorum muzarabicorum*, 1:84: "Item precessores nostri Eugenius, Hildefonsus et Iulianus Toletane sedis antistites in suis dogmatibus ita dixerunt in missam de cena Domini: 'Qui per adobtiui hominis passione, dum suo non indulgit corpori, nostro demum,' id est, iterum, 'non pepercit.'" Elipandus quotes the same version in the letter to Alcuin (*Corpus scriptorum muzarabicorum*, 1:102), invoking the testimony of the Toledan bishops, as mentioned above.

97. Toledo BC 35.6, fol. 16r: "qui per adoptiui hominis passionem, quasi quasdam in presentis populi adquisitione maniebas" (part of the *pax* prayer "Dignum et iustum est, uere salutare nobis, atque conueniens gratias agere, laudes impendere, intelligere munera").

98. Madrid, BN 13053, p. 30: "Nota haec uerba ab Elipando in Epistola ad Pps. Francofordienses allegata."

99. Burriel also noted this separately in his notes on the manuscript in Madrid, BN 13054, fol. 5.

100. "Placeat, dilectissimi fratres" in Toledo BC 35.3, fol. 152r, and Toledo BC 35.6, fol. 96. For a transcription from Toledo, BC 35.3, see Férotin, *Liber mozarabicus sacramentorum*, cols. 322–23.

101. Madrid, BN 13046 (copy of Toledo, BC 35.3), p. 542: "Hanc periodum allegat Elipandus in Epistola ad P. P. Francofordienses, eam que S. Ildefonso tribuit, eum que hujus Misse auctorem facit." Madrid, BN 13053 (copy of Toledo, BC 35.6), p. 215: "Haec ipsa periodus est, quam in Epistola ad Francofordienses Patres allegat Elipandus, tamquam a B. Ildefonso conscriptam." The attribution to Ildefonsus is in *Corpus scriptorum muzarabicorum*, 1:90 ("secundum Hildefonsum qui dicit").

3 | A Gem Worthy of a King
The Facsimile of a Mozarabic Chant Book

Some professors of music, both of the holy Church of Toledo (where there are and
have always been excellent ones) and of this court, to whom I showed the musical
points of the Visigoths, confess openly that they do not understand them, and thus
one from Toledo, {who} looked at them {as he} heard the Mozarabic Chaplains
sing, and not finding any correspondence, or not understanding what the notes
had to do with the letters, for lack of clefs and lines, became more doubtful and
confused than before carrying out this observation.

—Francisco Xavier de Santiago y Palomares,
Polygraphia Gothico-Española

With these words Palomares described the lack of any evident connection
between the chant of the early modern Mozarabic liturgy and the medieval
manuscripts widely thought to preserve its melodies. His statement is a rare
acknowledgment before the twentieth century that the link between the two
traditions had been lost. As seen in the introduction, the cantorales created
under Archbishop Cisneros for the Mozarabic Chapel in Toledo Cathedral
were thought to contain the melodies of the chants preserved for centuries
by the Mozarabic community. It appears, however, that most of the melodies in the cantorales were either borrowed from the Roman rite or newly

composed, as they usually differ in contour from the corresponding chants in the medieval manuscripts.[1] Various explanations for this divergence have been proposed. Given the greatly diminished number of Toledan Mozarabs in the late fifteenth century, any survival of their oral chant tradition at that time is uncertain at best.[2] Even if it had been a continuous living tradition, we do not know how it related to the extant medieval manuscripts. Furthermore it is not clear how the oral and notated traditions could have been combined (or reconciled) for rendering in the modern notation of the cantorales created for the use of the Mozarabic chaplains.

The nature of the relationship between oral chant traditions and their written records is a notoriously vexed question, particularly with regard to the early history of Latin chant in the West.[3] By the late fifteenth century the written and oral transmissions of Gregorian chant melodies were closely intertwined; singers tended to perform chant from books. However, at this point in history the Gregorian chant was a long-standing, continuous oral tradition supported by literate modes of learning. By contrast the Mozarabic chant tradition had been interrupted and diminished, perhaps entirely discontinued. Even if the melodies sung in the Mozarabic parishes had survived throughout the Middle Ages, it is unlikely that clerics around 1500 would have had at their disposal techniques for transcribing music that had never before been written in a decipherable notational system. Indeed Ortiz, in his preface to the *Missale mixtum*, does not mention the music of the Mozarabic rite at all.[4] The question of rhythm is equally troubling: the chants in the cantorales are written in black mensural notation of the previous century, but we do not know whether the Mozarabic chant in the oral tradition would have been sung in proportional rhythm.

Consequently the musical legacy of the Cisneros cantorales remains somewhat difficult to assess. Divergences between the texts in the cantorales and those in the medieval manuscript sources have been identified through comparative analysis, but such analysis is more challenging for the melodies, which mostly lack clear Old Hispanic antecedents or models. Some of the melodies in the Cisneros cantorales are clearly derived from the style of Gregorian chant, while others have a more archaic flavor, leading to speculation that they represent vestiges of Mozarabic chant.[5] Vito Imbasciani hypothesized that after the texts were assembled, Gregorian melodies were applied to those chants that had them (texts that were also sung in the Roman rite and chants borrowed from the Roman rite for services that did not exist in the Old Hispanic rite). According to Imbasciani, the other melodies were composed soon before the compilation of the choir books, and in some cases might have been partly based on the configurations of neumes in the medieval manuscripts of Toledo Cathedral. Imbasciani notes, however, that the rite itself was very likely obsolete in the fifteenth century.[6] Characterizing the promotion of the Mozarabic rite under Cisneros as a restoration or renewal obfuscates the fact that it was necessary to reinvent some aspects of the tradition.

Given the many unquestioned suppositions layered upon the neo-Mozarabic chant since 1500, it is all the more remarkable that Palomares, who was neither a musician nor a historian but rather a lay scribe and calligrapher, so clearly perceived the gap between the living neo-Mozarabic tradition and the silent music of the Visigothic neumes. While the texts in the liturgical books could be transcribed for modern readers, the only way to transmit the content of the neumes was to copy them exactly. As described in chapter 2, Palomares executed many pen-and-ink drawings of neumes to accompany transcriptions of manuscripts. Most of these copies were intended for study; an accurate likeness of a page served to illustrate Burriel's description and analysis of the manuscript and constituted a convenient record for quick reference later on in the Commission's work. In 1752, however, Palomares had occasion to demonstrate the full extent of his skill in reproducing the original appearance of a manuscript. In that year, at the request of Burriel, he executed an opulent full-size, full-color parchment facsimile of Toledo, BC 35.7, a book of masses and offices for Marian feasts and for the Christmas-Epiphany cycle.[7] Burriel considered this the earliest extant Toledan chant book; he dated it to the reign of Alfonso VI, and specifically to the period around 1085.[8] More recently the paleographer Anscari Mundó has dated the manuscript to around 1100 or slightly later and has localized it to the Mozarabic parish of Santa Eulalia. Copious annotations in later hands show that the book was in use through at least the thirteenth century.[9] The extensive time and effort expended on the production of the facsimile itself can be explained in part by the fact that it was intended for presentation to the king.[10] For Burriel, Toledo, BC 35.7, must have seemed exceptionally important not only as a witness to the liturgy of the Toledan Mozarabic community, but also to the historical identity of Toledo itself. Taking into account the symbolic valence of the medieval manuscript in the eighteenth century, this chapter reconstructs the meanings of the facsimile as an artifact.

The Old Hispanic Rite as Patrimony

Burriel perceived the Toledan manuscripts in Visigothic script as a national legacy that was all too often overlooked by his contemporaries. It rankled him that the Old Hispanic rite received more attention abroad than at home, even though so many important medieval sources were located in Spain. He viewed the relationship between the liturgical traditions as competition, not only because the Roman rite had displaced the Old Hispanic liturgy, but also because of the national affiliations of modern liturgical scholars: French and Italian historians were behind the majority of eighteenth-century publications on the Old Hispanic rite, and several of the most influential works were based on a manuscript that was not preserved in Spain at all, but rather was housed in the library of Verona's cathedral chapter (Verona, Biblioteca Capitolare, LXXXIX).[11] Manuel C. Díaz y Díaz dated the textual contents of this orationale to the late seventh century and the copying of the manuscript itself to around 711. The text may have been copied in the northwestern Iberian peninsula or in the area of Narbonne from a Toledan manuscript adapted to the liturgical use of Tarragona. An annotation in Lombard script that can be dated to 731–32 suggests that the book was already in northern Italy by that time.[12] Two Italian priests wrote commentaries on this venerable codex: Gaetano Cenni (1698–1762) from Pistoia and Giuseppe Bianchini (1704–64) from Verona, who also transcribed the text.[13]

As director of the Commission on the Archives, Burriel hoped to make the Visigothic manuscripts in Toledo Cathedral's library better known in Spain and abroad, an aim he stated in a letter of 1752 to the royal confessor, Francisco de Rávago:

> It makes me ashamed that foreigners have not made known our Visigothic and Mozarabic liturgies in so many ways. . . . For this reason, I have resolved to collect as much as I can here for the honor of our Spanish liturgies in all their branches. Here there are eleven Visigothic volumes in parchment that contain various pieces of Visigothic or Mozarabic liturgy. The missal and breviary published by Cardinal Ximenez for the use of the churches were composed using these [manuscripts]: however, the manuscripts are very different in substance and organization, and if there is anything of utility to be done with them, it would be to print them *prout stant*, as has been done for the Gallican missals and the Gregorian and Leonine sacramentaries, the *ordo romanus*, etc.[14]

The model for future publications to which Burriel alludes here is probably Muratori's edition of 1748, the second volume of which contains reprints from Tomasi's editions and Mabillon's *De liturgia gallicana*.[15] Burriel advocated printing a diplomatic edition of the Old Hispanic liturgical manuscripts (transcribing their contents *prout stant*, "as they stand") because the

Ortiz editions had transformed the texts so extensively. In a letter written two years later to his colleague Pedro de Castro, Burriel placed in the context of national rivalry both the edition of Muratori and the need to publish the little-known manuscripts in Toledo:

In the library of this holy church there are preserved the eight manuscripts in parchment and Visigothic script that Father Jean Pien described in his treatise on this liturgy, through the report of Don Pedro Camino, my friend who is still alive and currently the presider of the Mozarabic Congregation, and there are also three others that Camino has not seen, besides some fragments of others. Although Father Manuel Acevedo reprinted in Rome, with new notes, the Mozarabic missal and breviary of Cardinal Cisneros, it would be very good to do with these Visigothic manuscripts the same that many authors of all nations have done, and that Muratori has just done, in 1748, with the manuscripts of the ancient Roman liturgy, printing in two volumes the sacramentaries of Saint Leo, Saint Gelasius, Saint Gregory, and others, exactly as they appear in the same ancient manuscripts, with brief annotations. In the first volume of the new edition of the works of Cardinal Tomasi (which has been sold here as well, divided into two volumes with different title pages and dedications, as if they were separate works), Bianchini incorporated a Visigothic manuscript that is preserved in the chapter library of Verona. . . .[16] Our Visigothic, Mozarabic or Isidoran liturgy can compete in every way with that of any other nation; just the library of this primatial church of Toledo offers us eleven volumes: ours is the Gothic Missal that Mabillon printed and that Muratori reprinted; ours the cited codex of the Chapter of Verona; ours the Visigothic volumes of Cardeña . . . and I do not doubt that in other monasteries of Spain there are preserved, as in that of Cardeña, many Visigothic liturgical books, enough to compose a collection so ample and complete that no other nation could offer a similar one.[17]

Here Burriel claims as a legacy of the Spanish nation some liturgical manuscripts preserved outside the Iberian peninsula. He groups the early liturgical codices of Toledo Cathedral in Visigothic script not only with the Verona orationale, but also with what he calls a "Gothic missal" that had been printed by Mabillon and then reprinted by Muratori. The missal in question is probably an early Burgundian sacramentary now known to liturgists as the "Missale Gothicum" (Vatican City, BAV, Reg. Lat. 317).[18] By calling such a book "ours," Burriel alluded to Mabillon's attribution of the Vatican manuscript to the ecclesiastical province of Narbonne, which had been part of the Visigothic kingdom. The repetition of "ours" (*nuestro*) in his letter amounts to an affirmation of continuity between the Visigoths and the Spaniards of the eighteenth century, an idea that was common in the historical discourse of the time.

For Burriel the Toledan liturgical manuscripts in Visigothic script were artifacts of a lost ritual tradition and functioned as symbolic objects representing the religious identity of the historical Mozarabic community in Toledo. In the early modern period the Mozarabs and their rite had taken on a heightened significance within an emerging vision of the transhistorical "Spanish" nation, a vision founded, in part, on the fiction of a continuous line of Catholicism from the Visigoths to the Mozarabs of medieval Castile. The modern Toledan Mozarabs were in turn seen as heirs to the legacy of the medieval community, and particularly to the privileges and exemptions granted them and reconfirmed by a long series of kings, beginning with Alfonso VI in 1101.[19]

The Mozarabs in Eighteenth-Century Toledo

In eighteenth-century Toledo the juridical status of the Mozarabs was the subject of renewed debate, in the course of which the charter of 1101 was studied and published.[20] The foremost proponent of the Mozarabs' privileges was Pedro Camino y Velasco, who in 1740 published the *Noticia historico-chronologica de los privilegios de las nobles familias de los mozarabes de la imperial ciudad de Toledo*, an annotated historical compilation of documents that appeared soon after Philip V had confirmed the privileges and exemptions of the community earlier in the year.[21] The *Noticia* contains a chronological summary of all the privileges granted the Mozarabs from Alfonso VI to Philip V, and includes a transcription and translation of the 1101 charter (the original of which is now lost), along with later charters that supported the payment of tithes to the Mozarabic parishes.[22] The volume begins with a dedication that dwells at length upon the venerability of the "Visigothic or Mozarabic mass" in the context of the antiquity of the Hispanic church. Dedicated to the infante Luis Antonio Jaime de Borbón e Farnesio, who was titular archbishop of Toledo from 1735 to 1754, this text conveys the signal importance of the early rite of Toledo to the man who was both the head of the Toledan church and a member of the Bourbon royal family. Camino's insistence on the validity of the traditional privileges and exemptions enjoyed by Mozarabic parishioners was nonetheless challenged in court, as it had the effect of reducing tax revenues. In response to such objections

Camino wrote a detailed defense of the Mozarabs' privileges in 1744; this text is preserved at the end of a manuscript containing Burriel's compilation of liturgical excerpts from printed breviaries.[23] Since Camino's text survives among Burriel's papers, the Jesuit probably consulted it and possibly even requested the copy to be made for his own use.

Burriel took an interest in the contemporary debate regarding the status of the Mozarabs.[24] A remark in the "Apuntiamientos" of 1749 makes his position on the matter clear: "In Toledo, where I lived for seven years, a thousand attempts were made to do away with the foundations of Ximénez and to invalidate the concessions given to the Mozarabs, when they only needed to correct the abuses that there were: and moreover all should agree to maintain that which I judge to be the greatest and most solid glory of the nation."[25] This reference to the conflict in Toledo regarding the Mozarabs' exemptions suggests that there may have been grounds for challenging their traditional privileges. Burriel appears to have studied the matter rather closely. The text that immediately precedes his copy of Camino's *Defensa* sets forth the perspective of the Toledan Mozarabs themselves.[26] In this undated document the clergy of the six Mozarabic parishes request royal patronage (*patronato real*) and an income to support their performance of the traditional rite. The petition must be addressed to Ferdinand VI, for it refers to Philip V as deceased. Citing Philip V's attendance at mass in the Mozarabic Chapel of Toledo Cathedral in 1723, the petitioners invite Ferdinand to hear their rite celebrated in Toledo. Appealing to the status of the Old Hispanic liturgy as a national treasure, they refer to the rites, ceremonies, and prayers of the Visigothic liturgy as "the most glorious crest and shield that could be made for Spain . . . the envy of foreign nations."[27] This description matches Burriel's own characterization of the rite as "the greatest and most solid glory of the nation."

The petition mentions the numerous court cases since 1500 challenging the Mozarabic parishes' rights to their traditional tithes. According to the petition, the priests and prebendaries charged with observing the rite cannot keep up with growing costs, "nor maintain themselves with the decency owed to their character and Ministries, given the extreme scantiness to which their income is reduced, which is notorious. They see themselves obliged (although with the greatest pain) to abandon the said Churches, leaving the holy and most ancient Mozarabic Rite exposed to total extinction."[28] According to the petitioners, no one could be found "who for a lean stipend would want to study and learn such an exceedingly difficult rite and chant, or take upon himself the immeasurable effort of celebrating the mass and all the daily and nightly canonical hours."[29] Thus despite the measures taken by Cisneros to endow the Mozarabic Chapel in Toledo Cathedral and its chaplaincies, the parishes apparently had difficulty sustaining the old rite.

The preservation of the petition in Burriel's papers along with Camino's *Defensa* indicates the Jesuit's familiarity with the manner in which the Mozarabic parish clergy invoked their rite's uniqueness and antiquity so as to reaffirm their special status. He also must have known Camino's *Noticia*, another text that invokes the liturgical tradition of the Mozarabs as historical justification for their special status in Toledo. The sentiments reflected in these texts, and the contemporary debate concerning the status of the Mozarabs, could have influenced Burriel's own approach to the history of the

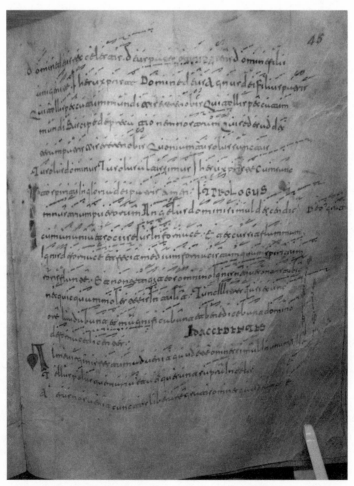

FIGURE 3.1 Toledo, BC 35.7, fol. 45r. Copyright © Archivo y Biblioteca Capitulares, Catedral Primada de Toledo.

Toledan community and perhaps played a role in his decision to commission from Palomares a facsimile of Toledo 35.7.

Reproduction, Transcription, and Commentary

In his facsimile copy (Madrid, Palacio Real, Biblioteca, II/483) Palomares faithfully rendered nearly every detail of the original and subsequently claimed to have reproduced the script, neumes, and even the binding so

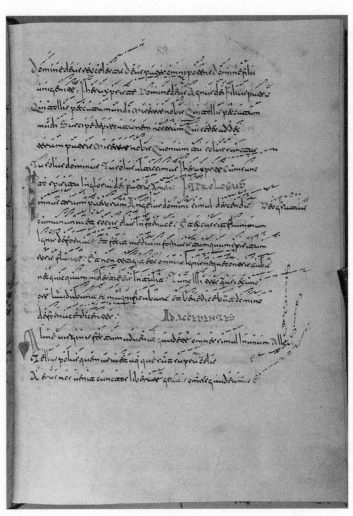

FIGURE 3.2 Madrid, Palacio Real, Biblioteca, II/483, p. 89. Copyright © Patrimonio Nacional.

accurately as to make the copy practically indistinguishable from the medieval manuscript on which it was modeled. Years later, in his request for a royal pension, he wrote (speaking of himself in the third person):

> He made an exact copy of the entirety of a Mozarabic-Gothic missal in parchment from [the manuscripts] preserved in that library, on which he worked incessantly for about six months, and the result was so similar to the original, not only in the idiosyncratic character of the Visigothic letters, [and] the particular nature of the musical notation (which until now no one has understood) but also in the material of its binding and its condition, that when the Dean and other canons of that holy church saw [the copy], it was judged identical to the original, and some even thought that there should be a certification that the petitioner made this copy, so that later on it would not be taken for the original.[30]

Burriel likewise emphasized the excellence of the reproduction in his letter to Francisco de Rávago:

> Furthermore, I have undertaken to have [the liturgical books] copied in their entirety; three volumes have already been copied. One of them (because it contains the masses of Saint Ildefonsus for the eight days before Christmas, and those from Christmas to Epiphany) not only has been copied, but also reproduced in Visigothic script with its colors and with the same Visigothic notation and rough parchment, so similar to the original that I was told it would be necessary to put a certification as to which is the original, and which the copy, so that later on there will be no doubt when the parchment of the copy becomes tarnished by time and handling. It is a gem worthy of the King for whom it was made.[31]

The painstaking care with which the facsimile was prepared is eloquent testimony to Palomares's skill (Figures 3.1 and 3.2). Palomares omitted some of the late medieval additions to the manuscript, such as the chant added in Aquitanian notation in the lower margin of fol. 46v; the lower margin of the copy for that page is blank (Figure 3.3). Perhaps this was a conscious choice to elide later, non-Hispanic elements in the manuscript. If so, Palomares might have made this omission for the same reason that Burriel's preface to the facsimile does not mention the liturgical reform. The facsimile is otherwise remarkably faithful to the original, even incorporating subtle details such as the different shade of ink in which a slightly later hand (using a finer pen nib and more delicate strokes) added a second layer of musical notation, as can be seen in Figure 3.3.[32]

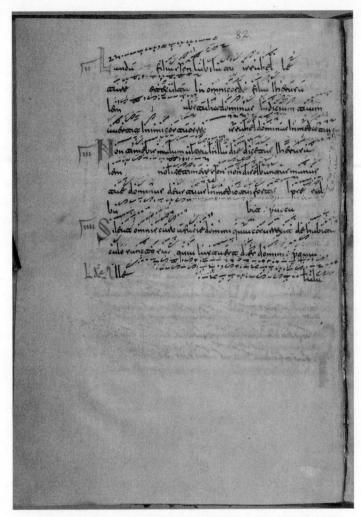

FIGURE 3.3 Madrid, Palacio Real, Biblioteca, II/483, p. 82. Copyright © Patrimonio Nacional.

To render the textual contents of the manuscript accessible to an eighteenth-century reader, Palomares made a complete transcription into modern script. The first version of this transcription, now preserved with Burriel's other papers in the Biblioteca Nacional in Madrid, appears to be a working draft made in preparation for diffusion; it begins with a title page that, according to José Janini, signals Burriel's intention to publish the text.[33] A presentation copy of this transcription was presented to the king along with the parchment facsimile, and the two manuscripts are still preserved together in the library of the Royal Palace in Madrid.[34]

The working draft of the transcription contains numerous annotations in Latin by Burriel, including remarks on the chants and their notation. Commenting on "Alme virginis festum," an *ad accedentes* chant sung while the congregation approached the priest to take Communion, Burriel described its musical structure (see the first part of the chant in Figures 3.1 and 3.2): "The word 'Alleluia' is divided into responses to the versicles. 'Alle' is the only response to the first versicle, and the music is notated. For the remaining versicles, except for the last, the response is simply 'e,' and over this vowel the music is notated; it is not always the same, but variable, and wonderfully rendered. The response to the last versicle is 'eluia,' with music notated over each vowel."[35] This composition is remarkable for several reasons, and Burriel's interest was piqued. First, it is a rare, and possibly the oldest, instance of a sequence in the Old Hispanic rite. Since it is not rubricated as a sequence, however, Burriel apparently did not recognize it as such; its genre was first pointed out by Louis Brou, who identified the model as a Mozarabic office chant.[36] Second, the chant's structure, which Burriel aptly describes, incorporates a performance practice known as "neumatizing," in which the melodies of successive verses of a sequence are repeated without text after the texted verse has been sung.[37] Burriel's description of the notation of "Alme virginis" shows an awareness of musical contour as conveyed by the unheighted neumes of the Toledan manuscript.

Burriel's commentary on another folio likewise indicates close attention to the musical notation and analysis of the script, and the facsimile executed by Palomares captures its appearance with the same precision as Burriel's description (Figures 3.4 and 3.5). The colophon is written across the page in a single column; the layout then changes to two columns for a prayer followed by psalm antiphons in the left column.[38] Burriel described the page thus:

> After the end of the copied-out manuscript and the signature of the scribe Sebastian on the same page, there follows immediately the prayer *De eterna rerum*, then antiphons for the canonical psalms in the same Visigothic script in which the entire codex is written, so that they can be considered of the same hand. The antiphons, moreover, bear the same type of musical notation that is seen throughout the manuscript. After this, on the same page there follow certain rubrics for the office of the Nativity with elements that are not Visigothic, but Gallican, and these are written in the script not used for books or privileges but rather the script used for letters, accounts, and other monuments of common commerce, and royal decrees of minor importance,

in the late thirteenth century and throughout the fourteenth century. The language in which these same rubrics are notated is partly Latin and partly the vernacular of the time, both of these barbarous.[39]

Although Burriel's disparaging assessment of the Latinity of the rubrics is characteristic of early modern disdain for medieval forms of Latin, his comment reveals that he had carefully studied both the handwriting and the textual contents of the page. The continuation of this annotation treats the matter of chants and their notation in further detail, addressing the verso containing slightly later additions, which like "Alme virginis" are *ad accedentes* chants (Figures 3.6 and 3.7). Observations on both text and content led Burriel to draw conclusions about the date of the manuscript on paleographic grounds; his opinion has been confirmed, in its general outlines, by Mundó (cited earlier).

> Then on the reverse page of the same folio there follow certain antiphons ornamented with music that appear to belong to [the genre of] *Ad accedentes* for the Communion in the mass of the Assumption of Holy Mary. Both the notation and the script are Visigothic, although perhaps not of the same hand that wrote the codex. Since these antiphons were written at the end of the manuscript after the rubrics were written, which were executed in the thirteenth or fourteenth century, it clearly establishes that the Toledan Mozarabs did not abandon the use of Visigothic script in writing their liturgical books during those centuries. Still, no one should infer from this that the entire codex was written in the thirteenth or fourteenth century. For inasmuch as I can form a hypothesis from the close inspection of this same codex, from collating it with other very early dated Visigothic [manuscripts], and having considered all the additions, even the most minimal ones, I am convinced that this is the oldest of all the liturgical manuscripts that are preserved in the library of the church of Toledo, although I believe that it was written in Toledo not before the deplorable Moorish domination, but either during the time of that same captivity, or some time after the city was restored to the Christian religion.[40]

Burriel adduced the date of the manuscript from close examination of the textual and musical hands, employing a kind of paleographic analysis that had never before been applied to the early Toledan chant books. His comparison of the layers of musical notation also represents a new approach to this material. His annotation links the codex to the Toledan Mozarabic

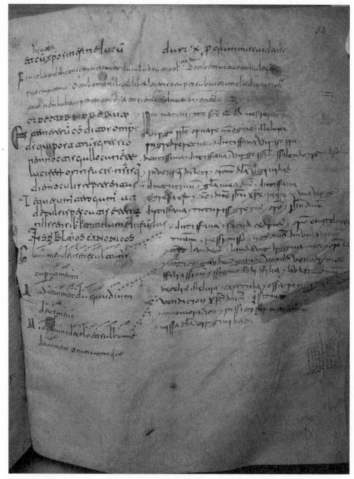

FIGURE 3.4 Toledo, BC 35.7, fol. 54r. Copyright © Archivo y Biblioteca Capitulares, Catedral Primada de Toledo.

community's liturgical observances, as well as to its manuscript production. One imagines that Palomares's copy of the page, seen here in Figure 3.7, was a part of the process of study.

Burriel's Preface for Ferdinand VI

The presentation of the facsimile and transcription to Ferdinand VI took place in 1755, when the Commission on the Archives was faced with desuetude after a period of upheaval in the Spanish government. After the Concordat of 1753, which more or less achieved the goals of the lengthy negotiations

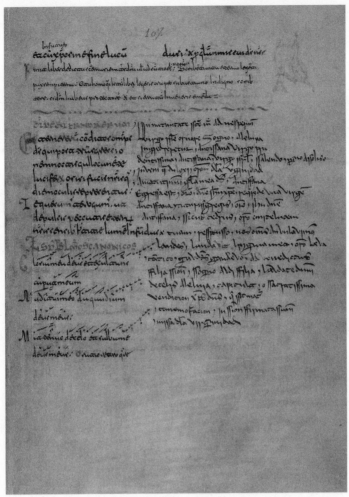

FIGURE 3.5 Madrid, Palacio Real, Biblioteca, II/483, p. 107. Copyright ©
Patrimonio Nacional.

between the Spanish government and the Vatican, the Commission on the
Archives essentially lost its relevance for the ministers of Ferdinand VI. The
subsequent dismissal of Burriel's patrons, the Marques de la Ensenada and
Francisco de Rávago, greatly diminished the Commission's support at court.
The gesture of offering the facsimile to the king as a fruit of the Commission's
labors may have been a vain attempt to convince the monarch that the team
in Toledo was doing something crucial for the glory of the nation.[41]

To that end the facsimile includes a preface by Burriel, explaining the
historical significance of the rite as a link in an unbroken tradition of belief
and ritual practice connecting the monarch to his "ancestors," the Visigothic

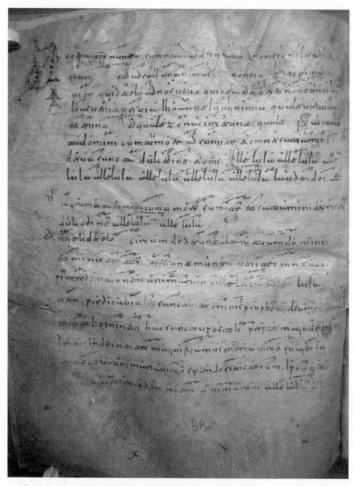

FIGURE 3.6 Toledo, BC 35.7, fol. 54v. Copyright © Archivo y Biblioteca Capitulares, Catedral Primada de Toledo.

kings. Forging an imaginary link between the Visigoths and the Bourbons (two dynasties that in reality were remote from one another in every possible way) was a common enough historiographical strategy in the Spanish Enlightenment. Burriel's approach, however, was distinctive in that he constructed this fictive narrative of continuity through the history of the liturgy, employing as evidence an arcane manuscript that had been painstakingly reproduced in all its recondite graphic specificity. It is significant that Burriel chose to insert this text in the facsimile itself rather than in the accompanying volume containing the transcription of the text. The preface serves as a framing device, one that reveals the meaning of this ancient book, which was surely different from anything the king had ever seen.

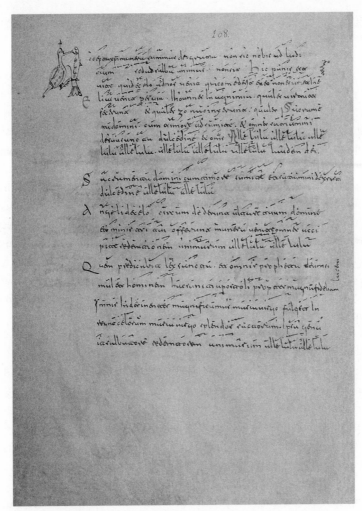

FIGURE 3.7 Madrid, Palacio Real, Biblioteca, II/483, p. 108. Copyright ©
Patrimonio Nacional.

Sire: Among the many manuscript tomes that are kept in the Library of the Holy Church of Toledo, the Primate of Spain, which I
have examined by order of Your Majesty, are found eleven volumes
written on parchment in Visigothic script, which contain different
parts of the Office and Liturgy called, with various names, Visigothic,
Isidoran, Toledan, and Mozarabic, which was common in Spain in the
times of the Visigoths, and of the Moors until the eleventh century,
and which since then had been preserved without interruption in the
Mozarabic parishes of Toledo, to which has been added a chapel in the

Primatial Church in which the liturgy is sung every day. These precious manuscripts are an inestimable monument of the faith and religion of Spain, because with their authenticity and venerable antiquity they demonstrate the marvelous uniformity and harmony of our present beliefs with that which the ancient Spaniards believed from the earliest times of Christianity until now, and the uninterrupted continuity, by the grace of God, of Catholicism in Spain throughout the centuries from those times until our own. These books are so many witnesses worthy of veneration for their antiquity, and greater than all others in their authenticity, for they proclaim and affirm that Your Majesty believes, confesses, and worships with all his Spanish Catholic vassals the same that the Kings, ancestors of Your Majesty, have believed, confessed, and worshipped since the Catholic Kings Saint Hermengild and his brother the Catholic King Reccared, for more than twelve hundred years and all the vassals that they had, ancestors of those of us who have the fortune to be vassals of Your Majesty today.[42]

Here Burriel presents the pre-Roman-rite liturgical manuscripts of Toledo Cathedral as the link between Hermengild (a Visigothic prince) and Ferdinand VI (the first Spanish Bourbon to be born in Spain). Hermengild, a convert from Arianism to Catholicism, was revered as a martyr; Ferdinand was known for his personal piety.[43] Accounts of the king's daily attendance at church services reached the public through print media such as the *Gaceta de Madrid*, a periodical publication that functioned as a form of court propaganda.[44] In the eyes of Burriel, Ferdinand's piety and devotions made him a fitting heir to the Catholic princes of Visigothic Spain. It is striking that Burriel refers to the Visigothic kings with the term "progenitores" ("ancestors"); Alfonso VI's diploma of December 18, 1086, similarly uses the word "progenitores" (albeit in Latin) to describe the Christian kings who had once ruled in Toledo.[45] Both texts imply continuity of descent between the Visigoths and the medieval Leonese kings, an ideology that has been dubbed "Neo-Gothicism."[46] While Burriel situated the distinctive features of the Toledan Mozarabic manuscripts within the historical setting of the "Reconquest," he also construed them as a metaphorical bridge across the centuries, linking the reigning monarch to the Visigothic kings as well as to the medieval kings of Castile and León.[47] Other contemporary instances of the term "progenitores" addressed to Ferdinand VI in relation to the Mozarabic rite appear in the petition from the clergy of the Mozarabic parishes. The petitioners refer to the "principal purpose of the sainted holy kings that were

Your Majesty's progenitors" as honoring the ancient liturgy.[48] The clergy refer to the call upon the king's piety and religious zeal, which are compared with those of his predecessors ("progenitores").[49] These invocations of the king's ancestors place him in a long line of royal patrons who favored the Mozarabs with privileges. The facsimile of the liturgical book, like the petition from the clergy of the Mozarabic parishes, sought to increase the currency of the old rite with the reigning king of Spain.

The facsimile reproduction also created a seductive fantasy of historical continuity. Burriel's preface leaves out the suppression of the Old Hispanic rite (as well as the Arianism of the Visigoths before the conversion of Hermengild). The liturgical books take their place alongside the other manuscripts from the early Middle Ages: Bibles, patristic writings, canon law and church councils, papal decretals, Visigothic law codes, and the martyrologies and passionaries from which the lives and deeds of the saints were read aloud in the divine office. The Toledan liturgical manuscript not only bears witness to traditions of sacral kingship, but also provides evidence for the primacy and antiquity of the Spanish church. Despite the vicissitudes to which the Old Hispanic rite was subject over the centuries (asserted Burriel), the substance of its belief and observance, as represented by these books, was unchanging. Along with the entire range of textual genres studied by the Commission on the Archives, the evidence combined to form a "river of authority" affirming the venerable tradition of Spanish Catholicism:

If to such illustrious testimony is joined that provided (with marvelous harmony among them) by the copies of the Bible, written more than a thousand years ago, before the Moorish invasion, the works of the saints and Spanish fathers of the church preserved in very ancient volumes; the canon law collection composed of councils, papal decretals, constitutions, and the decisions of prelates; the collection of secular law, from the *fuero-juzgo* of the Visigothic kings with all the legal codes, reports from parliament, decrees, and other laws up to those decreed by Your Majesty; the martyrologies, and passionaries in which are contained the lives and deaths of the holy martyrs and confessors that are part of the divine office, its mutations and variations in various centuries, without changing the substance of belief and cult; and finally our ancient chronicles and histories, supported by authentic documents from each period, of which a great number are still preserved in our archives, they form a river of authority with only Spanish springs in favor of the Catholic religion, and the firm tradition of our faith, which is more than enough to stifle all the heresies at once.[50]

The metaphor of the river is a telling one; rivers flow continuously but, as the saying (attributed to Heraclitus) goes, one cannot step into the same river twice. Burriel's preface seems to imply a continuity inherent in the rite itself; it makes no direct reference to the liturgical reform of the eleventh century or the introduction of the Roman rite. Admittedly what may appear to be a rhetorical strategy could instead be attributed to the fact that the preface centers on the manuscript itself rather than on the historical circumstances surrounding its production. According to Burriel, Toledo, BC 35.7, was produced during the reign of Alfonso VI of Castile and after the Christian conquest of Toledo in 1085, the period in which the Roman rite was introduced at Toledo. As we saw in the introduction, the change of rite in 1086 caused a rupture in the ritual community of the city by essentially excluding the Mozarabs from the Cathedral. Burriel's account of this event in his *Paleografía Española* makes it clear that he knew its ultimate significance for the status of the Mozarabs and their liturgy.[51]

In Burriel's preface to the facsimile his insistence on the centuries-long continuity of the rite may indicate a desire to attenuate the importance of the historical watershed that separated the liturgical traditions of Visigothic Spain (which he assumed to live on in the Old Hispanic rite of the Mozarabs) and the Roman rite observed by his contemporaries. Despite the symbolic power of the "restored" rite celebrated in the Mozarabic Chapel of Toledo Cathedral, Burriel knew that the neo-Mozarabic rite was an invention and that the medieval rite of the Mozarabs was largely forgotten. By invoking the Visigoths as the ritual and national predecessors of the Bourbons, however, Burriel rewrote history, establishing a fictive parallelism that inherently reinforced the authority of both. Seen from this teleological vantage point, the relationship between the two dynasties is no longer an anachronistic leap across the intervening centuries but has become both reasonable and logical.

In the remainder of his preface Burriel describes the contents of the liturgical book itself, stating that Ildefonsus of Toledo had a role in the creation of the Visigothic liturgy:

So that Your Majesty may have the pious pleasure of seeing what these Visigothic tomes look like and how they are written, I arranged for Don Francisco Xavier de Santiago y Palomares, a native of this city of Toledo, a youth of extraordinary ability in drawing and in imitating all sorts of ancient scripts, to copy the volume that appears to be the oldest and the most significant of all. It is composed of two parts, or two codices, in which many leaves are missing at the beginning, at the end, and in the middle. In the first part is the majority of the treatise written by Saint Ildefonsus in defense of the perpetual virginity of Our Lady the Virgin Mary, divided into seven *missae*, or seven parts that were read to the people at mass. There follows the proper mass of the day of the Annunciation of Our Lady, or the Incarnation of the eternal Word in her most pure form, which, by decree of the tenth Council of Toledo, which Saint Ildefonsus attended, was celebrated in Spain on the 18th of December, and was the principal feast of Saint Mary the Virgin, the Mother of God. Part of this mass is a very devout sermon of the saint, which was recently published for the first time by Father Henrique Flórez. Perhaps they repeated the same mass for the seven subsequent days, and in the place of the sermon was read part of the saint's [i.e., Ildefonsus's] treatise. Apart from this, in the same first part [of the manuscript], besides other minor things there is the office and mass of the Assumption of Our Lady. In the second part of the volume are the offices and masses that were celebrated from the day of the Nativity of the Lord until [the] Epiphany, and they are for Christmas itself, Saint Stephen, Saint John the Evangelist, the Circumcision, New Year's, and the Epiphany to the Kings. It is stated in the testimonies of Saint Julian and of Elipandus, successors to the holy doctor Ildefonsus in the see of Toledo, that the saint composed some masses, offices, and sermons. In the encomium attributed to Cixila, also archbishop of Toledo, which apparently he composed as a prologue for a manuscript of the masses of Saint Ildefonsus, and which is found copied in many very ancient manuscript volumes in the Escorial, Toledo, and elsewhere, it is said that the holy doctor not only composed but also set to music some offices and masses. The sermon, which in this manuscript appears anonymous, incorporated into the mass of the Annunciation, is found also with other sermons and separated from the mass under the name of Saint Ildefonsus in the manuscript from which the abovementioned Father Flórez published them. All these things together lead us to believe that all the offices and masses contained in this volume were composed and set to music by the holy prelate and doctor Ildefonsus, most tenderly devoted to Our Lady of all the holy doctors and ancient fathers [of the church].[52]

The sermon to which Burriel refers at the end of this passage is Ildefonsus of Toledo's treatise on the perpetual virginity of the Virgin Mary, a text found in Toledo, BC 35.7, divided into liturgical readings.[53] As if to reinforce the attribution of the sermon to Ildefonsus, the facsimile includes an author portrait of the bishop writing his treatise while gazing raptly upon an apparition of the Virgin and Child.[54] The insertion of an author portrait is a framing device that functions in the same manner as Burriel's preface, by associating the manuscript with a venerable father of the Spanish church and linking it to the Visigoths. As we have seen, just as Palomares had done in his own account of the copy, Burriel pointed out the faithful rendering of the neumes in the facsimile. Moreover he stated that Ildefonsus had composed the melodies as well as the texts of the chants, a point that may have been calculated to capture the attention of Ferdinand VI, whose love of music was well known:

> The Visigothic musical notes were likewise reproduced as they appear in the original. This volume is worthy of the highest esteem above all the other manuscript volumes of the office, and the Visigothic or Mozarabic liturgy, for its content and for its author; to which it should be added that of all this only a small part was printed in the Mozarabic missal and breviary that the venerable Cardinal Archbishop of Toledo, Francisco Ximenez de Cisneros, a man of immortal memory, had copied and printed.[55]

Even without a particular interest in history, Ferdinand could appreciate the idea that the religious music he knew and appreciated was distantly related to the curious signs in the manuscript facsimile. Unlike the repertory of the king's chapel, however, this was silent music: the neumes could not be performed, but could only be presented to the ruler in writing. Although music is customarily described as a sounding object, in this case its visual trace could be interpreted as a meaningful connection to the times of the Visigothic bishop Ildefonsus.

Why did the team in Toledo devote such painstaking labor to creating a precise copy of an eleventh-century manuscript that served no apparent purpose beyond nostalgia and display? What motivated the reproduction of a liturgical manuscript in the context of an archival enterprise purportedly concerned solely with diplomatics? Burriel's preface, and Palomares's subsequent account of the presentation to Ferdinand VI, both refer to the king's desire to *see* (*ver*) an example of the religious legacy of his realm.[56] Central to the presentation copy, then, was the gesture of reproduction. The textual contents were made available in the transcription, but Burriel presented the essence of this legacy from the time of the Visigothic kings as immanent in the graphic appearance of the manuscript, as if the physical artifact itself symbolized the history that he sought to recover, preserve, transmit, and explain. By interpreting the Visigothic liturgical manuscripts as a window onto the history of the Spanish nation, even while applying modern critical and comparative methods to the neo-Mozarabic editions,

Burriel created a historiography that was ultimately no less mythographic than that of his predecessors. Palomares's facsimile copy was an essential component of this process.

Notes

Francisco Xavier de Santiago y Palomares, *Polygraphia Gothico-Española* (Madrid, RAH 9/4752), p. 21: "Algunos profesores de la Musica, assi de la Santa Iglesia de Toledo en donde los hay, y ha havido siempre muy excelentes, como de esta Corte, à quienes hè mostrado los puntos de la Musica de los Godos confiessan llanamente, que no los entienden, siendo assi que uno de Toledo, teniendolos presentes oyò cantar à los Capellanes Muzaraves, y no hallando corespondencia, ò no entendiendo la que tenian las notas con las voces por falta de claves y de rayas, se quedò mas dudoso y confuso que antes de hacer esta observacion."

1. González Barrionuevo, "La música litúrgica," 182–85; Imbasciani, "Cisneros," 12; Rojo and Prado, *El canto mozárabe*, 103–7.

2. Imbasciani states that, as far as one can tell from Ortiz's comments, the medieval Mozarabic manuscripts in Toledo Cathedral were not used for performance ("Cisneros," 7).

3. For several different points of view on this subject, see Boynton, "Orality," 99–167; Levy, *Gregorian Chant*; Treitler, "Oral, Written, and Literate Process," 471–91; Treitler, "Reading and Singing," 135–208; Treitler, "The 'Unwritten' and 'Written' Transmission,'" 131–91. Many pertinent articles have been reprinted in Kelly, *Oral and Written Transmission in Chant*.

4. See Imbasciani, "Cisneros," 6; for the preface to the *Missale Mixtum* of 1500, see 187–88.

5. See, for instance, González-Barrionuevo, "La música litúrgica," 183–84.

6. Imbasciani, "Cisneros," 138–40.

7. For the contents, see Janini and Gonzálvez, *Catálogo*, 103–4.

8. See Burriel's comments in the transcription of the manuscript in Madrid, BN 13060, fol. 31v.

9. Mundó, "La datación," 14–15.

10. Although the facsimile was completed by the end of 1752, it was presented to Ferdinand VI by the Duke of Alba only in 1755, apparently in order to satisfy the king's wish to see one of the early liturgical books in the cathedral. This is stated in the fair copy of Palomares's request to Charles III for a royal pension (London, BL, Egerton 588, fol. 159v). The presentation is also mentioned in the annotations in two manuscript copies of one of Burriel's letters: Madrid, RAH, 9/5921, fol. 104r (in Burriel's hand); Madrid, Real Biblioteca, II/2838, fol. 184v.

11. For the text see Vives, *Oracional visigótico*.

12. Díaz y Díaz, "Consideraciones," 13–29. See also Vivancos, "El oracional visigótico," 121–44.

13. Gaetano Cenni, "Antiquissimi ritus gothico-Hispani CL Viri Cajetani Cenni sacrosancte basilice vaticane presbyter beneficiati de libello orationum gothico-hispano codicis veronensis judicium Tomo I de antiquitate Ecclesie Hispanie pag. 28 et seqq.," excerpted from his *De antiquitate Ecclesiae hispanae dissertationes*; Bianchini, "Adnotationes." Both are in the compound publication *Liturgia antiqua, Hispanica, Gothica, Isidoriana, Mozarabica Toletana Mixta illustrata* (Rome: H. Mainardi, 1746).

14. Letter of December 22, 1752, in Burriel, *Cartas eruditas*, 243–44: "Causame verguenza que los Extrangeros no hayan ilustrado de tantas maneras nuestras Liturgias Gotica y Muzarabe. . . . Por esto me he resuelto à recoger aquí quanto pueda para la ilustracion de nuestras Liturgias Espanolas en todos sus ramos. Once tomos Goticos en pergamino hay aqui, que contienen diversos pedazos de Liturgia Goda ó Muzarabe. De ellos se compuso para uso de las Iglesias el Misal ó Breviario que imprimió el Cardenal Ximenez; pero los manuscritos tienen mucha diferencia en substancia y órden, y si de ellos se ha de hacer alguna cosa de provecho, será imprimirlos todos *prout stant*, como se ha hecho con los Misales galicanos, Sacramentarios, Gregorianos y Leonianos, *ordo romanus*, etc."

15. Muratori, *Liturgia romana*; Mabillon, *De liturgia gallicana libri III*. See Vismara, "Muratori alla 'Scuola Mabillona,'" 135–52.

16. Bianchini, *Josephi Mariae*.

17. Burriel, *Cartas eruditas*, 268–69: "Conservanse en la libreria de esta santa Iglesia los ocho tomos manuscritos en pergamino, y letra Gótica, de que hace memoria el Padre Juan Pinio, en su tratado de esta Liturgia, por relacion de Don Pedro Camino, mi amigo que aún vive, y es hoy Presidente de la Congregacion Muzarabe, y tambien se conservan otros tres, que Camino no vió, fuera de algunos fragmentos de otros. Aunque el Padre Manuel Acebedo reimprimió en Roma con notas el Misal y Breviario Muzarabe del Cardenal Cisneros, convendria mucho hacer con estos tomos Góticos manuscritos, lo mismo que han hecho muchos autores de todas naciones, y ahora acaba de hacer el Muratori año de 1748 con los códigos de la Liturgia Romana antigua, imprimiendo en dos tomos los Sacramentarios de San Leon, San Gelasio, San Gregorio, y otros; segun se hallan en los mismos códigos antiguos á la letra, con notas breves. En el primer tomo de la nueva edicion de las obras del Cardenal Tomasi (que acá se ha vendido tambien, repartido en dos volumenes con diverso frontispicio y dedicatoria; como si fuera cosa diferente) incorporó Blanchini un codigo de Liturgia Goda, hallado en la librería del Cabildo de Verona. Nuestra Liturgia Goda Muzarebe ó Isidoriana por todas razones puede competir con la de qualquiera otra nacion. sola la libreria de esta Iglesia primada de Toledo nos ofrece once tomos: nuestro es el Misal Gótico, que imprimió Mavillon y reimprimió Muratori; nuestro el citado código del Cabildo de Verona; nuestros los tomos Góticos de Cardeña . . . y yo no dudo, que en otros Monasterios de España se conservarán, como en el de Cardeña, muchos tomos Góticos Liturgicos, bastantes á componer una colleción tan amplia y completa, que no sé si podrá ofrecerla semejante otra nacion alguna."

18. The two modern editions of the text are *Missale Gothicum*, edited by Henry Marriott Bannister, and *Missale Gothicum: E codice Vaticano Reginensi Latino 317 editum*, edited by Els Rose.

19. On the 1101 *fuero* of the Mozarabs granted by Alfonso VI, see the introduction.

20. Hitchcock, *Mozarabs*, 81–83.

21. On opposition to the renewal of the Mozarabs' privilege, see Hitchcock " An Examination," 126–27. I am extremely grateful to the author for sending me part of his unpublished dissertation.

22. Camino y Velasco, *Noticia*.

23. Camino y Velasco, *Defensa*, Madrid, BN 13059, fols. 208–223v. For a list of the liturgical contents of Madrid 13059, see Janini and Serrano, *Manuscritos*, 171–75.

24. On Burriel's "Memorias auténticas de las santas vírgenes y mártires sevillanas Justa y Rufina," see chapter 2.

25. Burriel, "Apuntamientos," in Echánove Tuero, *La preparación intelectual*, 270. See chapter 1.

26. Madrid, BN 13059, fols. 204r–205r, copied by the same hand as Camino's *Defensa*.

27. Madrid, BN 13059, fol. 204r: "tymbre y blazon el mas glorioso, que pudo hacer a España, son embidia de las Naciones estrangeras."

28. Madrid, BN 13059, fols. 204v–205r: "ni mantenerse con la decencia debida a su character y Ministerios, a vista de la suma cortedad a que estan reducidas sus rentas, que es notoria; se veran precisados (aunque con gravissimo dolor suyo) a desamparar dichas Iglesias, y dejar expuesto el sagrado antiquissimo rito mozarabe a una total extinccion."

29. Madrid, BN 13059, fol. 205r: "porque no se allara quien por un tenue emolumento, quiera aplicarse a aprehender el rito y canto sumamente dificiles; ni tomar sobre si el imponderable trabajo de la asistencia al exercicio de la Missa, y de todas las horas canonicas diurnas, y nocturnas."

30. London, BL Egerton 588, fol. 159r–v ("Relación breve de los servicios hechos por Don Francisco Xavier de Santiago Palomares, natural de la Ciudad de Toledo"): "Hizo una copia al vivo de todo un Missal Gothico Muzarabe en pergamino de los que se conservan en aquella Bibliotheca, en que trabajo incesantemente cerca de seis meses, y saliò tan parecido al Original, no solo en lo raro de los Caracteres Gothicos, notas particulares de la Musica (que hasta ahora ninguno hà entendido) sino aun en lo material de su enquadernación, y circunstancias, que haviendolo visto el Dean, y otros Canonigos de aquella Santa Iglesia, mereciò la aprobación de identica con el original, y aun pensaron algunos en que se dejase Certificación de haver hecho el Suplicante esta Copia, para que en lo subcesivo no se equivocase con los originales."

31. Letter of December 22, 1752, in Burriel, *Cartas eruditas*, 244: "He emprendido, pues, la copia entera de ellos; tres tomos están ya acabados de copiar; y uno de ellos porque contiene las Misas de San Ildefonso para los ocho dias antes de Navidad, y los de Navidad hasta Reyes, no solo se ha copiado, sino dibujado al vivo en letra Goda, con sus colores, y con la misma musica Goda, y pergamino tosco, tan semejante al original, que se me ha prevenido que se ha de poner certificacion de quál es el original, y quál la copia, para que en adelante no se dude quando el pergamino de la copia esté deslucido del tiempo y manos. Es alhaja digna del Rey para quien se ha hecho."

32. On this manuscript in the context of the other Toledan manuscripts containing multiple notational styles, see Zapke, "Notation Systems," 209.

33. Madrid, BN 13060, fols. 1–117. The title page is on fol. 1r. See Janini and Serrano, *Manuscritos*, 175–76.

34. The presentation copy containing the transcription is now Madrid, Biblioteca del Palacio Real, II/482.

35. Madrid, BN 13060, fol. 16r: "Nota. Vox Alleluia partitur in responsionibus versiculorum. Primao versiculo respondetur Alle tantum, et notatur musica. Reliquis versiculis praeter ultimum respondetur tantum e, et notatum supra hanc vocalem musica; at non semper eadem; sed diversa, mireque modulata. Ultimo denique versiculo respondetur eluia, cum musica supra unamquamque vocalem notata." Burriel here is referring to Toledo 35.7, fol. 45r–v.

36. Brou, "Séquences et tropes," especially 29–30, 33–35.

37. Kruckenberg, "Neumatizing the Sequence," 243–317.

38. Toledo, BC 35.7, fol. 54r; facsimile in Madrid, Palacio Real II/483, p. 107.

39. Madrid, BN 13060, fol. 31r: "Post codicis excripti finem, Sebastianique descriptoris subscriptionem in eadem pagina continuo subsequuntur tum oratio De eterna rerum, tum Antiphone de Psalmos canonicis iisdem caracteribus gothicis, quibus totus codex conscriptus est, ita ut ejusdem manus censeri possunt. Antiphonae vero idem musicis genus, quod in toto codice conspicitur, adnotatum habent. Post haec in eadem pagina subsequuntur rubricae quaedam de Officio Nativitatis elementis non gothicis, sed Gallicanis, iisque, quibus non libri, aut Privilegia; sed quibus epistole, reddituum rationes, reliquaque vulgaris commercii monumenta, et regia minoris momenti decreta labente saeculo XIII et integro saeculo XIIII conscribebantur. Idioma vero, quibus eaedem rubricae notantur, partim est latinum, partim eo tempore vulgare, utrumque vero barbarum."

40. Madrid, BN 13060, fol. 31r–v (referring to Toledo 35.7, fol. 54v): "Deinde in avorsa ejusdem folii pagina subsequuntur Antiphonae quaedam, musica ornatae, quae uidentur Ad accedentes, ad communionem in missa de Assumptione Sanctae Mariae pertinere. Tam musica, quam caracter gothicus est; licet non ejusdem fortasse manus, quae codicem conscripsit. Cum vero eae Antiphonae ad calcem codicis post Rubricas conscriptae fuerint, saeculo XIII aut XIV exaratas, plane constat, toletanos Muzarabes Gothicorum caracterum usum in describendis liturgicis suis libris minime istis saeculis dereliquisse. Caeterum ne inde inferat quisque, codicem integrum his eisdem XIIIo aut XIVo saeculis fuisse descriptum. Ego enim, quantum conjectura assequor possum, ex accurata ipsius codicis inspectione, ex collatione cum alijs Gothicis vetustissimis anno signatis, et ex omnibus etiam minutissimis verum adjunctis attente perpensis, persuasum habeo, codicum liturgicorum omnium quotquot in Bibliotheca Toletanae Ecclesiae asservantur, hunc esse vetustissimum; licet ipsum non ante miserandam Maurorum dominationem, sed vel ipso captivitatis tempore, vel paulo post urbem christiano cultui restitutam, Toleti fuisse conscriptum, credam."

41. This motivation for the production of the copy was first suggested by Maria Luisa López Vidriero in "Camino de perfección," 2–11.

42. Madrid, Biblioteca del Palacio Real, II/483, fol. 3r–v: "Señor. Entre los muchos tomos manuscritos, que guardan en la Libreria de la Santa Iglesia de Toledo, Primada de las Españas, que hè reconocido de orden de Vuestra Magestad, se hallan onze volumenes escritos en pergamino, y letra gothica, que contienen diferentes partes del Oficio, y Liturgia llamada con diferentes nombres Gothica, Isidoriana, Toledana, y Muzárabe, que fuè general en España en los tiempos de los Godos, y de los moros hasta el Siglo XI, y que desde entonces acà se hà conservado sin interrupcion en las Parroquias Muzárabes de Toledo, à que se hà añadido una Capilla en la Iglesia Primada, en que se canta todos los dias. Estos preciosos manuscritos son un monumento inestimable de la Fè, y Religion de España, porque con su authenticidad, y antiguedad venerable prueban evidentemente la maravillosa uniformidad, y consonancia de nuestra actual creencia con lo que creyeron los antiquos Españoles desde los primeros tiempos de la Christiandad hasta ahora, y la continuacion no interrumpida por la misericordia de Dios del Catholicismo en España por toda la serie de los Siglos desde aquellos tiempos hasta los nuestros. Estos libros son otros tantos testigos dignisimos de veneracion por su vejez y mayores de toda excepcion por su authenticidad que claman, y guitan, que V. Magestad cree, confiesa, y adora con todos sus Vasallos Catholicos Españoles lo mismo, que desde

los Catholicos Reyes San Hermenegildo, y su hermano el Catholico Rey Reccaredo, han creydo, confesado, y adorado por mas de 1200 años todos los Reyes Progenitores de V. Magestad con todos los Vasallos, que tuvieron, ascendientes de los que hoy tenemos la dicha de serlo de V. Magestad."

43. Collins, *Visigothic Spain*, 57–59; Rodríguez G. de Ceballos, "La piedad," 361–74.

44. Torrione, ed. *Crónica festiva*.

45. Gambra, *Alfonso VI*, vol. 2, *Colleción diplomatica*, 227. I am grateful to Liam Moore for pointing out that the diploma of 1086 employs the term "progenitores."

46. On neo-Gothicism see Deswarte, *De la destruction à la restauration*, 17–25, and more recently Moore, "Religious Language," 226.

47. On Burriel's description of the Reconquest of Toledo in his *Paleografía Española*, see chapter 1.

48. Madrid, BN 13059, fol. 204v: "objeto principalisimo de los santos reyes glorioso progenitores de V. Magd . . . en las seis referidas Iglesias: se dignaron tambien de pasar en persona a Toledo, y decoralas, oyendo la missa de este sagrado rito, y honrando a sus ministros."

49. Madrid, BN 13059, fol. 205r: "Este le libramos en el Catholico celo, religion, y Piedad de V. Magd. Augusta. En cuyas virtudes, no siendo V. Mag. Inferior a ninguno de sus gloriosos progenitores."

50. Madrid, Biblioteca del Palacio Real, II/483, fol. 3v: "Si à tan ilustre testimonio se junta el que dan con maravillosa harmonia entresi los exemplares de la Biblia, escritos mas hà de mil años antes de la invasion de los Moros, las obras de los Santos, y Padres españoles conservadas en volumenes antiquisimos, la serie del Derecho Canonico compuesto de Concilios, Epistolas Decretales de los Papas, constituciones, y determinaciones de los Prelados, la serie de Leyes seglares desde el Fuero-Juzgo de los Reyes Godos con todos los Codigos Legales, Quadernos de Cortes, Decretos, y Pragmaticas hasta las que ha dispuesto V. Magestad, los Martyrologios, y Passionarios, en que se contienen las Vidas, y muertes de los Santos Martyres, y Confesores, que eran parte del Oficio Divino, las mutaciones, y Variaciones de este en diversos Siglos, sin mudarse la substancia de la creencia, y del culto, y finalmente nuestras antiguos Chronicas, y Historias apoyadas de Documentos authenticos de cada tiempo, que aun se guardan un mucho numero en nuestros Archivos, se forma un Rio de authoridad con solas las fuentes de España à favor de la Religion Catholica, y de la firme tradicion de nuestra fè, que es sobrado para ahogar de una vez todas las heresias."

51. On the *Paleografía Española*, see chapter 1.

52. Madrid, Biblioteca del Palacio Real, II/483, fol. 3v–4r: "Porque V. Magestad tenga el religioso gusto, de ver, como son, y de que manera estan escritos estos tomos Gothicos de la Liturgia Muzárabe, he dispuesto, que Don Francisco Xavier de Santiago, y Palomares, natural de esta Ciudad de Toledo, Mozo de extraordinaria habilidad en el dibujo, y remedo de toda suerte de letras antiguas, copiase al vivo el tomo que parece mas antiguo, y es el mas apreciable de todos. Componese este de dos partes, ò dos Codigos, en que faltan muchas hojas al principio, al fin, y en el medio. En la primera se halla la mayor parte del tratado escrito por San Ildefonso en defensa de la perpetua virginidad de nuestra Señora la Virgen Maria, dividido en siete Missas, ò siete partes que se leîan al pueblo en la Missa. Siguese la Missa propia del dia de la Annunciacion de Nuestra Señora, ò Encarnacion del Verbo eterno en sus purissimas entrañas, que por decreto de Concilio Toledano

Decimo à que asistiò San Ildefonso, se celebraba en España el dia 18 de Diciembre, y era por antonomasia la fiesta de Santa Maria Virgen, y Madre de Dios. Parte de esta Missa es un devotissimo Sermon del Santo, que se imprimiò poco ha la primera vez por el P. Fray Henrique Florez. Acaso se repetia la misma Missa en los siete dias siguientes, y en lugar del Sermon se leîa una parte del tratado del Santo. Demas de esto en la misma primera parte fuera de otras cosas menores se halla el Oficio, y missa de la Assumpcion de Nuestra Señora. En la segunda parte del tomo estan los oficios, y Missas, que se celebraban desde el dia de la Natividad del Señor hasta la manifestacion à los Santos Reyes, y son de la misma Natividad, de San Esteban, de San Juan Evangelista, de la Circuncision, del principio del Año, y de la Aparicion a los Reyes. Consta por los testimonios de S. Julian, y de Elipando, succesores del santo doctor Ildefonso en la Silla de Toledo, que el santo compuso algunas Missas, Officios, y Sermones. En el elogio que se atribuye à Cixila Arzobispo tambien de Toledo, que parece se formò, para que sirviese de Prologo à algun Codigo de Missas de S. Ildefonso, y el qual se halla copiado en muchos volumenes manuscritos muy antiguos del Escurial, de Toledo, y otras partes, se dice que èl Santo Doctor no solo compuso, sino puso tambien en Musica algunos Oficios, y Missas. El Sermon, que en este Codigo se halla sin nombre de Autor incorporado en la Missa de la Annunciacion, se encuentra tambien junto con otros Sermones, y separado de la Missa, à nombre de S. Ildefonso en el manuscrito de donde los imprimiò el citado Padre Florez. Todas estas cosas juntas hacen creer prudentemente, que todos los officios, y Missas, que contiene este Volumen son compuestos, y puestos en Musica por el santo Prelado y Doctor Ildefonso, ternisimamente devoto de Nuestra Señora entre todos los Santos Doctores, y Padres antiguos." Earlier, Burriel had stated that the Assumption liturgy in this manuscript was not by Ildefonsus (see p. 71).

53. Ildefonsus of Toledo, *Ildefonsi Toletani Episcopi*, 147–263.

54. The composition comes from the early modern iconography of the saint rather than from the medieval tradition. For a reproduction see Boynton, "Writing History with Liturgy," 199. On the images in a manuscript of Ildefonsus's treatise, copied around 1200, probably in Toledo, see Raizman, "A Rediscovered Illuminated Manuscript," 37–46. Iconography of the saint in Toledo Cathedral is discussed in Pérez Higuera, "Escenas de la vida," 797–811. See also Dodds, "Rodrigo," 239–41. I am grateful to Colum Hourihane for enabling me to consult this study before its publication.

55. Madrid, Biblioteca del Palacio Real, II/483, fol. 4r: "Las notas musicales gothicas van tambien copiadas al vivo, segun se hallan en el Original. Es pues este tomo digno de summo aprecio sobre todos los demas Tomos manuscritos del Officio, y Liturgia Goda, ò Muzárabe por su contenido, y por su Autor; à que se añade, que de todo esto solo se imprimio una pequeña parte en el Missal, y Breviario Muzarabe, que hizo ordenar, y dar à luz el Venerable Cardenal Arzobispo de Toledo Don Fray Francisco Ximenez de Cisneros, varon de immortal memoria." On Ferdinand's love of music, see the introduction and chapter 4.

56. Palomares stated that the presentation was "to satisfy the desire that His Majesty had to see this relic, one of the most celebrated of the Church of Toledo" (London, BL, Egerton 588, fol. 159v: "el gusto que S.M. tenia de ver esta antigualla de las mas celebres de la Iglesia de Toledo").

4 | Alfonso X in the Age of Ferdinand VI

Copying the Cantigas de Santa Maria

As Burriel noted in his "Apuntamientos para fomentar las letras" of 1749, in the 1740s he had seen in the library of Toledo Cathedral a manuscript of the *Cantigas de Santa Maria*, a thirteenth-century collection of sacred songs in Galician-Portuguese attributed to King Alfonso X of León and Castile.[1] This manuscript, usually called the "Toledo codex," has been in the Biblioteca Nacional in Madrid since the nineteenth century (Madrid, BN 10069).[2] In 1755, while working with Burriel in Toledo Cathedral, Palomares made a copy of the Toledo codex and dedicated it to Barbara de Braganza. However, the copy (now Madrid, BN 13055) apparently never reached the queen; it remained in Burriel's personal library until his death.[3] Perhaps a more luxurious presentation volume was planned, for which the copy was supposed to be a preparatory work.[4]

It is tempting to see the copy of the Toledo codex as a pendant to the facsimile of the liturgical book presented to the king in the same year (see chapter 3). Although they are very different in appearance, these two books share several important features. Each includes a complete textual transcription and a complete, highly accurate rendering of the musical notation in its respective exemplar, and each prefaces the painstakingly reproduced contents of the medieval manuscript with drawings that situate the copy squarely in the present. Moreover both the *Cantigas* copy and the facsimile of the liturgical book share a theme of devotion to the Virgin Mary that is illustrated by the textual contents and the prefatory images. As seen in the facsimile of Toledo, BC 35.7 (chapter 3), the portrait of Ildefonsus of Toledo gazing upon an image of the Virgin refers to the presence in the manuscript of Ildefonsus's treatise on the perpetual virginity of Mary.[5] The association of Ildefonsus with this seminal text of Marian doctrine inspired Alfonso X in his own tribute to the Virgin; the second *Cantiga* relates a widely diffused miracle story, in which Mary gave Ildefonsus an alb to wear on her feast days and Saint Leocadia appeared to Ildefonsus to inform him that the Virgin lived through him.[6] As we will see, in his copy of the Toledo codex of the *Cantigas*, Palomares added a representation of Alfonso singing to the Virgin Mary that subtly evokes qualities of Ferdinand VI. Both the reproduction of the Toledan liturgical book and the copy of the Toledo codex of the *Cantigas* are cultural and political objects whose meanings are further enriched by their functions as gestures of homage to royal patrons. In addition to representing exceptional artifacts of eighteenth-century interest in the Middle Ages, these copies constitute significant elements in the construction of the monarchs' public personae.

Because historians have until now considered the Palomares copy of the *Cantigas* only in relation to the medieval original, the copy's rich significance in its own eighteenth-century context has essentially been overlooked. Nonetheless the copy has its own story to tell about the philological and political concerns of the moment in which it was made. In this chapter I address the cultural meanings of the copy as a product of Enlightenment historicism, resituating it in the trajectory of modern scholarly reception of the *Cantigas*.[7] In taking this approach to the Palomares copy, I apply to an eighteenth-century manuscript the kind of interdisciplinary analysis that has recently become more common in the study of medieval manuscripts. Such an investigation employs a multifaceted approach, according all parts of the book, including additions and annotations, equal status, considering the motivation for and the historical context of compilation, and taking into account a manuscript's intended and actual audience, readership, and reception. Furthermore in order to understand a manuscript as an object, it is necessary to displace the focus of attention from the author as the source and origin of the text to the various scribes and compilers who took part in the creation of the whole.[8]

The Toledo Codex

The Toledo codex is both the most visually understated and the least understood of the four *Cantigas* manuscripts.[9] Whereas the other three preserve as many as four hundred cantigas, the Toledo codex contains a cycle of only one hundred cantigas, along with two prologues and a supplement.[10] Unlike the two manuscripts now preserved in the Escorial library, the Toledo codex features no figural decoration, its only illumination consisting of flourished initials in blue and red.[11] Scholars' views on the date of the manuscript are inextricably linked to their understanding of the processes of composition and compilation that resulted in the diverse collections of cantigas represented by the extant manuscripts.[12] Both the time and place in which the Toledo codex was produced thus remain subject to debate and speculation, and the date of its acquisition by the library of Toledo Cathedral is likewise unknown.[13]

There is consensus, however, that the Toledo codex represents a state of the Alfonsine collection corresponding to the earliest stage of compilation.[14] Recent scholarship has been based on paleographic and codicological analysis of the manuscript itself, lending greater weight to internal evidence— a departure from the methods used by earlier generations of scholars, who based their assessments of its date primarily on comparisons with other manuscripts of the thirteenth and fourteenth centuries. Stephen Parkinson contends that the Toledo codex was the first manuscript of the *Cantigas* to be compiled and written.[15] Manuel Pedro Ferreira argues that it is an early copy, made no later than 1280, of an exemplar from around 1270.[16] Others see it as a late copy of an earlier compilation, an argument that places the manuscript in the late thirteenth or early fourteenth century, possibly after the death of Alfonso X in 1284.[17]

One of the principal difficulties in dating the Toledo codex is its distinctive musical notation. Higini Anglès, the first musicologist to transcribe the *Cantigas* in full, maintained that the Toledo codex employed a form of mensural notation typical of the very late thirteenth century and early fourteenth. Thus, he argued, it could not have been notated as early as the middle or third quarter of the thirteenth century, the date that had been more or less accepted since Burriel's commentary on the manuscript was published in 1755 in the *Paleografía Española*. Anglès's assessment was based on comparisons with French manuscripts of the same period.[18] As Ferreira has pointed out, however, musicologists' traditional reliance on manuscripts of French polyphony for dating the Toledo codex has been an impediment to close study of the notation itself. Ferreira argues that the notation of the Toledo codex represents the alternation of brevis and semibrevis with signs based on the forms of virga and punctum found in the square notation used for Gregorian chant in the thirteenth century (the short-stemmed virga and both the square and rhomboid forms of the punctum). According to Ferreira, the Toledo codex could have been notated as early as 1270–75, with square notation as a model for its distinctive notational system.[19] One of the reasons for the variety of dates assigned to the manuscript is that, having no clear antecedents or counterparts in the musico-poetic collections of the period, it appears to have emerged from a vacuum.[20] As a fully notated manuscript with a prologue attributing the collection to a single author, the Toledo codex is quite unlike the roughly contemporaneous chansonniers of the troubadours and trouvères.

The Palomares Copy in Context

Palomares transcribed the texts in a contemporary hand but, as was his practice in copies of liturgical manuscripts, rendered the appearance of the original musical notation as faithfully as possible. Such close attention to the notation of vernacular song in a medieval manuscript was rare in the middle of the eighteenth century. Scholars in France were gradually rediscovering the music and poetry of the trouvères and, to a lesser extent, the songs of the troubadours. In the 1720s and 1730s French antiquarians made or commissioned copies, anthologies, and comparative tables of chansonniers that they owned or borrowed from the Royal Library.[21] Most of these copies were actually transcriptions that did not imitate medieval script or notation, and the medieval manuscripts from which they were made were treated with considerably less veneration than would be the case today. Owners of medieval chansonniers in the first half of the eighteenth century did not hesitate to annotate them, even filling staves that had been left empty with new melodies written in an approximation of the manuscripts' notational style (which led musicologists to assume, until recently, that the added melodies had been notated in the Middle Ages).[22] Those examining the chansonniers of troubadour and trouvère song in the early eighteenth century seem to have taken a particular interest in mensural notation, which indicates the duration of notes.[23]

Medieval mensural notation seems to have attracted the attention of, among others, Jean-Jacques Rousseau. In 1749, in one of his articles on music for the *Encyclopédie* of Diderot and d'Alembert, Rousseau announced that he would publish transcriptions of music from manuscripts of the thirteenth and fourteenth centuries, along with commentary that would demonstrate to others how to decipher early musical notation. He never accomplished this goal. Although his articles refer to Machaut manuscripts (presumably at least some of them the ones now preserved in the Bibliothèque Nationale de France), it seems that Rousseau relied primarily on treatises of music theory for his information on medieval notation, perhaps because he found the notation of the original manuscripts difficult to understand.[24]

The efforts of Rousseau, Palomares, and the aristocratic owners of the chansonniers to transcribe, copy, and otherwise disseminate medieval notation were, however, isolated cases. Because early musical notations were reproduced in print only rarely, by the eighteenth century they had not yet become part of a widely diffused body of scholarly knowledge. Only a few melodies of vernacular song were published with reproductions of their original notation during the first half of the eighteenth century. The earliest printed example of a trouvère melody that imitates the medieval notation appears in the first volume of the *Istoria della volgar poesia* by Giovanni Mario Crescimbeni (1663–1728).[25] An appendix to the edition of Thibaut de Navarre's songs by Levesque de la Ravallière, first published in 1742, also mimics the original notation.[26] According to John Haines, the reproductions printed by Crescimbeni and de la Ravallière were precocious attempts within the larger framework of the antiquarian study of secular song. In France as elsewhere more sustained treatments of medieval music would not appear until later in the century. Engravings of medieval French songs reproducing their original notation were included in large surveys, such as Jean-Benjamin de Laborde's *Essai sur la musique* of 1780, as well as in volumes of more limited scope, such as the *Mémoires historiques sur Raoul de Coucy* of 1781.[27] Likewise Martin Gerbert's *De Cantu et Musica Sacra*, which appeared in 1774, contained some of the first engravings of medieval chant notation.[28] In this context it is all the more remarkable that Palomares, who was neither a historian nor a musician, so faithfully reproduced the musical notation in a type of manuscript that was far less common in Spain than the chansonniers of the trouvères were in Italy and France. Perhaps it was his very ignorance of the notation in the Toledo codex that led him to copy it so carefully. He did not attempt to transcribe or to explain it.

The Palomares copy also shows Burriel's interest in the texts of the *Cantigas*. Although it is now assumed that the original language of a poetic text is itself of intrinsic historical and aesthetic value, in the eighteenth century this presupposition was not widely applied to medieval vernacular literature. Most philologists of the time saw fit to "improve" the texts they published by altering them considerably or presenting them exclusively in paraphrase or translation. Even the foremost eighteenth-century French scholar of vernacular texts, Jean-Baptiste de La Curne de Sainte-Palaye (1697–1781), considered the manuscript versions of medieval troubadour poems stylistically and linguistically inferior to contemporary French as regulated by the Académie Française.[29] The remarkable care with which Palomares transcribed the Toledo codex of the *Cantigas* and reproduced its notation, on the other hand, suggests that he aimed to convey as much of the manuscript's appearance and language as its contents. In other words, his approach was more antiquarian than philological in nature.

Bringing the Cantigas into the Eighteenth Century

The title page of the copy clearly links the medieval manuscript to the person of Alfonso X as well as to that of the reigning queen of Spain: "Poems in the Galician, or old Portuguese language, by Don Alonso the Tenth, called the Wise, King of Castile, and of León, copied from a tome in parchment in the Library of the Holy Church of Toledo, corrected, it seems, by the hand of the King himself . . . offered to the Queen, our lady, by Father Andrés Burriel of the Society of Jesus."[30] The dedication of the copy to Barbara de Braganza could be meant to allude both to the fact that her native language was Portuguese (and thus related to the literary language of the *Cantigas*) and to her celebrated cultivation and patronage of music.

Barbara was particularly renowned as a keyboard player. Most of the sonatas of Domenico Scarlatti, her music teacher, were written for her own performance. As Sara Gross Ceballos has recently argued, these compositions can be interpreted as musical portraits of the queen, reflecting her skill at the keyboard, her rich and varied musical tastes, and her passion for dancing.[31] Barbara's lifelong devotion to music may be the reason for the particular emphasis on musical notation in Palomares's copy of the *Cantigas*. This tribute is comparable to the homage offered to her by the renowned music theorist and teacher Giovanni Battista Martini (1706–84) in his *Storia della Musica*; the first volume, dedicated to Barbara, features a frontispiece that is generally considered to be an allegory of her musical persona and that is clearly indebted to the iconography of Saint Cecilia.[32]

As a retrospective document the Palomares copy of the Toledo codex extends into the eighteenth century the original cultural project represented by the *Cantigas*, which constitute a tribute to Alfonso X as patron, creator, and poetic subject. The Palomares copy begins with an author portrait, signed by Palomares in 1755, depicting King Alfonso singing to an apparition of the Virgin and Child (Figure 4.1). The insertion of the portrait endows the text with the visual icon of a unitary author, providing one example of the ways in which the construction of Alfonso's agency has shaped the reception of the *Cantigas* over the centuries.[33] Alfonso himself, in his *General Estoria*, set forth his understanding of a king's role as "author": "A king makes [writes] a book, not because he wrote it with his own hands, but because he composes its arguments, and emends them, and makes them

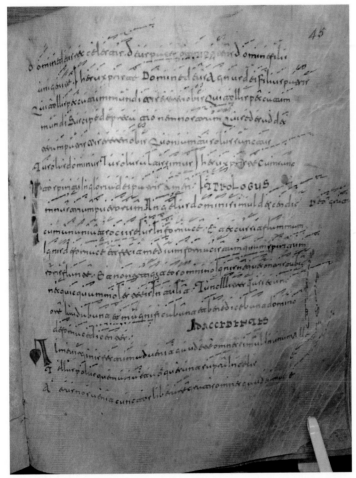

Toledo, BC 35.7, fol. 45r. Copyright © Archivo y Biblioteca Capitulares, Catedral Primada de Toledo.

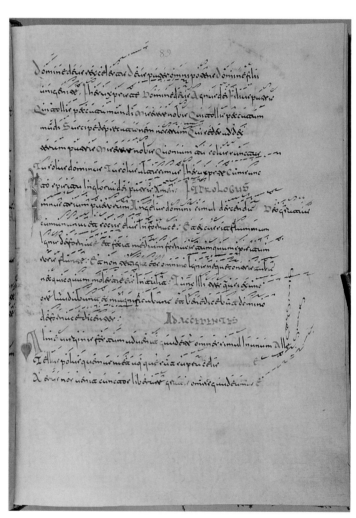

Madrid, Palacio Real, Biblioteca, II/483, p. 89. Copyright © Patrimonio Nacional.

FIGURE 4.1 Madrid, BN 13055, unpaginated. Copyright © Biblioteca Nacional de España.

uniform, and rectifies them, and shows the way they should be done, and thus he whom he [the king] orders writes them, but we say for this reason that the king writes the book."[34]

Because the Toledo codex lacks figural decoration altogether, it contains no image of the king. The addition of an author portrait in the Palomares copy allies it with the practice of Alfonsine representation found in the Escorial manuscripts of the *Cantigas*, which include several images of the king as patron and poet, as well as an expanded collection of poems.[35] Explicit textual invocations of Alfonso's "presence" in the *Cantigas* are more frequent in the Escorial collections than in the more limited repertory of one hundred cantigas transmitted by the Toledo codex. As Joseph T. Snow has argued, over time Alfonso became increasingly prominent in the texts and miniatures of the *Cantigas*, which were gradually transformed into a personal narrative of the king, despite the involvement and intervention of multiple compilers.[36] It is likely that Palomares saw the two Escorial manuscripts of the *Cantigas* in the late 1750s, when he assisted Francisco Pérez Bayer with the inventory of the manuscripts in the Escorial library.[37] We do not know whether Palomares had already seen other *Cantigas* manuscripts when he drew the portrait of Alfonso X in his copy of the Toledo codex, but it is possible that he had already consulted the manuscripts at the Escorial or had heard about them.

The iconography of the author portrait would have been rich with meaning for viewers of the eighteenth century, and particularly for its royal audience (see Figure 4.1). Indeed the *Cantigas* copy and the image of Alfonso can be understood as a form of indirect tribute to the king as well as to the queen. By interpreting the drawings in the context of other visual culture associated with the court, one can situate these images within contemporary discourses on the Bourbon monarchy and the role of Ferdinand VI in the history of Spain.

In the portrait Alfonso holds a scroll on which is visible a form of musical notation resembling that in the Toledo codex; his laurel crown and the inkwell signal his status as poet. The two crowns on the table and the lion and castle on the robe (and in the coat of arms at the bottom of the image) symbolize the kingdoms of León and Castile, first joined under one king in 1037 by Ferdinand I.[38] Certain elements in the author portrait evoke both the renowned wisdom of Alfonso "El Sabio" and the renewal of the arts and sciences during the reign of Ferdinand VI, which, as we have seen, was consolidated through the foundation of learned academies and celebrated in literature associated with the court. Below Alfonso's feet appear several symbols of learning and science: the caduceus, a globe, and an open book showing geometrical figures, as well as a compass and ruler, which complement the armillary sphere placed on the table next to the king's right hand. Armillary spheres are instruments that represent the structure of the universe for the purposes of astronomical observation or measurement. In the visual arts armillaries (as they are also called) function as emblems of astronomy and signal erudition. Early modern armillaries illustrate the Copernican theory of the earth rotating around the sun, which is represented by a globe like the one seen in the portrait.[39] Medieval armillaries based on the Ptolemaic geocentric theory were known in western Europe beginning in the twelfth century; it is possible that Palomares knew of the one described and depicted in the second book of the *Libros del saber de astrología*, compiled in the middle of the thirteenth century for Alfonso X and copied in his scriptorium.[40]

In addition to symbolizing Alfonso X's interest in astronomy and astrology, the attributes in this portrait can be read as signs of the scientific erudition cultivated during Ferdinand's reign. The globe, for instance, suggests the eighteenth century as much as the thirteenth, and perhaps alludes to the significance of geography in the context of Spain's colonial project.[41] The presence of the armillary sphere may refer to the new importance that astronomy attained under Ferdinand VI, who gave the Seminary of Nobles a collection of scientific instruments for instructional purposes.[42] Demonstrational armillary spheres were used in the eighteenth century to teach the principles of astronomy.[43]

The choice of objects can be linked even more closely to the maker of the image himself. According to Burriel, Palomares's father (also named Francisco de Santiago y Palomares) constructed scientific instruments, including globes, armillary spheres, and an astrolabe. In 1744 Palomares senior employed his own instruments in the daily observation of a comet, and his measurements were approved by a professional mathematician.[44] The portrait of Alfonso X thus makes reference to actual eighteenth-century scientific practices and objects that would have been known firsthand to Palomares from his father's experiments a decade before the copying of the Toledo codex.

The iconographic attribute of Alfonso X that can be linked most directly to Ferdinand VI is the caduceus. This symbol alludes to wisdom in the person of the god Mercury, who is also invoked in a poem by José Antonio Porcel (1715–94) celebrating Ferdinand's accession to the throne.[45] An even more direct association between the king and Mercury can be found in Martín Sarmiento's program for the decoration of the new Royal Palace in Madrid: in his proposal for one of the two principal staircases, the statue of the king was to be flanked by statues of Mercury and Ceres. Sarmiento described Mercury as holding the caduceus in one hand and a purse in the other. He goes on to explain the association of Ferdinand VI with Mercury:

> This god and goddess symbolize the happy state of a monarchy under an Octavian Peace. In the other folders of the *Sistema* which my smallness has conceived for the sculptural decoration of the Palace, I proposed as a base the characteristic gift of His Majesty, which is to be peaceful: "Ferdinand [is] the reconciler of peace." In the caduceus, peace signifies the arts and sciences; in Mercury, it signifies commerce in his purse; in Ceres, peace means the cultivation of the earth, and the cornucopia stands for abundance.[46]

The caduceus also appears in the foreground of a portrait of Ferdinand VI (now in the Academia de Bellas Artes de San Fernando in Madrid) by Antonio González Ruiz. Painted in 1754, this portrait depicts the king as protector of the arts and sciences. The allegorical figure of Agriculture extends the caduceus to the monarch, creating a linkage of Mercury and Ceres very much like the one proposed in Sarmiento's *Sistema*. Given the context of symbolism in cultural products of the 1740s and 1750s associated with the court, it seems clear that the attributes of Alfonso X employed by Palomares in the author portrait are intended to link the book of the *Cantigas* generally to the accomplishments of Bourbon Spain and to associate the medieval king specifically with Ferdinand VI. Not only the iconography, but also the composition of the image evokes eighteenth-century conventions of portraiture such as the neoclassical architectural details, the Rococo style of the table, and the curtain drawn back illusionistically by a cord to enhance the dramatic appearance of Alfonso's vision.

The other prefatory image in the copy can also be seen as a distinct gesture toward the concerns of the Bourbon government. On the page preceding the prologue, a trio of cherubs symbolizes the joining of Science, Religion, and Military Skill or Prowess, with Religion as the dominant figure in the group (Figure 4.2).[47] The cherub representing Science is accompanied by attributes of navigation, which can be interpreted as an allusion to the development of the Spanish navy under Ferdinand VI.[48] The modern attributes of the scientific cherub, as well as the noticeably relaxed appearance of the martial cherub positioned at the opposite end of the trio, combine to suggest that the image associates the *Cantigas* with the values promoted by Ferdinand's government; in the 1750s his reign was celebrated in official literature as an auspicious moment of peace in which the arts and sciences could flourish.[49]

The network of allusions to the reigning monarch in these two illustrations is strengthened by the cross and the flaming altar, the attributes of the cherub representing Religion. Compositions drawing upon similar iconography were common to many allegorical images of the seventeenth and eighteenth centuries. The same elements also appear in a contemporary work produced for the Spanish court, one of Corrado Giaquinto's frescoes for the stairway of the Royal Palace in Madrid, depicting "Spain Rendering Homage to Religion and the Church." The best preserved rendition of this composition is the oil sketch now in the Prado.[50] Giaquinto's three allegorical figures are female; the figure meant to personify Bourbon Spain is dressed as Minerva, the goddess of war, the figure representing the Church holds a cross, and the figure of Religion sits behind a flaming altar (Figure 4.3).[51] The altars exhibit a classicizing appearance both in Giaquinto's composition and

FIGURE 4.2 Madrid, BN 13055, fol. 16r. Copyright © Biblioteca Nacional de España.

in the Palomares copy of the *Cantigas*. This minor stylistic detail may reflect the symbolic interpretation of the altar in the influential iconological treatise of Cesare Ripa, who stated that the flaming altar refers to its use in sacrifices before the coming of Christ.[52]

My comparison of the drawing of the three cherubs to Giaquinto's "Spain Renders Homage to Religion and the Church" is based on iconographic elements that suggest a common thematic basis underlying the two compositions, rather than any visible stylistic affinity. Despite the clear differences between the trio of cherubs and the composition by Giaquinto, both are cultural products shaped by the court propaganda of the time, which

FIGURE 4.3 Corrado Giaquinto, "Spain Rendering Homage to Religion and the Church," oil sketch. By permission of the Museo Nacional del Prado, Madrid.

emphasized the royal couple's piety. The meaning of the image in the Palomares copy is deepened when understood in relation to the visual allegory of the Bourbon dynasty commissioned by the king.

Ferdinand's and Barbara's renowned devotion to music appears in other works of Corrado Giaquinto as well, such as a painting commissioned by the royal couple that portrays Saints Ferdinand and Barbara, along with Saint Cecilia, in front of the Virgin Mary.[53] This *sacra conversazione* links the saints whose names the monarchs bore while also emphasizing their relationship to Saint Cecilia, the patron saint of music.[54] Marian devotion, the central theme of the *Cantigas*, was also culturally important in eighteenth-century Spain.[55] The image of the sainted King Ferdinand III gazing at the Virgin parallels the figure of Alfonso X singing to the Virgin in Palomares's author portrait. The connection between the two figures is further enhanced by the fact that Ferdinand III was Alfonso's father. Both kings, depicted as literally uplifted by their devotion to the Virgin, were models for Ferdinand VI.

Another tribute to Ferdinand's and Barbara's devotion to music—one no less symbolic than Giaquinto's *sacra conversazione*—appears in one of the first works the artist completed upon his arrival in Madrid in 1753, the famous portrait of the castrato Farinelli dressed in the insignia of the military order of Calatrava, which had been conferred upon him in 1750 for his service to the crown. Here the king and queen do not appear, as it were, in person, but are represented symbolically in a picture within the portrait, a roundel borne aloft by angels.[56] Farinelli's military garb, in addition to signaling the singer's importance at court, is a visual reminder of the costumes he wore on the opera stage while performing the roles of military heroes from ancient history and Greco-Roman mythology.[57] Like the portraits of Ferdinand and Barbara, the Farinelli portrait demonstrates how aptly Corrado Giaquinto's works for the Spanish court represent the cultivation of religious and courtly arts during the reign of Ferdinand VI.

By day the notoriously pious king and his musical consort attended church services; by night they attended performances of opera in the royal theater. Both of these court rituals featured the highest level of musical performance, and both functioned as mirrors of the monarchy, reported along with the court's other activities by the widely diffused periodical *Gaceta de Madrid*.[58] Moreover many of the operas performed and produced by Farinelli constituted a form of indirect homage to the king, as the glorification of royal patrons and the affirmation of their sovereignty were central to *opera seria*, the predominant music-theatrical genre in the eighteenth century.[59] Beginning in the 1730s libretti by Pietro Metastasio (1698-1782), the court poet of Vienna, became increasingly popular texts for musical settings by Spanish opera composers; indeed Metastasio, at the request of Farinelli, revised some of his works specifically for performance in Madrid.[60] The plots of Metastasian libretti would have been understood by audiences as implicitly linking Philip V and Ferdinand VI to illustrious rulers of history and mythology.[61] It is in this broad context of music and art as carefully crafted constructions of the monarchs' images that we should understand the Palomares copy of the Toledo codex.

Given the musical interests of the dedicatee, it is probably no coincidence that the copy carefully preserves the appearance of the original musical notation. (Compare Figure 4.4 to Figure 4.5.) Neither Burriel nor Palomares could interpret the musical notation, but they both apparently considered it to be integral to the work as a whole. They shared this conviction with Alfonso X himself, who apparently considered the music a crucial element

FIGURE 4.4 Madrid, BN 10069, fol. 9v. Copyright © Biblioteca Nacional de España.

of the *Cantigas*. Unlike most medieval collections of Galician-Portuguese lyric, the other manuscripts of the *Cantigas* contain musical notation as well. According to Martha Schaffer, the musical notation functioned in the same manner as diagrams in the Alfonsine scientific manuscripts, conveying crucial information that words alone could not provide.[62]

The fact that Burriel and Palomares were fully aware of the importance of the notation is all the more striking because this music was, for them, inevitably silent: in the mid-eighteenth century the Toledo codex had not yet been studied by any scholars of music. Without a system for translating the

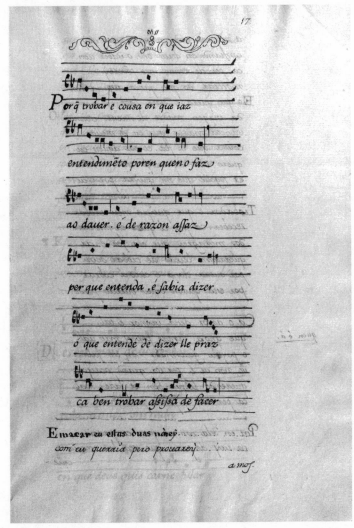

FIGURE 4.5 Madrid, BN 13055, fol. 17r. Copyright © Biblioteca Nacional de España.

rhythms of the notation in the Toledo codex into a modern form of notation, only the pitches of the melodies could be determined from the staff notation. As far as we can tell, the decision to copy the notation so carefully seems to have had no implications for reconstituting the *Cantigas* as sounding music. Although they did not attempt transcription or reconstruction, such a task would have been theoretically possible because the note shapes bear comparison to the square notation used in the chant manuscripts that were still being produced in Spain in the seventeenth and eighteenth centuries.

In spite of the fact that the music of the *Cantigas* remained unsounded and unheard, both Burriel and Palomares took active roles in the transmission of the manuscript's contents, and sometimes even "corrected" them. For instance, when he saw that the refrain was omitted between two coplas in the original manuscript, Burriel wrote it in himself.[63] In general Palomares reproduced the nuances and subtleties of the notation quite accurately. It is not clear whether he understood the function of the custos at the end of each line of music, and he was probably not aware of the potential rhythmic or metrical implications of the stems on the notes, but he nonetheless captured most of the manuscript's notational conventions. Although he appears to have misinterpreted some aspects of the notation, he did not hesitate to make minor changes and corrections to the melodies to ensure the accuracy of the result. In one case, for example, Palomares saw that the custos concluding the first line of music was written in the space above the top staff line. Because the original had only four lines at that point, he added a fifth line in the copy, so that the last note of the first line of music is a C, which he judged from the space between it and the previous note, an A. The custos for this line appears to have been erased in the Toledo codex (part of the staff line is missing).[64] In several instances Palomares added a staff line to those used in the original manuscript.[65]

The few outright mistakes Palomares made in copying the medieval notation can be attributed to an understandable ignorance of its symbols. For instance, in one case he separated the vertical strokes from a set of rhomboid notes, suggesting that he did not realize they should be appended to the notes themselves; in the copy they look like rests.[66] In those cases where a note overlaps with the text and descends below the lowest staff line, he sometimes wrote the note on the lowest staff line instead of in the space.[67] Palomares also altered the format of the music in his copy by introducing a double bar to separate the refrain from the first part of the copla (which comprises two musically identical phrases). This detail could suggest that he understood the structure of the music, or conversely it may indicate his awareness of the poetic form.

Palomares took a different approach altogether to the text of the Toledo codex, writing the first unnotated verse in a rather poor imitation of the thirteenth-century Gothic script, a striking contrast with his virtuosic copies of manuscripts in the Visigothic scripts of earlier centuries. In the remainder of the text, written in a modern hand, he sometimes included abbreviations without resolving them; they were resolved in the margins by a later annotator, presumably Burriel. The transcription of the text into modern script is generally quite accurate. In the course of transcribing the entire text Palomares omitted one complete copla, two individual lines, and two individual words; however, he supplied even more elements that had been omitted in the medieval original (two individual coplas, five individual lines, and six individual words). Most of the changes involve the addition or omission of diacritical accents, which are relatively inconsistent in eighteenth-century usage. Most of the orthographic alterations are semantically insignificant; double consonants are replaced with single ones and vice versa, and "v" is replaced with "b" (a Castilianism). Liquid consonants are treated as interchangeable with one another, as are sibilants (especially ç and z).[68] The few morphological changes that are evident errors suggest inadvertent Castilianization of the text, such as the substitution of "de seda" for "da seda" in the third copla of Cantiga 16, *Por nos de dulta tirar*.[69]

Palomares's gesture of textual transcription can be seen as a kind of translation or transposition of the medieval manuscript into a more modern and therefore a more accessible written idiom. The transcription is comparable to the complete textual transcription of the liturgical book that accompanied the parchment facsimile presented to Ferdinand VI (see chapter 3), but there are important differences between the two. Whereas Barbara would have understood the poetry of the *Cantigas* to some extent, it is unlikely that Ferdinand would have comprehended all of the Latin texts in the manuscript. Nonetheless the transcription afforded him a relationship to the texts similar to the one he had to the liturgical texts that he experienced on a daily basis. Moreover although Burriel added no explanatory introduction to the *Cantigas* copy, presumably because the work itself begins with a poetic prologue, his vernacular preface to the facsimile volume provides still another level of access to its contents by explaining and contextualizing them. The prefatory drawings added by Palomares to the *Cantigas* copy fulfilled the same function as Burriel's vernacular preface by providing a visual link between a medieval king of León-Castile and the modern Bourbon monarchy.

The differing approaches that Palomares took to music and text suggest that he and Burriel considered transcription an adequate account of the textual contents for their immediate purposes. Palomares was, after all, demonstrably far less interested in the Gothic bookhand than in the Visigothic script of the earlier Toledan manuscripts, and reproducing the script of the Toledo codex would have been a far more time-consuming task than transcribing the text.[70] He was far more inclined to perform such a labor of love for a monument in the Visigothic script than in the later forms of handwriting that were marked by the incursion of foreign elements into Spain. Textual transcription was a pragmatic way to render the *Cantigas* available to a modern reader.

Burriel added several marginal comments to the copy, mostly corrections or observations on the medieval annotations to the text.[71] Although he did not speculate on the provenance of the manuscript, he took particular interest in textual emendations and mentioned the type and usually also the age of the script in which they were recorded in the margins of the Toledo codex.[72] Burriel also noted the annotations associating certain cantigas with liturgical use, such as "Des quando Deus" for the feast of the Assumption.[73] However, he seems to have misunderstood the import of an (admittedly enigmatic) annotation below the first line of the final copla of "Pos que dos reys."[74] The marginal note associates this cantiga with the feast of Palm Sunday, but the name of that feast is crossed out and "do batesmo" is written above it by a contemporary hand. As pointed out by Martha Schaffer, in the Palomares copy of the Toledo codex Burriel copied the annotation with "a festa dos ramos," neglecting to note that Palm Sunday had been replaced in the original manuscript by a reference to baptism.[75]

Burriel's Dating of the Toledo Codex

The most consequential of Burriel's many comments on the copy addresses an annotation below the twelfth copla of Cantiga 77 in the Toledo codex.[76] A copla was added in a cursive script in the lower margin, perhaps not long after the manuscript was produced; the same hand crossed out the corresponding text with light diagonal strokes (Figure 4.6). The added copla is the one that appears in the main body of poem in the other manuscripts of the Cantigas, and presumably was copied from one of them. In the Toledo codex, this copla reads thus:

> E a Virgen escolleita
> tragian eno meogo
> da companna, que dereita
> mente a el veno logo,
> et dissele "sem sospeita,
> dim una ren, eu te rogo,
> que de ti saber quería."[77]

The original copla in the Toledo codex is not found in any of the other manuscripts, but differs only slightly from the added one:

> E a Virgen corõada
> tragian eno meogo

que mui ferament yrada
veno pera ele logo
i disse: "Pois m'as leixada
una cousa eu te rogo,
me di que saber querria."[78]

Valeria Bertolucci has pointed out that the substitute copla, which corresponds to the readings in Escorial manuscripts B.I.2 and T.I.1, removes the description of the Virgin Mary as "yrada" (angry) and also serves the purpose of altering the end rhyme in lines 1, 3, and 5 to *-eita*. The *-ada* rhyme used in the original text repeats the rhyme sound employed at those positions in the first copla of the poem; the change, which varies the rhyme, is stylistically preferable.[79] For Burriel, however, the date and possible attribution of the hand were more important than the reason for the change. In one of his annotations to the Palomares copy he commented, "This copla is written in the lower margin in a broad cursive script, perhaps in the hand of King Alfonso himself, and serves as a correction for the copla that is signaled and crossed out in the body of the work."[80] Thus just as Palomares's portrait introduced a degree of Alfonsine representation into the copy, so Burriel's annotations linked the manuscript to the king's person. It was presumably on Burriel's instructions that Palomares's transcription of this cantiga substituted the marginal text for the original one, thereby according the annotation special authority. By placing in the body of its text what the medieval manuscript had suggested in the margins, the eighteenth-century copy thus continues the process of revision that can be observed throughout the medieval textual tradition of the *Cantigas*.

The substance of Burriel's commentary on this substitution appeared in the *Paleografía Española*, which was published for the first time in the same year as the production of the copy (1755). Once disseminated in print, his words exerted a lasting influence on the reception of the Toledo codex. Burriel seems to have been the first paleographer in the early modern period to study the manuscript closely, and his opinions on the dating of the Toledo manuscript substantially determined its later reception.[81] His assessment was all the more influential for being illustrated by two of Palomares's engravings. Plate 8 of the *Paleografía* reproduces two lines of the musical notation of the prologue from the Toledo codex, immediately over the annotation in cursive script that Burriel had tentatively attributed to Alfonso X (Figure 4.7). This illustration seems to be the earliest publication of medieval mensural notation in Spain. The commentary on this plate in the *Paleografía* reinforces further the connection between the manuscript and the persona of the king:

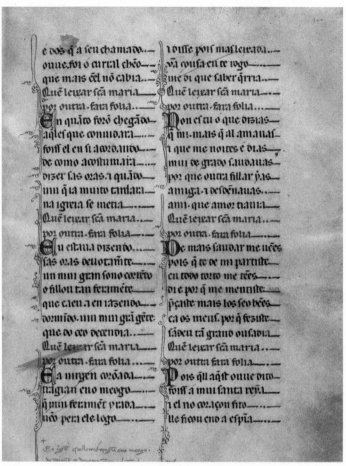

FIGURE 4.6 Madrid, BN 10069, fol. 100r. Copyright © Biblioteca Nacional de España.

In plate 8, number 1 shows the beginning of the prologue to a volume of poems by King Alfonso the Wise, which contains one hundred *Cantigas*, in Galician or Portuguese, of the miracles and praises of Saint Mary, five of her feasts, five of the feasts of Our Lord Jesus Christ, and sixteen other miracles of the same Lady. It is written on vellum-like parchment in a careful hand, illuminated with color throughout, and each *Cantiga* has music notated on the first copla and the refrain, which almost all of them have. The work opens with the index, at the beginning of which the author reveals himself in several coplas. . . . Among the titles appears that of King of the Romans, hence he must have composed the book after his unfortunate election, realized only in name.[82]

Here Burriel cites Alfonso's reference to his own election as Holy Roman Emperor in 1257, which was never confirmed.[83] This attention to historical detail finds an analogy in Palomares's attempt (seen in the plate) to imitate the flourished initial letter P in the prologue to the *Cantigas*, "Porque trobar," which he had not incorporated into his manuscript copy of the *Cantigas*. In most of the copy Palomares used very simple stylized vegetal motifs, a combination of leaf sprays and tendrils, to evoke the much more formal initial letters in the Toledo codex, in some cases adopting a different convention altogether to indicate the hierarchy of initials that distinguished between the refrain, which opens each cantiga, and the first part of the copla.

The next section of Burriel's commentary in the *Paleografía Española* brings the Toledo codex even closer to the person of Alfonso X:

> In this volume of poetry there are some emendations in cursive script, and it seems possible that they are from the hand of the king himself, as it would seem that a codex of such richness and delicacy could have been written for him alone. One of these emendations, made in the margin of Cantiga 77 (substituting one entire copla, more harmonious, for another with the same meaning) is depicted in number 2. It tells of an apparition of Saint Mary, accompanied by saints and angels, and should be read as follows:

> E á Virgen escolleita
> tragian en o meogo
> da compaña, que dereita-
> mente á el veno logo,
> édissele sin sospeita,
> dim una ren, eu te rogo,
> que de tí saber quería.[84]

Burriel's argument that only the author of the *Cantigas* would have added the substitute copla exemplifies the modern understanding of the *Cantigas* as a unified work by a single author who had the sole authority to make changes to the text. The attribution of the entire collection to Alfonso himself, however, is now widely recognized as a fiction,[85] and scholars tracing the development of the collection from the state represented in the Toledo codex to the more ample corpus of the later manuscripts have noted that the process of compilation reflects the work of many different "authors." Manifold too were the medieval readers and performers who shaped the reception of the text. In the Middle Ages, then, the *Cantigas* were apparently not considered so venerable as to preclude significant alterations such as the

FIGURE 4.7 Burriel, *Paleografía Española*, plate 8. By permission of Columbia University, Rare Book and Manuscript Library.

textual substitutions in the Toledo codex. Martha Schaffer has argued to the contrary that such marginal annotations in the Toledo codex reflect active use related to performance, and that the manuscript, which she sees as a later copy of the first *Cantigas* collection, was "converted to use as either a working exemplar or a personal copy for an individual involved in composition, compilation, and/or performance."[86] Schaffer advocates understanding the later *Cantigas* manuscripts as all equally valid witnesses to a process of re-compilation and evolution, not as better or worse copies of a unified work.[87]

The Palomares copy, with its prefatory illustrations, not only furthered Burriel's historiographic goals, but also reflected his own experience of the manuscript as a link to the past. The copy and Burriel's commentary on the Toledo codex in the *Paleografía Española* attest to the uses of the Middle Ages by intellectuals associated with the court of Ferdinand VI. The visual fusion of Ferdinand's persona with that of Alfonso X, and the combination of medieval notation and modern script, are both amalgamations of past and present that typify the construction of history cultivated within the Spanish Bourbon cultural program. Thus the copy takes on a new meaning in the context of the artistic projects promoted by the government of Ferdinand VI in the mid-eighteenth century. As we have already seen, explicit connections between Ferdinand VI and medieval rulers also shaped the visual structuring of history in Martín Sarmiento's program of decoration for the new Royal Palace in Madrid, which juxtaposed Visigoths with the medieval kings of Castile and the Bourbons.[88] Likewise Burriel's history of the liturgy in the preface to the parchment facsimile of Toledo, BC 35.7, linked Ferdinand VI to his seventh-century antecedents. The Palomares copy of the *Cantigas* presents yet another example of a medieval king functioning as a symbolic bridge between past and present. Given the favor enjoyed by music at the court of Ferdinand VI, it is particularly fitting that the connection is made through the copy of a book of song associated with a royal singer.

Notes

Parts of this chapter appeared in Boynton, "Reconsidering the Toledo Codex."

1. Burriel, "Apuntamientos," in Echánove Tuero, *La preparación intelectual*, 288.

2. For a complete online description and bibliography (continually updated) on the Toledo codex as a whole and on its contents, see http://sunsite.berkeley.edu/Philobiblon/BITAGAP/1067.html (accessed June 10, 2009). It is not known when the manuscript entered the cathedral library; it appears late in the inventories. See Ramón Gonzálvez Ruiz, *Hombres y libros*, 578, who hypothesizes that Gonzalo Pérez Gudiel, archbishop of Toledo from 1280 to 1299, could have brought it into the collection.

3. The copy of the *Cantigas* is the first item in the inventory of Burriel's books made at his death in 1762, and the description of the Toledo codex there states that it was "corregido al parecer de mano del mismo Rey." See Galende Díaz, "Repertorio bibliografico," 245.

4. It is possible that the presentation copy survives, as yet unidentified, in a Portuguese collection; Barbara's library did not remain in Spain after her death.

5. On this text, see chapter 3.

6. For information on this text, the manuscript, and the various sources for the miracle see the entry in the Oxford Cantigas de Santa Maria Database, http://csm.mml.ox.ac.uk/index.php?p=poemdata_view&rec=2 (accessed June 10, 2009).

7. A description of the copy can be found in Higinio Anglès, *La música de las Cantigas*, 2:19–21.

8. Some recent examples of scholarship in this vein include Taylor, *Textual Situations; The Whole Book.*

9. The other manuscripts are Real Monasterio de San Lorenzo El Escorial, B.I.2; Escorial T.I.1; Florence, Biblioteca Nazionale, Banco Rari 20. On the Toledo codex in the context of the other manuscripts see Gonzálvez Ruiz, *Hombres y libros*, 571–78.

10. I refer to the entirety of the cycle as "the *Cantigas*," and to unspecified examples of this genre as "cantigas" (without italics).

11. The most recent detailed study of the manuscript is Stephen Parkinson, "Layout and Structure," 133–53.

12. On the processes by which these collections were formed, see most recently Parkinson and Jackson, "Collection," 159–72.

13. Schaffer, in "Los códices," 130–35, points out the difficulty of determining the character and location of the scriptoria in which the Alfonsine manuscripts were copied, in the absence of information regarding the circumstances of production.

14. For a brief summary of scholarly debates on the manuscript, see Monteagudo, "'Cantares,'" vii–xiii.

15. Parkinson, "Layout and Structure," 133.

16. Ferreira, "The Stemma," 97 (where the dates given are between 1264 and 1276).

17. This was the conclusion of Malcolm Parkes and Sonia Scott-Fleming as reported in "Round Table," 214–20. David Wulstan, in "The Composition," 154–95, also contends that the Toledo codex is a late copy of the original compilation.

18. Anglès, *La música de las Cantigas*, 2:24–26. See also Anglès and Subirá, *Catálogo*, 160.

19. See Ferreira, "Understanding the *Cantigas*." I am grateful to the author for sharing this study with me before its publication.

20. On the codicological context in other medieval Galician-Portuguese *cancioneiros* see Ferreira, "The Layout of the *Cantigas*," 47–61.

21. Haines, *Eight Centuries*, 120–24.

22. Aubrey, "Medieval Melodies," 17–34.

23. Haines, *Eight Centuries*, 124.

24. See Duchez, "Jean-Jacques Rousseau," 39–111. I am grateful to Nathan J. Martin for bringing Rousseau's interest in medieval notation to my attention.

25. Crescimbeni's six-volume *Istoria* was first published in Rome in 1698 and reprinted numerous times in the eighteenth century, often with Crescimbeni's commentaries and expansions. For an illustration of the musical example from the 1702 edition, see Haines, *Eight Centuries*, 110 (example 3.4).

26. Appendix to Levesque de la Ravallière, *Les Poësies, Eight Centuries*, 112 (example 3.5).

27. Haines, *Eight Centuries*, 112–16.

28. Gerbert, *De Cantu*.

29. Kendrick, "The Science of Imposture," 101–5.

30. "Poesias en lengua gallega, ò portuguesa antigua de Don Alonso Decimo llamado el Sabio, Rey de Castilla, y de León. Copiadas de un Tomo en pergamino de la Libreria de

la Santa Iglesia de Toledo, corregido al parecer de mano del mismo Rey . . . Ofrecidas a la reyna nuestra señora por El Padre Andrès Burriel de la Compañia de Jesus."

31. Ceballos, "Scarlatti and María Bárbara," 197–223.

32. *Storia della Musica*. See also *Un reinado bajo el signo de la paz*, 19. On the iconography of Saint Cecilia see Connolly, *Mourning into Joy*.

33. I am grateful to Martha Schaffer for pointing out to me the symbolism of this portrait. For the question of authorship in the *Cantigas* and Alfonso's role in their production see particularly Ferreira, "Alfonso X, Compositor," 117–37; Mettmann, "Algunas observaciones," 355–66; Scarborough, "Autoría o autorías," 331–37; Schaffer, "Questions of Authorship," 17–30.

34. "El rey faze un libro, nonparquel el escriua con sus manos, mas porque compone las razones del, e las emienda et yegua, e enderesca, e muestra la manera de como se deuenfazer, e desi escriue las qui el manda, pero dezimos por esta razón que el rey faze el libro." Text and translation from Cárdenas, "Alfonso's Scriptorium," 92.

35. On the visual representation of Alfonso X in Escorial T.I.1, see Domínguez Rodríguez, "Imágenes de un rey trovador," 229–39. Wulstan, in "The Composition," 167–68, points out that in this manuscript the king appears to be dictating from a book to scribes who are writing on scrolls.

36. Snow, "Alfonso X y las 'Cantigas,'" 159–72.

37. On Palomares's collaboration with Bayer in this period, see chapter 5.

38. The name that Ferdinand I shared with Ferdinand VI might have suggested the connection to viewers. On Ferdinand I see Viñayo González, *Fernando I*.

39. See Schechner Genuth, "Armillary Sphere," 28–31; www.hps.cam.ac.uk/starry/armilldemon.html (accessed November 10, 2010).

40. The treatises on the armillary are edited in volume 2 of the *Libros del saber de astronomia del rey D. Alfonso X de Castilla*. For a recent discussion of the *Libros* in this context see García Avilés, "Alfonso X," 83–103.

41. On the linkage of the visual arts with Spain's overseas endeavors, see Schulz, "Spaces of Enlightenment," 189–227.

42. Navarro Brotóns, "Science and Enlightenment," 393. According to Navarro Brotóns, Burriel himself is thought to have emphasized the modernization of science teaching as *director supernumerario* of the seminary in 1746–47. On Burriel's years at the seminary, see the preface.

43. Treatises on the use of the armillary sphere appeared in the eighteenth century, including Benjamin Martin, *The Description and Use of Both the Globes, the Armillary Sphere, and Orrery, Exemplified in a Large and Select Variety of Problems in Astronomy* . . . (London, 1758).

44. Letter of June 12, 1745, to Gregorio Mayans in Mayans y Siscar, *Gregorio Mayans y Siscar, Epistolario. II*, 150.

45. Porcel y Salablanca, "Canción Heroica," lines 91–92: "Dando ya al viento velas por talares / Mercurio fiel frecuentará los mares" (Already giving sails to the wind instead of his [winged] heels / Faithful Mercury will frequent the seas). See also Bonet Correa, "Introducción," 2–3. I thank Ronald Surtz for help with the translation of the couplet.

46. Sarmiento, *Sistema de adornos*, 220: "Este dios y diosa, como símbolos, significan el estado feliz de una monarquía, sobre el pie de una Paz Octaviana. En los otros pliegos, que

contienen el Sistema que mi cortedad ha ideado para los adornos de escultura de Palacio, propuse como basa la prenda característica de S.M., que es el ser pacífico: Ferdinandus reconciliator pacis. La paz significa en el caduceo las Artes y Ciencias; en Mercurio, el comercio en su bolsa; el cultivo de la tierra, en Ceres, y la abundancia de todo, en la cornucopia."

47. I am grateful to Louise Rice for her initial identification of these figures.

48. The Marques de la Ensenada made the development of the Spanish navy a high priority in the first half of the 1750s; see Barton, *A History of Spain*, 143; Lynch, *Bourbon Spain*, 176–78.

49. On this theme, see most recently *Un reinado bajo el signo de la paz*, 1–9, 31–49.

50. On this composition, see Cioffi, "Corrado Giaquinto at the Spanish Court," 332–35.

51. See Pérez Sánchez, *Corrado Giaquinto y España*, 228–33 (cat. 61).

52. Ripa, *Iconologia*, 429–32 (description of altar on 432). I thank Catherine Puglisi for referring me to Ripa's treatise as well as providing references to relevant comparanda for the composition by Corrado Giaquinto.

53. Pérez Sánchez, *Corrado Giaquinto y España*, 192–93 (cat. 45).

54. For a useful discussion of the term "sacra conversazione," designating the representation of the Virgin Mary with other saints, see Humfrey, *The Altarpiece*, 12–13. I am grateful to Bill Barcham for this reference.

55. On the interaction between elite and popular Marian devotion in Spain in the eighteenth century, see Saugnieux, "Ilustración católica," 275–95. On the devotional life of Ferdinand and Barbara, see *Un reinado bajo el signo de la Paz*, 361–69.

56. The portrait is in the Civico Museo Bibliografico Musicale in Bologna; see Pérez Sánchez, *Corrado Giaquinto y España*, 154–55 (cat. 28). On the musical references in the portrait, see Heartz, "Farinelli Revisited," 430–48. On its place in the iconography of Farinelli, see Joncus, "One God," especially 460, 485.

57. I am grateful to Karen Hiles for pointing out this connection.

58. Entries in the *Gaceta de Madrid* for 1747–58 are edited by Margarita Torrione in *Crónica festiva*, 245–333. For a recent synthesis of Torrione's extensive work on opera at the Spanish court in this period, see Torrione, "La sociedad de Corte," 165–95.

59. Feldman, *Opera and Sovereignty*.

60. Kleinertz, "Music Theatre in Spain," 413. On the help that Metastasio gave to Farinelli's endeavors in Madrid, see Savage, "Getting By," 387–409.

61. On early reception of Metastasio in Spain see Kleinertz, *Grundzüge*, 1:77–112.

62. Schaffer, "Los códices," 141–42.

63. As in Madrid, BN 13055, f. 108v (which corresponds to Madrid, BN 10069, fol. 56v).

64. "Santa Maria sempros seus aida," Madrid, BN 13055, fol. 117v–118r (corresponds to Madrid, BN 10069, fol. 61v–62r).

65. As in Madrid, BN 13055, fols. 128r, 143v.

66. Madrid, BN 13055, fol. 123v (which corresponds to Madrid, BN 10069, fol. 64v). Palomares omitted the plicated D above the syllable "o"; perhaps he did so because it is partly erased, but he included the immediately preceding D on the second syllable of the word "quiser," which is just as faded and erased as the plicated D.

67. An example is the melody for the word "seus" in the third musical system of Cantiga 64 (Madrid, BN 13055, fol. 154v, compared to Madrid, BN 10069, fol. 82v).

68. My summary of the verbal differences between the copy and the original is based on the results of Sean Hallowell's exhaustive comparison of their textual contents.

69. Madrid, BN 13055, fol. 51v; Madrid, BN 10069, fol. 27r.

70. On Palomares's view of the history of handwriting in Spain, see chapter 5.

71. Burriel's annotations to the Palomares copy are reproduced in Anglès, *La música de las Cantigas*, 2:20–22. The annotations in the Toledo codex are printed in Monteagudo, "'Cantares,'" and analyzed in Schaffer, "Marginal Notes," 65–84.

72. For instance, on fol. 178r of Madrid, BN 13055, Burriel wrote, "This copla is emended in the margin with two lines of old cursive script, thus . . ." ("Esta copla està emendada en la margen en dos lineas de letra cursiva antigua asi . . ."). On fol. 193r: "This verse is corrected in a cursive script, thus . . ." ("Este verso està corregido de letra cursiva asi . . ."). On fol. 218r: "It said *razonador*, but is emended by an old cursive script in the margin to *Aiudador*" ("Decia *razonador*; pero esta enmendado de letra cursiva antigua en el margen *Aiudador*." An unusual reference to a noncursive script is on fol. 287v: "added in italics" ("añadido de letra bastardilla").

73. Fol. 275r: "Al pie de esta llana hai de letra antigua cursiva una Nota, de donde se colige, que estas coplas sirvieron de motetas en la Iglesia, pues dice assi: 'A vigia de Sancta Maria dagosto seia dita *Des quando Deus sa Madr. aos ceos levou, i no dia seia dita Beneita es Maria filla madre dada.*'" This note indicating liturgical use of the cantiga for the Vigil of the Assumption corresponds to the annotation in Madrid, BN 10069, fol. 143r. See Schaffer, "Marginal Notes," 69–70.

74. Madrid, BN 13055, fol. 278r: "Al pie de esta llana hai una nota de letra cursiva antigua, que dice asi: 'Pois desta deue seer â festa dos ramos. Aver non poderia lagrimas que chorasse.' Este es el estrivillo de la Cantiga Lª que es de los *siete Dolores*."

75. Schaffer, "Marginal Notes," 69–71.

76. Cantiga 77 in the Toledo codex (with the refrain "Quen leixar Santa Maria") corresponds to Cantiga 132 in the standard numbering, which is based on the Escorial manuscripts of the *Cantigas*. For the most recent critical edition of the text see Alfonso X, el Sabio, *Cantigas*, 2: 91–96.

77. Madrid, BN 10069, fol. 100r: "They were conducting the Virgin, the chosen one, in their midst. She came directly to him and said to him: 'I pray you, tell me in all honesty something I would like to know from you.'" Translation modified from *The Songs of Holy Mary*, 164.

78. "And they bore in their midst the crowned virgin, who was very angry, and she said 'Since you have abandoned me, I pray you, tell me something I would like to know from you.'"

79. Bertolucci Pizzorusso, "Primo contributo," 118.

80. Madrid, BN 13055, fol. 187r: "Nota. Esta copla està escrita en la margen inferior de letra cursiva rasgada, acaso de mano del mismo Rey Don Alonso y sirve de correccion à la que està en el cuerpo de la obra tildada, y borrada."

81. Burriel published commentary on the Toledo codex in his treatise *Paleografía Española*, on which see below. Whereas Henrique Monteagudo, in "'Cantares con sões saborosos de cantar,'" vii, states that the commentary on the Toledo codex in *Paleografía Española* was Martín Sarmiento's, in fact Sarmiento's account of the *Cantigas* in his posthumously published *Memorias para la Historia de la Poesía* clearly demonstrates that he paid attention only to the language of the text. (Sarmiento is known for

his pioneering work in Galician philology.) See Sarmiento, *Obras posthumas*, 270–71. Agustín Millares Carlo, in *Tratado de Paleografía Española*, 1:313, states that Sarmiento wrote this treatise in 1741.

82. Burriel, *Paleografía Española*, 71–72: "En la lamina 8ª muestra el num. I° el principio del Prologo de un tomo de Poesías de el Rey Don Alonso el Sabio, que contiene cien *Cantigas*." Endnote: "Canciones, que se hacian para cantar en Lengua Gallega, ó Portuguesa de *Milagros, y loores de Santa Maria*: cinco de sus Fiestas: cinco de las de N. S. J. Christo: y diez y seis de otros milagros de la misma Señora. Está escrito en pergamino avitelado de letra primorosa, iluminado todo de colores, y cada *Cantiga* tiene notada la musica sobre la primera copla, y estrivillo, que trahen casi todas. La Obra empieza por el Indice, en cuya frente se descubre el Autor en varias coplas. . . . Entre los titulos pone el de *Rey de Romanos*, por donde consta haber compuesto el Libro despues de la malograda eleccion, que de él hicieron por sola su fama."

83. On the election and the lengthy conflicts that followed, see O'Callaghan, *A History of Medieval Spain*, 362; O'Callaghan, "Image and Reality," 24–26; O'Callaghan, *Learned King*, 200–233.

84. Burriel, *Paleografía Española*, 74–75: "En este tomo de Poesía hay algunas enmiendas de letra cursiva, y parece creible, que son de propria mano del Rey, para el qual solo, al parecer, pudo escribirse Codigo de tanto coste, y primor. Una de ellas, hecha en el margen de la *Cantiga LXXVII* (substituyendo una copla entera mas harmoniosa por otra del mismo sentido) se ha retratado en el num. 2. Habla de una aparicíon de Santa Maria, accompañada de Santos, y Angeles, y debe leerse asi: E á Virgen escolleita/tragian en o meogo / da compaña, que dereita/mente á el veno logo, / édissele sin sospeita, / dim una ren, eu te rogo, / que de tí saber quería."

85. See the acknowledgment of this fact in, for instance, Snow, "Alfonso as Troubadour," 126–40.

86. Schaffer, "Marginal Notes," 66–67.

87. Schaffer, "The 'Evolution' of the *Cantigas*," 186–213.

88. See chapter 1.

5 | Palomares and the Visigothic Neumes

Palomares continued to reap the intellectual benefits of his collaboration with Burriel in Toledo Cathedral's archives and library long after the work of the Royal Commission on the Archives concluded in 1756. The supervision of the Jesuit had a profound influence on the young calligrapher, amounting to an apprenticeship of sorts that served to consolidate the latter's paleographic skills and shape his subsequent career. In addition to his own copies of manuscripts from the cathedral, Palomares drew upon his experience of working with Burriel as the foundation for his later treatise on paleography.[1] This chapter focuses on the contribution of Palomares to the history of paleography, with particular emphasis on his interest in neumes. Although his most important work on medieval manuscripts remains unpublished, it illustrates a method based equally on long familiarity with manuscripts in Visigothic script and on an extraordinary ability to copy them. In this regard Palomares possessed knowledge and skills that were unmatched in his lifetime. Most significantly, he understood something frequently overlooked: musical notation is a graphic element that should be fully integrated into paleographic study.

Palomares after the Royal Commission on the Archives

Palomares described his professional activities of the 1750s and early 1760s in a petition to Charles III, which he wrote in the hope of obtaining both the patronage of the monarch and a government pension.[2] According to this autobiographical account, Palomares had been employed by the Contaduría Principal de Rentas Provinciales since 1751. From 1751 to 1756 he had taken a leave of absence to assist Burriel in Toledo, where he perfected his knowledge of and ability to copy early documents and scripts. With great effort, Palomares wrote, he produced highly accurate drawings of documents and royal seals that remained little known in Spain because they had never been reproduced in print. He stated that the drawings remained in the possession of Burriel, who could attest to their accuracy. This detail indicates that the petition must date to the period between 1759 (when Charles III succeeded to the throne) and 1762 (when Burriel died). Palomares also mentioned the parchment facsimile he made of the chant book Toledo 35.7, which had been presented to Ferdinand VI.[3]

After the termination of the Commission on the Archives in 1756, Palomares returned to Madrid with Burriel, where he worked for the Contaduría while attempting to improve his situation. According to his account of this period in his petition, he turned first to various government ministers, showing them his copies of maps and other works that displayed his exceptional ability at drawing. After failing to obtain a new position in this manner, he wrote directly to the king to request a royal appointment as copyist in a government ministry, or as calligraphy instructor to one of the royal princes, or as a manuscript restorer in the Royal Library. If none of these positions was available, he hoped nonetheless to obtain a higher salary than he could earn in the Contaduría.

The petition was accompanied by an outline for a new history of paleography that corresponds loosely to the contents of the *Polygraphia Gothico-Española*, a treatise Palomares completed in 1764 on the history of writing in Iberia from late Roman cursive to the late twelfth century.[4] This text survives in the library of the Royal Academy of History in a folio-size volume written and illustrated entirely by hand.[5] Each style of script is depicted in extraordinarily accurate drawings with a trompe-l'oeil presentation that mimics engraved plates. These examples represent texts taken from manuscripts, coins, and inscriptions, as well as tables of letters and abbreviations. The obvious model for such a presentation is the *De re diplomatica* of Mabillon, though Palomares's treatise focuses more on manuscripts than on charters, which are the subject of Mabillon's treatise.[6]

Virtually all of the illustrations for the *Polygraphia* are based on Palomares's drawings of manuscripts in Toledo Cathedral and in the library of the royal monastery of San Lorenzo at the Escorial. Palomares had first copied pages from the Escorial manuscripts in 1762 and 1763, while assisting Pérez Bayer (with whom he had already worked in Toledo for the Commission on the Archives) in preparing an index of the monastery's renowned collection of manuscripts. In February 1763, however, conflicts between the two men caused Palomares to quit. The story of this failed collaboration can be gleaned from documentation apparently assembled by Palomares, including copies of letters and a narrative account of the episode, all preserved together in the same manuscript that contains his request for royal patronage.[7] According to Palomares, when he completed the second volume of the index and Bayer presented it to Charles III, Bayer obtained an additional pension only for himself. Palomares went on to finish the third volume of the index, which was presented to the king and approved. He was then nominated for a position in the Royal Library that the king wished to grant him, but unbeknown to Palomares, Bayer scuttled the appointment. When Palomares realized that he would not gain any lasting advantage from his work at the Escorial, he goes on to say, he asked for a letter of recommendation and went to the royal palace of El Pardo to present himself to the king. His efforts, however, were in vain; he found out that Bayer had simply been augmenting his own income without promoting Palomares at court. In February 1763 Palomares refused to continue the index until Bayer agreed to recognize his contribution explicitly and to pay him a part of the additional income Bayer received for the index. Bayer became so incensed by this demand that he never completed the index. Nonetheless Palomares's work at the Escorial gave him access to manuscripts that formed the basis of his own monumental treatise.

The Polygraphia Gothico-Española *and the Old Hispanic Rite*

Among Palomares's motivations for the composition of his *Polygraphia* seem to have been self-promotion, homage, and competition. As seen in his request for a royal pension, in 1763–64 he was actively seeking a better standing. He clearly saw his treatise as an improvement on the only existing text of comparable scope, the *Bibliotheca Universal* of Rodríguez, which was left unfinished by its author and published in 1738 by Blas Nassarre, the royal librarian. This treatise happened to contain the only illustration of the Visigothic script printed since the early seventeenth century, a remarkably poor likeness of a manuscript in the library of Toledo Cathedral (Figure 5.1). The history of this image shows the ignorance of the Visigothic script that prevailed at least until the publication of Burriel's *Paleografía* in 1755. The plate is apparently based on a clumsy drawing by Pedro Camino y Velasco, whose calligraphy was inexpert at best. (Camino's lack of proficiency in Visigothic paleography is attested to by Burriel himself, in a copy that bears a Latin caption describing the medieval original as the property of Camino

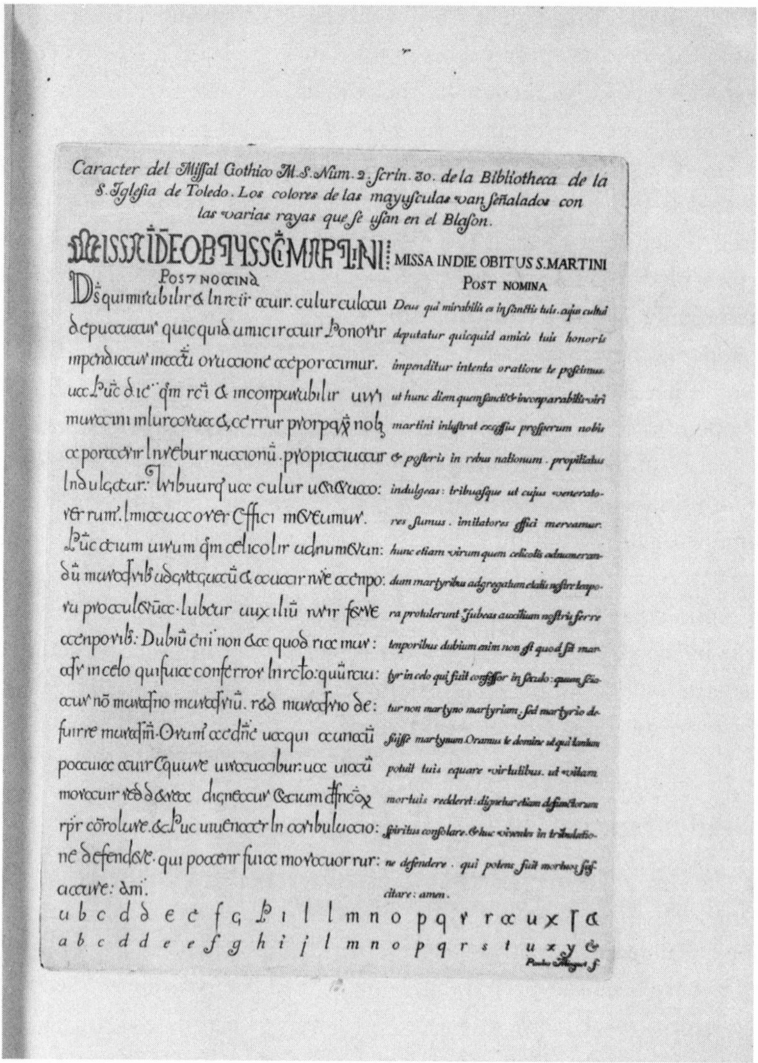

FIGURE 5.1 Christóval Rodríguez, *Bibliotheca universal de la polygraphia española*, plate 19. By permission of Columbia University, Rare Book and Manuscript Library.

Velasco, "a great scholar of these antiquities." Burriel has added a marginal note offering a more pragmatic assessment: "It cannot be used; he copied them badly. It must be corrected later.")[8] The drawing had been reproduced earlier, in the Bollandist Pinius's treatise *Liturgia Mozarabica*, which was first published in 1729 and then reprinted in 1740.[9] The illustration is followed by a postscript in Latin by Camino y Velasco, stating that he faithfully transcribed the *post nomina* prayer from the mass of St. Martin of Tours in a

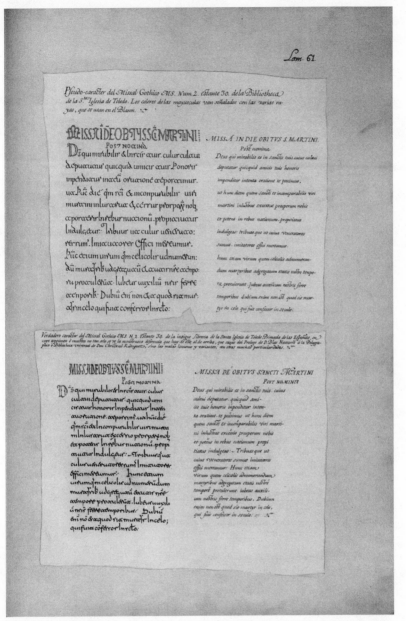

FIGURE 5.2 Palomares, *Polygraphia Gothico-Española*, plate 61. Copyright © Reproducción, Real Academia de la Historia.

manuscript provided by the cathedral librarian. The left column shows the prayer from Toledo 35.3, with a transcription in the right column. It seems that Blas Nassarre simply reused the plate from the Pinius treatise in his publication of the *Bibliotheca Universal*, altering it only slightly.[10]

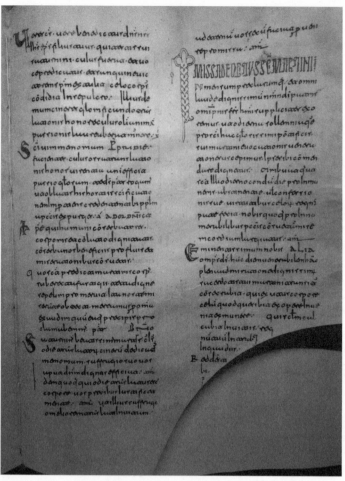

FIGURE 5.3A Toledo, BC 35.3, fol. 205r. Copyright © Archivo y Biblioteca Capitulares, Catedral Primada de Toledo.

In the preface to his *Polygraphia* Palomares criticized the *Bibliotheca Universal* roundly and at great length. In order to demonstrate the superiority of his own treatise, he went so far as to recount an anecdote about a canon of Toledo Cathedral who, it seems, had repeatedly asked Palomares how he could hope to improve upon Rodríguez's treatise. Palomares, annoyed that the ignorant canon's praise of the *Bibliotheca Universal* lent the treatise a degree of authority that went far beyond its actual merits, decided to enumerate its flaws graphically. First he showed the ignorant canon the manuscript page whose appearance was so grossly distorted in the plate published by Nassarre. Then he drew a perfect likeness of the plate from the *Bibliotheca* and juxtaposed it with his own, far more accurate rendering of

FIGURE 5.3B Toledo, BC 35.3, fol. 205v. Copyright © Archivo y Biblioteca Capitulares, Catedral Primada de Toledo.

the medieval manuscript. This comparison became a plate in the *Polygraphia* (Figure 5.2).[11] For the purposes of comparison with the illustration in the *Bibliotheca*, Palomares diverged from his usual practice, creating a composite image drawing on two different folios from the same manuscript, thus combining the rubric that begins the entire mass for Saint Martin (heading the right column of fol. 205r) with the text of the prayer itself, which begins on the reverse of the same leaf in the right margin (Figure 5.3).

While in Toledo Palomares had made an earlier copy of the same prayer, excerpting the same sentence for a plate in Burriel's *Paleografía*.[12] Burriel had chosen this prayer for illustration in the *Paleografía Española* because it was frequently cited by historians of the liturgy as evidence that the Old Hispanic rite dated to the fifth century. The text of the prayer appears to suggest that it was written soon after the death of Saint Martin in 397. As it appears in the Toledan manuscript, it can be loosely translated as "And the times of our age brought forth this man, who is to be numbered among those dwelling in heaven, and added to the martyrs."[13] As Burriel pointed out, this sentence was cited by the Italian cardinal Giovanni Bona (1609–74) as a sign of the text's early date.[14] Mabillon, however, maintained that the phrase "aetatis nostrae tempora protulerunt" might derive from a different, older liturgical text, and thus did not necessarily prove the antiquity of the Visigothic rite.[15] Mabillon's argument was refuted by Flórez, who maintained that the entire mass for Saint Martin dated to the first half of the fifth century.[16]

Although he was by no means an expert in liturgical history, Camino y Velasco likewise quoted the prayer in the dedication of his 1740 *Noticia* in order to argue that the mass was composed soon after Martin's lifetime: "There is no doubt that in 402 A.D., the year in which Saint Martin, Bishop of Tours, died in France, as soon as his glorious passing was known, our Spain composed in his honor the very devout mass and office that we have today in our missal and breviary, and we the Mozarabs celebrate his feast day with a liturgy of six copes, which corresponds to a duplex of the first class in the Latin Rite."[17] In a bid to reaffirm the community's privileges by promoting the historical validity of their traditions, Camino, unlike other eighteenth-century commentators on the prayer for Saint Martin, self-consciously uses the text to establish a connection with the modern liturgy of the Mozarabs in Toledo.

But even Palomares's ironic narrative of the genesis of the comparison plate in the *Polygraphia* confirms the importance of this short excerpt from a single brief prayer in nearly all early modern discourses on the Old Hispanic rite. The prayer in fact stood in for the rite metonymically, just as the page from the manuscript was universally treated as a representative of the Visigothic script. In this way the histories both of liturgy and of paleography were intertwined. And it was not only the few and flawed impressions of the Visigothic script circulating prior to the publication of Burriel's *Paleografía* that made the case for the early dating of the Old Hispanic rite: Burriel himself quoted and reproduced this prayer from the mass of Saint Martin as evidence for the liturgy's antiquity. The historical arguments concerning this single, truncated text reveal their authors' convictions about the linkage of past to present through the liturgy. Camino connected the ancient rite directly to the contemporary Toledan Mozarabs, while Flórez, who aimed to prove the priority of Hispanic religious traditions, maintained that the Visigothic liturgy predated the Roman rite in Spain. Burriel and Palomares interpreted the Old Hispanic rite as part of a transhistorical Spain. Both Palomares's *Polygraphia* and Burriel's *Paleografía* stress the correspondence between the history of liturgical books and that of the Hispanic church in Castile, framing Toledo and its book production in relation to the story of the Spanish nation. In fact the principal focus of the *Polygraphia* is on Castile; other parts of the Iberian peninsula are included as secondary in importance to Toledo. Thus a considerable portion of Palomares's *Polygraphia* is dedicated to the history of the Old Hispanic rite and its fortunes in Toledo.

Clearly influenced by his work with Burriel, Palomares understood the development of manuscript bookhands as coterminous with the history of the liturgy, which he always viewed through the lens of national identity. The introduction of the Roman rite in León-Castile involved the importation of liturgical books written in late Caroline minuscule, a development that was seen by Palomares (as well as by his contemporaries) as an encroachment by French clerics upon Spanish culture. As in Burriel's *Paleografía*, Palomares emphasizes the Frenchness of this style of handwriting and states that it was diffused through the process of liturgical reform, which brought about the need to copy new manuscripts based on the French exemplars. Indeed in a long paragraph on the origins of the Old Hispanic rite (called here the Visigothic-Mozarabic rite) and its survival in Toledo, Palomares presents the liturgical reform of Castile as a deliberate campaign by the French (*franceses*) to introduce their own liturgy there:

> The city of Toledo having been recovered by the glorious Emperor Alfonso VI, son of King Ferdinand the Great, when it came time to restore and reestablish religious observance there, for this purpose and at the invitation of the same Emperor came a legate of Pope Gregory VII called Richard, Abbot of Marseille, who sought to introduce the liturgy composed by the same Pope Gregory,[18] which at that time was used in France (and is the same we have today in Spain), and he sought the abolition of the very ancient Visigothic or Isidorian liturgy. This legate insisted incessantly with the King that his desire be accomplished, inflaming with his persuasions Queen Constance and Archbishop Bernard, who, being French, wished to instill the liturgy of their homeland, so effectively that King Alfonso, to please the Queen, legate, and Archbishop, agreed.[19]

The connection Palomares implies between Constanza of Burgundy (who was the niece of the abbot of Cluny, Hugh of Semur) and liturgical reform seems to derive from the chronicle of the thirteenth-century archbishop of Toledo, Rodrigo Jiménez de Rada, who repeatedly states that

Constanza coerced Alfonso VI into adopting the Roman rite.[20] According to Palomares, even though Jiménez de Rada presented the introduction of the Roman rite as an initiative of the queen, the idea for the liturgical reform actually came from Bernard of Sahagún, the Cluniac archbishop of Toledo installed by Alfonso VI.[21]

The chronicle of Jiménez de Rada also appears to have been the source for an anecdote in Palomares's introduction, which recounts two famous symbolic contests between the Old Hispanic and Roman rites, one enacted through a judicial duel and the other in the form of a trial by fire, or ordeal. These widely diffused narratives were not devised by Jiménez de Rada, but were derived from accounts in earlier chronicles written a century after the events they describe, making it impossible to verify their historicity.[22]

The first known reference to the duel and the ordeal occurs in the Chronicle of Nájera, written in the late twelfth century.[23] All the early accounts situate the duel and ordeal in Burgos in 1077, after Alfonso had decided to introduce the Roman rite in his kingdom, but before the conquest of Toledo. In Palomares's version of the story, the duel occurred after the inhabitants of Toledo opposed the introduction of the Roman rite. The Toledan (meaning Mozarabic) side was deemed victorious over the Roman rite, which Palomares calls "French, or Latin, or Gregorian."[24] Palomares presents this as a battle in which numerous pairs of knights fought in single combat. Alfonso VI, dissatisfied with the outcome, then demanded an ordeal, and a liturgical book from each rite was thrown into a blazing bonfire. According to tradition, the Roman rite book (which Palomares calls "French or Gregorian") leaped out of the fire, while the Mozarabic one remained in the flames without burning.[25] Palomares concludes, "What is certain is that the French or Gregorian liturgy was received by the Spaniards with great abhorrence."[26]

The manner in which Palomares incorporates the story into the *Polygraphia* thus demonstrates both the centrality of Toledo to the narrative and the close association between liturgical reform and modern national identity, two themes widely in evidence throughout his text. The next section of the treatise, which quotes directly from Burriel's account of postconquest Toledo in the *Paleografía Española*, reinforces the idea that national identities shaped the city's new profile. Among the various groups in its diverse population, the Franks emerge predominant, appropriating not only the ecclesiastical center of power (the cathedral), but also the power of the written word, as the introduction of the new script (known in Spanish as the *letra francesa*) eventually renders the books in Visigothic script obsolete.

Having established this background for the introduction of the rite, Palomares introduces the letra francesa, which he claims originated in a style of writing that was left behind by the Visigoths in the Roman province of Gallia Narbonense. He states that an even better name for it than "frances" (French) is "Gothico-frances" (Visigothic French).[27] This historical appropriation for the Visigoths of a Caroline minuscule script is reminiscent of the way Burriel claimed for Spain all liturgical books written in any part of the former Visigothic kingdom (see chapter 1). At the same time, however, Palomares acknowledges that the Caroline minuscule had been used in the kingdoms of Navarre, Aragon, and Catalonia since the Carolingian period.[28] Using modern national categories, this style of script could perhaps be described as both French and Spanish, and it is these affiliations that underlie the account of the politics of postconquest Toledo that Palomares wove seamlessly into his paleographic narrative. He states that, because of the influence that Queen Constanza and Archbishop Bernard, "who were also French," exercised over Alfonso VI, "the Franks, or French" who had participated in the capture of the city were especially favored over the Castilians who had fought alongside them. For Palomares, indeed, the Caroline scripts seen in charters of the period suggested the presence of French hands in the royal chancery, the most immediate paleographic evidence that the French had penetrated the inner circles of power.[29]

The introduction to the plates concludes with the adoption of the letra francesa by the Castilian clergy of Toledo, who, according to Palomares, learned this script in the process of copying new liturgical manuscripts for the celebration of the Roman rite (here called the "liturgia francesa o Gregoriana"). Palomares points out that even some of his examples in Toledan Visigothic script contain features of late Caroline minuscule, suggesting the assimilation of the letra francesa by the Mozarabs themselves.[30]

Neumes in the Polygraphia

Of the many drawings of neumes Palomares executed for the Royal Commission on the Archives in Toledo, most were pen-and-ink copies of individual pages made to accompany complete transcriptions of manuscripts; none of these was published. The only printed example of neumes based on Palomares's copies was an excerpt of two lines from a chant with Toledan notation that appeared in Burriel's *Paleografía Española* (see chapter 1). In the *Polygraphia Gothico-Española* Palomares went beyond the example set by Burriel. He focused on a more limited chronological period that ended with the introduction of the late Caroline minuscule, the letra francesa, in the course of the liturgical reform at the end of the eleventh century. Moreover he

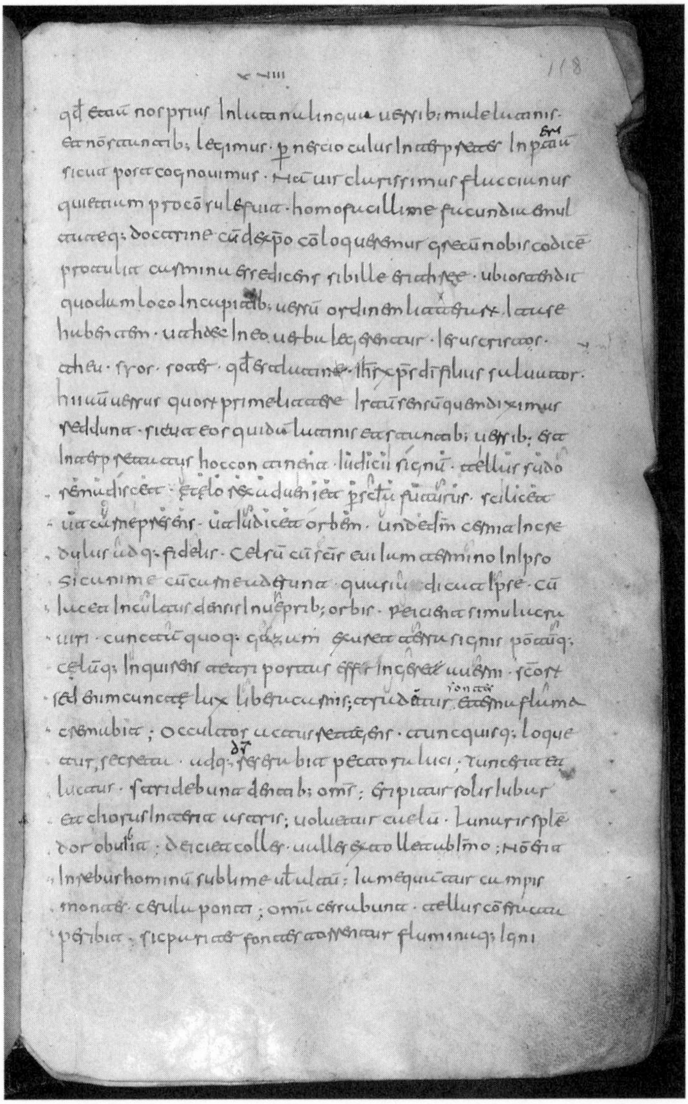

FIGURE 5.4 El Escorial, Real Monasterio de San Lorenzo, MS S.I.16, fol. 158r. Copyright © Patrimonio Nacional.

included numerous examples of liturgical manuscripts, illustrated neumes in two of his plates, and devoted an important section of his text to the origins of musical notation.

The ninth chapter, on neumes, follows one on orthography that includes the subject of accents. Consequently Palomares introduces neumes as a subcategory of accents:

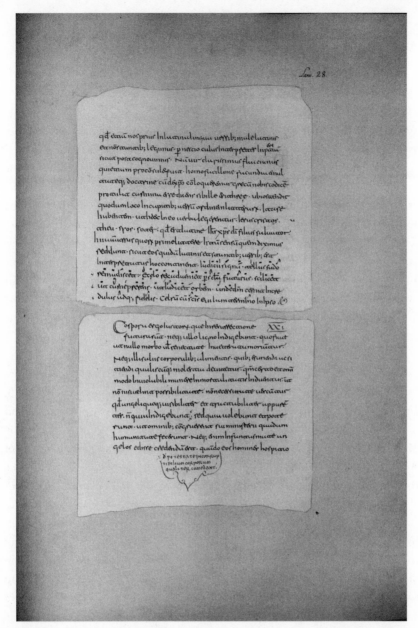

FIGURE 5.5 Palomares, *Polygraphia Gothico-Española*, plate 28. Copyright © Reproducción, Real Academia de la Historia.

The notes or musical points of the Visigoths seem to me to belong to the class of accents, or accentuation marks that change the sound of letters. They are so strange and different compared to modern ones and there are so many in the missals and other codices that, for my part, I think the reader will not be displeased by the strange manner in which they are arranged over the letters. Since none of the musicians of our time understand them, perhaps in the future someone will strive to comprehend them, and in the meantime the sight of them will divert the eye from the dryness and lack of amenity of my *Polygraphia*.[31]

Without citing any particular source for his interpretation of the neumes as accent marks, Palomares anticipates the long association of prosodic accent with early medieval notation. In the musicological scholarship of the nineteenth and twentieth centuries, one of the competing theories on the origins of neumes held that early neumes emerged directly from the prosodic accents of late antiquity. This theory, as originally formulated in the nineteenth century, has been largely discredited in recent decades because there is no consistent correspondence between the forms and functions of the accents and those of early neumes.[32] Charles Atkinson, however, has presented the evidence in the ancient grammarians and their Carolingian commentators for an understanding of prosodic accent that formed the background for the emergence of notation.[33]

Palomares's association between accents and neumes introduces the first example of musical notation in the *Polygraphia*, a plate with two copies from different parts of El Escorial, Real Monasterio de San Lorenzo, S.I.16, a ninth-century Augustine manuscript in Visigothic script (Figures 5.4 and 5.5).[34] The script was assigned to the late eighth or early ninth century by Millares Carlo.[35] The Escorial manuscript appears to be the earliest copy of Augustine of Hippo's *De ciuitate dei contra paganos* preserved in Spain.[36] Since this manuscript has been attributed to the region of Septimania (the ecclesiastical province of Narbonne), it does not belong, strictly speaking, to the textual tradition of Augustine in the Iberian Peninsula, even though it is part of the transmission of the text in the Visigothic script.[37] Instead the manuscript and its notation are an example of the widespread tradition of adding musical notation to the "Song of the Sibyl," a poem comprising twenty-seven Latin hexameter lines in book 18 of the *De ciuitate*, where Augustine presents it as a translation from Greek into Latin of prophetic verses attributed to the Erythraean Sibyl. The first letter of each Latin verse, when interpreted as its counterpart in the Greek alphabet, produces an acrostic, spelling "Jesus Christ, son of God, Savior," in Greek. Thus the acrostic is IESOUS CREISTOS THEOU UIOS SOTER in the Latin alphabet.[38] In the *Polygraphia* the upper part of plate 28 shows the passage in the Escorial manuscript containing the Sibylline verses (fol. 158r). The second example in plate 28 reproduces the lower half of fol. 30v. Palomares's commentary paraphrases the section of the *De ciuitate* in which Augustine recounts the origins of his translation. Palomares then states, "In this codex these verses have musical points over the vowels, exactly as depicted [in the example]."[39]

In the Escorial manuscript the first three verses and then selected phrases, words, and syllables are notated with neumes, as underlined below:

> The sign of judgment: the earth shall be moist with sweat.
> From heaven will come a future king for all eternity
> Present to judge all flesh and the earth,
> whereupon both the unbeliever and the faithful shall see God
> on high with the saints in that final moment of this age.
> Thus the souls in the flesh will come so that He may judge them.
> While [the earth] lies neglected in the dense bushes of the globe,
> They reject idols and all the treasure of man;
> Fire burns the earth and the sea and the sky,
> seeking to break open the gates of hideous hell.
> For the free light shall be given to the bodies of the saints;
> The eternal flame shall burn the guilty.[40]

> <u>Iudicii signum tellus sudore madiscet</u>:
> <u>e celo rex adveniet per secla futurus</u>,
> <u>scilicet ut carne presens ut iudicet orbem</u>.
> <u>unde deum</u> cernit incredulus <u>adque</u> fid<u>e</u>lis
> celsum cum <u>san</u>ctis eui iam ter<u>m</u>ino in ipso.
> <u>sic</u> anime cum carne aderunt quas <u>iu</u>dicat <u>ip</u>se,
> cum iacet in<u>cu</u>ltus densis in <u>ue</u>pribus orbis.
> <u>re</u>icient simulacra uiri cunct<u>am</u> quoque <u>ga</u>zam
> exurent <u>te</u>rras ignis pont<u>um</u>que celumque
> <u>in</u>quirens tetri portas effring<u>e</u>ret au<u>e</u>rni
> sanctorum sed enim cunct<u>e</u> lux <u>li</u>bera carni
> tradetur sontes eterna fl<u>am</u>a crem<u>a</u>bit.

The neumes were written after the text, in watery brown ink with a dull pen that caused the rectangular puncta to appear slightly rounded. (In Palomares's partial copy of the page, black ink and a sharper pen make the outlines of the neumes more distinct and angular.) The isolated neumes added after the first three completely notated lines of text are so much more faded that they seem to have been added at a different time, or at least with a different batch of ink.[41] It is difficult (if not impossible) to date such a small and idiosyncratic sample of notation, but the notation could have been added in the tenth century, the period from which the earliest known notated versions of the "Song of the Sibyl" survive. The rather archaic quality of the neume forms, as well as the absence of nuances that are found in eleventh-century Iberian notation, suggest an earlier date. The two forms of the torculus (both with and without loop) seen here appear in manuscripts copied before the mid-eleventh century in Catalonia, Castile, and León.[42] The notation in the Escorial manuscript closely resembles that in a fragment of a Catalan chant manuscript that has been dated to around 900 (Barcelona, Biblioteca de Catalunya, M. 1408/3 [80]).[43]

The Escorial manuscript may be the only known copy of the verses to transmit the neumes with the Augustinian text in its original context; I am not aware of other witnesses to *De ciuitate dei* containing musical notation.[44] The presence of early neumes in this manuscript raises the intriguing possibility (albeit one that is impossible to confirm) that the verses were first sung as part of the *De ciuitate dei* even before being separated from their original context. For the verses reported by Augustine were apparently sung; they are accompanied by musical notation in several manuscripts from the tenth century and later. The earliest examples of notated Sibylline verses appear in collections of sung poetry that are mostly nonliturgical. They form part of a broader tradition of neuming and performing late antique Latin texts that had the status of "classics" in the Middle Ages.[45] Two different hands, for example, notated *Iudicii signum* in a collection of *versus* (Paris, BNF, lat. 1154, fol. 122r).[46] The Sibylline verses are found notated with Beneventan neumes, perhaps added in the tenth century, in a ninth-century florilegium (Paris, BNF, lat. 2832, fol. 123v).[47] A tenth-century miscellany from Ripoll has neumes added in the eleventh century to just the first line.[48] The entirety of the text is notated with Catalan neumes in an eleventh-century fragment from the Cathedral of Vic.[49] It may be significant that several of these early examples come from the ecclesiastical province of Narbonne, which was also the region in which the Escorial Augustine manuscript originated.

Another performance context for the "Song of the Sibyl" emerged from the quotation of the Sibylline verses in the *Sermo de symbolo* "Vos inquam convenio o Iudei," which was attributed to Augustine in the Middle Ages but was probably written by Quodvultdeus, a fifth-century North African bishop.[50] By the central Middle Ages the sermon was used in many places as a reading for Matins on Christmas. Consequently the "Song of the Sibyl" appears with musical notation in numerous homiliaries, lectionaries, and breviaries from the Iberian peninsula and parts of what is now southwestern France. Most of the earlier manuscripts contain essentially the same melody, with various degrees of elaboration. The musical performance of the text was particularly widespread in the Iberian peninsula, where numerous vernacular versions survive, both as independent compositions and as a component of music dramas.[51]

Analysis of the notation in the Escorial manuscript shows that each of the first three lines of the text has its own distinct melody, as is also the case in the more complete musical settings of the Sibylline verses transmitted in later manuscripts.[52] Presumably the melody sung to the first line functioned as a refrain, while the contrasting melodies for the second and third lines formed a couplet that was repeated for all subsequent pairs of verses. After the first three lines of text only the compound and ornamental neumes are written in the Escorial manuscript. The neumes indicating single notes (the puncta and virgae) are omitted, presumably because they were taken by the scribe to be self-evident in the context of the repeated melody. The scribe's selectivity leads one to wonder why any neumes at all would be written for those verses in which the melody was repeated from previous parts of the poem. Furthermore what led the scribe to notate only certain parts of the text in these cases? By considering other examples of partial or intermittent notation in later manuscripts more light may be shed upon the function of the isolated neumes that appear after the first three lines of text in Escorial S.I.16.

The occurrence of intermittent notation in Visigothic manuscripts has been studied by Louis Brou, who argues that the practice of omitting repeated pitches was unique to scribes writing the melodies of the Old Hispanic chant.[53] Brou's examples comprise syllabic passages within chants that also had melismatic sections. Writing in 1952, however, he was unaware of a comparable phenomenon in several hymnaries of the mid-eleventh century that were notated at a time when the melodies of the office hymns were still predominantly an oral tradition.[54] For several reasons hymnaries offer more fitting analogies with the notation in Escorial S.I.16 than the examples considered by Brou. As in the musical settings of the Sibylline prophecy, the hymns are in Latin verse and their melodies have a repeating strophic structure. Likewise the same melody is sung to each distich in the "Song of the Sibyl." In the eleventh century most manuscripts made no allowance for the notation of the hymns; because the use of notation was not yet conventional for this genre, particular musical considerations led scribes to add notation between the lines of text. Partial notation seems to have fulfilled an explanatory function, demonstrating the linkage of melody and text at important junctures where misunderstanding could occur. Fitting the melodic contour to differing lines of verse entailed making adjustments that, however minuscule, are integral to the process of musical performance. Such adjustments seem to lie behind the partial notation of hymns, which consists principally of ornamental neumes (usually liquescence or quilisma) and any neumes representing more than one pitch. The decision to notate a liquescent neume in particular would be dictated by the changing consonants occupying a given metrical position in the text; liquescence, however, is not consistently notated, apparently because scribes did not feel obliged to indicate its every appearance.[55]

In the course of performing a predominantly syllabic melody remaining uniform over several successive strophes, even when the strophes varied in their number of syllables, singers might wonder about the placement of melismas. Shifting configurations of word lengths mean that compound neumes do not always occur in the same position; they can be sung to accented or unaccented syllables, and indeed to any part of a word, a technique that affects the shaping of individual phrases. The need to adapt to the changing structure of verse lines thus influences the perception of overall melodic contour.

In Escorial S.I.16 the neumes added occasionally after the first three lines are all composed of two or three notes. In addition to demonstrating the linkage of music and text, they convey essential information about melodic structure. The notation for the phrase "Unde deum," for example, in the fourth line of the poem, uses just two neumes to signal that this line of verse is to be sung to the second of the three melodies, differentiating it from the refrain melody used only for *Iudicii signum*. The clivis and torculus added to just one syllable of "adque" and "fidelis," respectively, provide further guidance for the singer in fitting the remainder of that line's melody to the verse. In the line "celsum cum sanctis" the smallest number of neumes necessary has been notated to show that it is sung to the third of the three melodies, thereby confirming that the second and third melodies alternate and that the musical structure of the whole song consists of a refrain followed by two contrasting melodies used for each subsequent pair of lines. Similarly the neumes for the line "Sic . . . ipse" confirm the return of the second melody. These neumes are placed on syllables that would have been accented when the verses were read aloud or sung. If indeed the notation of this passage functioned not only as a melodic sign, but also as a key to the proper accentuation of the verses, then we can better understand why Palomares chose such an atypical example to illustrate musical notation. As he states in the *Polygraphia*, he considered neumes to be a form of accentuation mark, and this passage from Augustine's *De ciuitate* illustrates well the linkage of notation and accent.[56]

One other plate in the *Polygraphia* illustrates neumes (Figure 5.6). Palomares describes it as representing "two other types of points, or musical notes, which seem different from those seen in plate 28. The first and second number [in the plate] represent the points that are found frequently in the missals and other books in Visigothic script that are preserved in the library of the Holy Church of Toledo."[57] The plate consists of three numbered parts, drawn by Palomares as if they were physically distinct pages. (Because the visual presentation of the illustration separates their contents, I will henceforth describe each of the three parts as pages.) Two different manuscripts supplied the material for this plate. Palomares states that the first two examples are from books in the library of Toledo Cathedral, and that the third is a Boethius manuscript from the Escorial. Although he did not identify the sources completely (which is quite unusual for Palomares), I have traced the first two pages in this plate to the first two flyleaves bound with Madrid, BN 10001.

The first two pages in plate 43 are partial copies from the bifolium bound as the front flyleaves in Madrid, BN 10001, fol. 1v (olim Toledo 35.1; Figure 5.7). This fragment originated in a different manuscript altogether and contains the form of neumatic notation generally identified with the north of the peninsula.[58] Palomares's approach to copying this notation merits extensive discussion. In general the writing angle of the neumes as they appear in his *Polygraphia* is more inclined to the right than in the original.[59] A similar slant of the pen is also discernible in a copy of the same bifolium that Palomares had drawn ten years earlier in Toledo. (He seems to have used his earlier drawings as the sources for illustrations in the *Polygraphia*.) The more inclined writing angle gives the notation a slightly hybrid character, combining the horizontal axis of Toledan neumes and the vertical axis of northern ones. Perhaps the horizontal axis was an acquired, unconscious habit that reflected the influence of Palomares's intensive work making a parchment facsimile of Toledo 35.7, for which he laboriously copied all the neumes in the entire codex. That ambitious project, which occupied six months in 1752, may have shaped his subsequent approach to copying neumes, endowing him with the graphic habits of a music scribe writing Toledan neumes.[60]

A detailed examination of this illustration in the *Polygraphia* is instructive, as it shows that Palomares's method at the time differed in some respects from his approach to copying in the 1750s, when he was working with the Commission on the Archives in Toledo. For Burriel's reference, Palomares executed highly accurate, literal copies; in the illustrations for the *Polygraphia* he rearranged the material to fit the text of the treatise and to make the images more internally consistent in format. The first page of plate 43 depicts most of the first column of Madrid, BN 10001, fol. 1v, which contains office chants and prayers for the end of Vespers and the beginning of Matins in

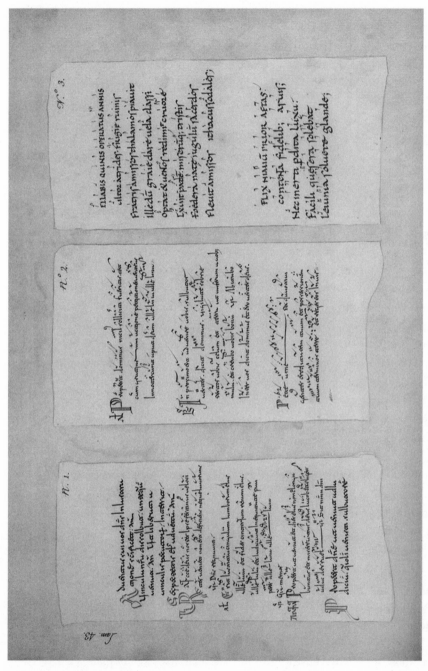

FIGURE 5.6 Palomares, *Polygraphia Gothico-Española*, plate 43. Copyright © Reproducción, Real Academia de la Historia.

FIGURE 5.7 Madrid, BN 10001, fol. 1v. Copyright © Biblioteca Nacional de España.

Advent (Figure 5.7). The copy makes slight adjustments to the original, such as writing the first line of text continuously, while the original contains a blank passage where an erasure occurred. Palomares also cleaned up the appearance of the original by copying all the text horizontally, whereas the medieval scribe had written the conclusions of two chants perpendicular to the main text block, in between the two columns. In the first chant text Palomares incorporates the unnotated incipit of the verse of the responsory, *Dominus regnavit*, following the respond, whereas in the medieval original (Madrid, BN 10001, fol. 1v) this verse had been inserted perpendicular to

the text in between the two columns. Similarly in the Alleluiaticus (an alleluiatic antiphon) he includes the incipit of the verse *Quia memor* as a separate
line, although in Madrid, BN 10001, this verse was likewise written later,
perpendicular to the text, between the two columns of the manuscript. In
this way Palomares "corrected" the presentation of the first two chants on
the page, making them conform to the layout of the third chant, *Prope est ut
veniat*, which is followed by the incipit of its verse, *Sit nomen Domini*. However, in the second page of the plate Palomares omits the incipit of the verse
for the Alleluiaticus *Prope est dominus*, which follows the chant and is written
within the line (not inserted later, perpendicular to the text).

Palomares's transcription of the Latin text, which faces the copy, also
shows attention to detail, but unlike his rendering of the chants' formats,
here he did not emend the contents of the original. He added the sign "%"
(meaning *ojo*, or "look") over the words *dissolbat* (for *dissolvat*), *pecatorum*
(for *peccatorum*), *Alleluia, misereuitur* (for *miserebitur*), *nicil* (for *nichil* or *nihil*),
abitabo (for *abitavo*), *cintoryum, davo* (for *dabo*), and *tivi* (for *tibi*). These spellings are typical of the Latinity of Iberian manuscripts, in which "b" and "v"
are frequently interchanged, and "ch" is often represented by "c" alone.[61]
Earlier in the *Polygraphia* he lists a number of such forms in his treatment of
orthography. There he designates them as "gothicismos": Gothic (meaning
Visigothic) features.[62]

The second page of plate 43 illustrates chants for the office of Matins in
Advent taken from the right column of the same bifolium employed in the
first plate (Madrid, BN 10001, fol. 1v and the right column of fol. 2r). In
this page of the example he extracted chants from their manuscript context;
the prayers surrounding the chants are not included (see Figure 5.7). Thus
the method he used to create this second page of the illustration differs significantly from the one he had employed in the first page, which presents a
rather faithful copy of an excerpt. While Palomares included both texts and
chants in an earlier copy of the material in this column, a drawing (probably from 1753) made for Burriel, his evident focus in the *Polygraphia* is the
notation of the chants.[63] Each chant is separated from the next by a blank
space, which calls attention to the fact that the chants are intentionally isolated examples rather than integral sections or segments of a manuscript page.
The mise-en-page appears all the more artificial because in this illustration
Palomares maintains the trompe-l'oeil effect (employed throughout the treatise) of presenting the excerpts on separated grounds that resemble variously
shaped, physically distinct leaves of parchment.

In the original manuscript all the chants presented in this example are
separated from each other by passages of text. The first two chants, the

alleluiaticus *Prope est dominus* and the psallendo *In proximo est advenire*, come from the right column of fol. 1v. Both of these chant genres are comparable to office antiphons in the Roman rite. In creating the illustration of *Prope est dominus* for the *Polygraphia*, Palomares made several subtle adjustments. He moved the first syllable of the word "innotescunt" (which is divided in the medieval original) to the next line, so that the word is written continuously, while at the same time omitting the neume that accompanies it in the original manuscript. In an earlier copy of this same chant (Madrid, BN 13054, written for the most part in 1753) he retained the original manuscript's syllabification and punctuation. He also copied four lines of the prayer text preceding it, which had the effect of reproducing the crowding of the first line of neumes by the text immediately above it. In the image of this page created ten years later for the *Polygraphia*, the first line of neumes has become the first line of the example. Palomares seems to have reused the earlier drawing, while rearranging its contents somewhat. The rendering in the *Polygraphia* is therefore a copy of a copy.

The third chant, the verse *Pete a me* for the *sono* of Christmas *Dominus dixit*, comes from the right column of the next flyleaf, fol. 2r, in Madrid, BN 10001.[64] While it is impossible to know the reasons for Palomares's choice of this chant rather than any of the others in the right column of fol. 1v, the extensive melisma near the beginning might have caught his calligrapher's eye. Moreover the manuscript page itself presents an interesting example of two different notational systems; the first three lines have been erased and replaced with chants in Toledan notation, a change that was probably made when the bifolium was already joined to the manuscript. Palomares copied only the first three lines of the chant, which occupies eight lines in the original.

The third page of plate 43 reproduces the beginnings of two poems excerpted from an eleventh-century manuscript of English origin containing the *De consolatione philosophiae* of Boethius (El Escorial, Real Biblioteca, e.II.1).[65] These poems, or *metra*, are notated with neumes that Palomares terms "Germano-Visigothic," and he points out that neumes appear only in the two excerpts he copied in the example.[66] As in the second page of plate 43, the two examples are separated from each other by blank space, reminding the viewer that they are excerpts removed from their original context. In the original manuscript the metra were accompanied by glosses, which Palomares omitted, presumably in order to focus on the notation alone. It is less clear why he left out the initial letters of both poems in an otherwise relatively accurate copy.

The first poem is the seventh metrum from book 4 of the *De consolatione* (*Tellabis quinis operatus annis*). As Palomares points out in his commentary, the entire metrum is notated, although he does not mention that the neumes were added by at least two different hands. The eight lines he copied are notated with staffless English neumes.[67] His rendering combines five lines from one page with three lines from the next, creating a semblance of continuity where, in the original, none exists.[68] The second example from this manuscript consists of five lines from the fifth metrum of book 2 (*Felix nimium prior aetas*), with Norman neumes of the late eleventh or twelfth century.[69]

The distinctive appearance of the neumes associated with manuscripts in Visigothic script caused Palomares to wonder about the origins of neumes in the Iberian peninsula, a question that continued to intrigue musicologists in the twentieth century.[70] He wrote, "It will not be easy to find out if the Visigoths learned from the Romans the points or musical notes in the missals and other ancient codices comparable to those I just cited, or if Saint Isidore, when he composed and ordered the Visigothic liturgy, took them from the ones being used in Spain, or in Italy, or if these points were common and customary in the entire Catholic Church."[71] This statement reflects the widespread attribution of the Visigothic liturgy to Isidore of Seville and presumes the existence of musical notation when the chant texts were first recorded in writing. Even in considering the earliest neumes, Palomares brings up the pervasive question of national origins, which also shaped the historiography of the liturgy. Just as scholars in the eighteenth century debated whether the Roman or Visigothic rite had priority in the Iberian peninsula, so Palomares wonders if the neumes of the Visigoths in fact originated in Italy. He notes that the only certainty concerning the history of notation was that staffless neumes differed completely from modern notation, which was thought to have been invented by Guido of Arezzo and perfected by Johannes de Muris.[72]

Other Liturgical Manuscripts in the Polygraphia

Several other plates in the *Polygraphia* contain copies of liturgical manuscripts from the Escorial and Toledo and exhibit remarkable accuracy when compared to the medieval manuscripts on which they are based, insofar, that is, as the latter can be identified. Plate 40 juxtaposes copies made from two different sources that represent the same style of Visigothic script. The first page contains the first page of the mass of Saint Vincent of Saragossa from a manuscript in the Escorial.[73] The second page of this plate is taken from an earlier drawing that Palomares made in Toledo of a fragment (now lost) owned by Camino y Velasco, from which Palomares excerpted a prayer from the mass for Saint Genesius of Arles.[74] Another fragment then owned by Camino y Velasco, a bifolium containing hymns, was copied in plate 33, which is also based on an earlier drawing. The Latin caption of the first drawing notes that the hymns are divided into their strophes.[75] A slightly shorter version of the same hymn text shown in the drawing *Iherusalem gloriosa mater* appears in the *Polygraphia* with a vivid yellow and green initial letter and is described in the caption as "part of a Mozarabic hymn for the feast of the holy martyrs Hadrian and Natalia."[76] Presumably this fragment, now also lost, attracted Palomares for its distinctive text format and illuminated letter.

A group of liturgical manuscripts from Toledo Cathedral, mostly lectionaries, homiliaries, and breviaries, is illustrated in plates 62 and 63. Whereas the plates with notation focused on the neumes, here the intention was to demonstrate the variety of Visigothic bookhands in texts designed for liturgical reading. The first page of plate 62 shows an unnotated verse for Lent from the main body of the breviary Madrid, BN 10001, omitting a notated antiphon that appears on the same page.[77] The second page shows a prayer for the feast of Saint Eulalia from a Toledan manuscript of the late eleventh or early twelfth century.[78] The third page combines excerpts from readings in two different Toledan manuscripts.[79] The fourth page, which shows a scriptural reading like the previous one, differs slightly from the original.[80]

Plate 63 comprises five small pages, one of them a horizontal strip. The first page is a very accurate copy of a short passage from a twelfth-century homiliary that was closely studied by Burriel.[81] The second page shows Psalm 119, verses 113–20 (*Iniquos odio habui*). The third page begins with four lines copied from an eleventh-century Toledan liturgical book, and continues with three lines taken from another source.[82] According to the caption on the facing page, the fourth and fifth pages of this plate were copied from a fragment of a missal owned in the eighteenth century by Palomares's father. Palomares identifies it as "containing a mass of Saint Leocadia," from which the prayer text in page 4 of the plate was copied.[83] While working for Burriel, Palomares had made a copy of the entire page containing this text.[84] The brief excerpt from the prayer in the *Polygraphia*, which has been taken out of its original context (where it was surrounded by notated chants), is thus analogous to the isolated chants that Palomares presented out of context in plate 43.

Comparing the plates in the *Polygraphia* to Palomares's earlier drawings of the same manuscripts draws attention to the contrasts in his copying methods in two different projects. In his work for the Royal Commission on the Archives, Palomares usually created a faithful record of a manuscript's format, which entailed copying the organization of elements in a given page. In his treatise, on the other hand, he sought to present distinct typologies of script and neumes, extracting the characteristics of specific hands in isolation, rather than demonstrating the graphic appearance of the whole. Both these approaches are integral to the discipline of paleography, and the *Polygraphia* was the first systematic study of the Visigothic script.

Palomares after the Polygraphia

As calligrapher and paleographer, Palomares was involved in several different projects of importance during the 1760s and 1770s. In 1764, the year in which he completed the *Polygraphia*, Charles III commissioned Palomares to assist the archivist Benito Gayoso in the organization and transfer of the archives of the Secretariat of State from the Buen Retiro palace to the recently completed Royal Palace. In 1766 Palomares was invited by the chief librarian of the Royal Palace, Juan de Santander, to consult with a team on the design of the Royal Library type foundry. Albert Corbeto argues that Palomares's influence can be discerned in the calligraphic appearance of the Spanish typeface that resulted from the design process.[85]

In 1776 Palomares published a calligraphy treatise, the *Arte nueva de escribir*, which was influential well into the nineteenth century.[86] In the 1770s at the Escorial he made a copy of the famous Codex Vigilanus or Albeldensis (Escorial d I 2), a manuscript completed at the monastery of Albelda in 976. Unlike most of his earlier copies, this one included illustrations in color.[87] From Palomares's hand-drawn plates four prints were made by the Madrid engraver Francisco Asensio in 1777.[88] This seems to have been the only time that a color facsimile by Palomares was reproduced mechanically.

Palomares also made color illustrations for a treatise, the *Ensayo diplomático*, by the Benedictine monk Manuel Abad y Lasierra (1729–1806). During the reign of Charles III, Abad carried out a survey of archival documents in Aragon that was comparable in scope to the survey undertaken by Burriel at Toledo for the Royal Commission on the Archives under Ferdinand VI.[89] Neither of these archival projects under royal patronage was completed, nor did either of them result in publications, but both yielded manuscript compendia that illustrate the development of manuscript studies in this period.

Abad began to study monastic archives in 1758, after entering the Benedictine monastery of San Juan de la Peña. He showed talent for archival studies and, beginning in 1765, received royal commissions to survey monastic archives in Navarre and Aragon. One result of his research was a prospectus for the *Ensayo* which he presented to the Royal Academy of History in 1781. The work was to be divided into three parts: diplomatics, bibliography, and paleography.[90] The prologue to this work acknowledges the assistance and expertise of Palomares, and the title page identifies him as a collaborator. Indeed in many ways Abad's treatise closely resembles the *Polygraphia Gothico-Española*, written less than two decades earlier. A sign of Palomares's influence on Abad is the latter's scant attention to the history of the Caroline minuscule in Spain. Abad did not envision including the script in his treatment of paleography, although he briefly mentions its use in Catalonia and Aragon because of French influence both before and after the liturgical reform. Given the prevalence of the Caroline minuscule in some of the northeastern areas of Spain in which Abad pursued archival research, it is odd that the *Ensayo* does not accord greater emphasis to the late Caroline and early Gothic scripts. If Palomares's own *Polygraphia* was the principal model and source for Abad's treatise, as I argue here, perhaps Abad privileged the Visigothic script because that had been the central focus for Palomares (albeit for different reasons). The title page suggests that the *Ensayo* was as much the work of Palomares as of Abad. In this context it is worth noting that Palomares became a member of the Royal Academy of History in 1781, the same year in which Abad presented his prospectus for the *Ensayo*.

Abad's *Ensayo* was never completed, but the illustrations it contains contribute significantly to our understanding of Palomares's career and demonstrate the calligrapher's long-standing interest in musical notation. As in his own *Polygraphia*, some of the pages have been colored to resemble darkened parchment, and the variable sizes of the images may be intended to represent the original dimensions of the manuscripts. Two of the plates feature musical notation and seem to have been chosen by Palomares for no other reason than his interest in neumes and liturgical texts. They do not relate to the text of the treatise in any discernible way; instead they seem to be superfluous. The first plate shows part of the Old Hispanic rite for the dedication of a church, taken from a breviary of the early eleventh century with Catalan neumes.[91] The second plate shows a page from a breviary in early Gothic script with Aquitanian neumes. The original seems to have been a manuscript of the late twelfth century copied for the Cathedral of Roda; the page reproduced contains part of Matins from the proper rhymed office for Saint Raymond, who was the bishop of Roda in 1104–26.[92] This is one of the rare cases in which Palomares copied a manuscript with script and neumes in the style he referred to as French, and it may be significant that the drawing was executed for a treatise that was not his own.

Palomares's entry into the Royal Academy of History in 1781 confirmed the lasting value of his contribution to the historical sciences. It was a fitting acknowledgment of his decades-long endeavors as a paleographer and calligrapher. Nevertheless he cuts a curious figure in the history of paleography and diplomatics as a discipline. He acquired impressive erudition but remains known today principally as a calligrapher. Among all the scholars who studied the medieval manuscripts of the Iberian peninsula, he was the sole layman, and yet his knowledge of early liturgical books was unsurpassed. Although not a musician, he was more familiar with the appearance of early musical notation than were most of his scholarly contemporaries, and thus it occupies an important place in his history of handwriting. Unable to understand the meaning of neumes, Palomares nonetheless copied them faithfully in all their variety, even though for him this music was silent, as it had been, and would remain, for centuries.

Notes

1. An overview of his life and works in this period can be found in Seniff, *Francisco Javier de Santiago y Palomares*, viii–xxvii. The most recent summary, with emphasis on his family and his testament, is Barrio Moya, "Noticias," 165–86.

2. A copy is preserved in London, BL, Egerton 588, fols. 158r–161r.

3. On this facsimile, see chapter 3.

4. The outline is preserved in London, BL, Egerton 588, fols. 1r–9v ("Indice de lo que se debe hacer para demostrar la Paleographia o Historia succesiva de nuestras Letras que es la vasa de la Diplomatica y Bibliographia Española").

5. The complete title of the treatise is *Polygraphia Gothico-Española. Origen de los caracteres o letras de los Godos en España; su progresso, decadencia, y corrupcion desde el siglo V hasta fin del XI en que se abrogò el uso de ellos, y sobstituyó la letra gothico-francesa: demostrada con variedad de abecedarios, abreviaturas, y otras curiosidades pertenecientes al perfecto conocimiento de ella, sacados de Monedas, Inscripciones, Libros, y semejantes Monumentos de la antiguedad que se guardan en las famosas Librerias de la Santa Iglesia de Toledo, y del monasterio de San Lorenzo del Escorial*, por D. Francisco Xavier de Santiago Palomares, Oficial en la Contaduria General de Renta Provinciales del Reyno, y natural de aquella Ciudad. Año 1764 (Madrid, RAH, 9/4752). A letter dated 1779 is bound with this volume; it refers to the preparation of a copy of the treatise, but it is not clear whether the manuscript itself dates from 1764, as indicated on the title page, or from 1779, as suggested by the letter.

6. Mabillon, *De re diplomatica*. On the influence of Mabillon in Spain, see chapter 1.

7. London, BL, Egerton 588, fols.123r–125r ("Relacion substancial de lo que ha ocurrido entre el Canonigo Bayer, y Don Francisco Xavier de Santiago Palomares sobre la Comision de San Lorenzo").

8. Madrid, BN 13054, fol. 121r: "Cuiusdam codicis vetustissimi, elementisque Gothicis exarati fragmen, id est duo unita folia membranacea, alicujus quaternionis, que apud D. Petrum Camino, et Velasco Presbyterum Toletanum, harum antiquitatum studiosissimo, quadam veluti relligione asservantur, que quidem, prout sequuntur, in paginas divisa ad marginem adnotantur." Marginal note in the hand of Burriel: "No sirve, le copió mal. Enmendose luego."

9. Pinius, *Liturgia Mozarabica*, cxi. On Pinius's work in Toledo, see the introduction.

10. Mayans noticed this already in 1746; see his letter to Blas Jover y Alcázar (quoted in the introduction), in *Gregorio Mayans y Siscar, Epistolario II*, 325–27.

11. Palomares, *Polygraphia*, vi–vii.

12. Burriel, *Paleografía española*, plate 15, number 5.

13. Toledo, BC 35.3, fol. 205v: "Hunc etiam uirum quem celicolis adnumerandum martyribus adgregatum etatis nostre tempore protulerunt"; emending *tempore* to *tempora* yields the version translated here.

14. Bona, *Rerum liturgicarum*, 68–69 (book 1, chapter 11); Burriel, *Paleografía*, 117–18.

15. Mabillon, *De Liturgia gallicana*, 31 (book 1, chapter 4).

16. Flórez, *España Sagrada,* 3: 217.

17. Camino y Velasco, *Noticia*, fourth page of unpaginated dedication: "Es sin disputa, que por los años de Christo de 402, en que falleció San Martin, Obispo de Tours, en Francia, nuestra España, inmediatamente que supo su transito glorioso, compuso en honor suyo la Devotissima Missa, y Oficio que hoy tenemos en nuestro Missal, y Breviario, y celebramos los Mozarabes en el dia de su Fiesta con Rito de seis Capas, que corresponde al doble de primera Classe en el Latino."

18. Palomares seems to have been unaware that the "Gregorian" chant was unrelated to Gregory VII.

19. Palomares, *Polygraphia*, 38–39: "Recuperada la Ciudad de Toledo por el glorioso Emperador Don Alonso VI hijo del Rey Don Fernando el Grande, como se tratasse de restaurar y restablecer en ella las cosas pertenecientes à la Religion, vino à estos Reynos para este fin y à instancias del mismo Emperador un Legado del Papa Gregorio VII llamado Ricardo Abad de Marsella, el qual solicitò introducir el oficio que compuso el nominado Papa Gregorio, que en aquel tiempo se usaba en francia (y es el mismo que hoy tenemos en España), y que se abrogasse el antiquissimo Gothico ù Isidoriano. Este legado insistaba incesantemente al Rey para complimiento de su deseo, inflamado de las persuasiones de la Reyna Doña Costanza y del Arzobispo Don Bernardo, que por ser Franceses de Nacion, deseaban substituir el oficio de su Patria, con tal eficacia que el Rey Don Alonso por complacer à la Reyna, Legado, y Arzobispo vino à consentir en ello."

20. Jiménez de Rada, *Historia*, book 6, chapter 25, 207–9.

21. Jiménez de Rada, *Historia*, 208; Palomares, *Polygraphia*, 39–40.

22. On the emergence of this narrative in the context of the liturgical reform see Hitchcock, "El rito hispánico," 19–41. I am grateful to the author of this study for bringing it to my attention.

23. *Chronica Naierensis*, 177.

24. Palomares, *Polygraphia*, 39.

25. Palomares, *Polygraphia*, 39–40.

26. Palomares, *Polygraphia*, 40: "Lo cierto es que el oficio Francès o Gregoriano fuè recibido de los Españoles con grande repugnancia."

27. Palomares, *Polygraphia*, 45.

28. Palomares, *Polygraphia*, 47.

29. Palomares, *Polygraphia*, 50.

30. Palomares, *Polygraphia*, 51.

31. Palomares, *Polygraphia*, 20: "En la classe de los accentos, ò apices que alteran el sonido de las voces me parece deben entrar las notas, ò puntos musicales de los Godos.

Son tan raros, y diferentes respecto de los modernos, y se hallan con tal abundancia en los Misales y otros codices que tengo para mi non desagradara al Lector su estraño modo di colocarlos sobre las voces, y à lo menos ya que entre los Musicos de nuestro tiempo no haya quien los entienda, puede ser que alguno se aplique à entenderlos en lo subcesivo, y entre tanto divertirà la vista por un rato entre la aridez y falta de amenidad de mi Polygraphia."

32. Levy, "On the Origin of Neumes," 59–90; Treitler, "Reading and Singing," 135–208.

33. Atkinson, *"De Accentibus*, 17–42; Atkinson, "Glosses, 199–215; Atkinson, *The Critical Nexus*, especially 41–46, 58–65.

34. The manuscript measures 325 x 200 mm and comprises 226 folios. The first eight books of Augustine's text are lacking. For a brief description with its contents see Antolín, *Catálogo*, 4:22–23.

35. Millares Carlo, *Corpus de códices visigóticos*, vol. 1, *Estudio*, p. 59 (number 61), vol. 2, *Album*, p. 62, plate 61, reproduces fol. 197r. Divjak, in *Die Handschriftliche Überlieferung*, 203, gives the date as "post med. s. VIII." Gorman, in "A Survey," 403, dates the manuscript to the mid-ninth century.

36. I base this assertion on the survey of the manuscripts of Augustine's works carried out and published under the aegis of the Austrian Academy of Sciences; for the manuscripts of the *De ciuitate dei* preserved in Spain see Divjak, *Die Handschriftliche Überlieferung*, 28–30, which suggests that Escorial S.I.16 is the earliest witness preserved in Spain; the second earliest is the tenth-century manuscript Madrid, RAH, 29.

37. Díaz y Díaz, "Agustín entre los mozárabes," 158, n5, states that the earliest peninsular codex of the *De ciuitate* is Madrid, RAH 29 (probably from San Millán de la Cogolla, with a note dated 977 in the hand of one of the main scribes). He excludes Escorial S.I.16 from his consideration of the transmission of the text in the Iberian peninsula because, although in Visigothic script, it was not copied in the Iberian peninsula.

38. Augustine, *Sancti Aurelii Augustini Episcopi De Civitate Dei*, 285–86.

39. Palomares, *Polygraphia*, 20: "En este codice se hallan estos versos con puntos de Musica sobre las vocales del mismo modo que representa al vivo la citada Lamina 28."

40. This translation is based on the text in the Escorial manuscript. The translation by R. W. Dyson, *Augustine: The City of God against the Pagans*, 850, renders the text with the Greek acrostic (IESOUS CREISTOS THEOUUIOS SOTER) but is less literal. Dyson's translation of the lines cited here reads thus: "In sign of the judgment, the earth shall be bathed in sweat. / Ever more to reign, a king from heaven shall come, / Sitting in judgment here, upon all flesh and the world. / Our God shall unbelievers and the faithful see / Uplifted with his saints on high when this age ends: / Souls, clothed in flesh, shall come to Him for judgment. / Choked with dense thorns, all the world lies untended; / Rejected are the idols and all the toys of men. / Every land, and all the sea and sky, shall burn with fire, / Invading even the dreadful gates of hell. / Salvation's light shall redeem the bodies of the saints / Though the wicked shall burn in everlasting fire."

41. Eric Marshall White at Southern Methodist University kindly suggested this interpretation of the inks to me (upon consultation of the manuscript in the Escorial library in June 2006). Michel Huglo seconded this opinion in July 2007.

42. Mas, "La notation catalane," 17, 28; Garrigosa i Massana, *Els manuscrits musicals*, 352. The forms of virga, clivis, and torculus in the Escorial manuscript resemble

those of the early Visigothic neumes in Paris, BNF, lat. 8093. On this manuscript in the larger context of early Hispanic/Visigothic notation see Michel Huglo, "La notation wisigothique," 19–26.

43. On this manuscript see Garrigosa i Massana, *Els manuscrits musicals*, 316–21, 445 (plate 3).

44. Descriptions of the manuscripts of *De ciuitate dei* do not mention musical notation. On the manuscript tradition see Gorman, "A Survey," who draws upon the earlier list, not yet superseded, in Wilmart, "La tradition des grands ouvrages," 279–92.

45. Ziolkowski, in *Nota Bene*, 31–32, sets the musical notation added to the Sibylline verses in the context of neumed postclassical Latin texts. On the medieval performance of ancient Latin texts see also Bobeth, *Antike Verse*; Bobeth, "'Cantare Virgilium'"; and Wälli, *Melodien*.

46. On this version, see Barrett, "Music and Writing," 91–95.

47. For a reproduction of this page, see Anglès, *La música a Catalunya*, fig. 77.

48. Barcelona, Archivo de la Corona de Aragón, 106, fol. 92v; see figure 20 in Maricarmen Gómez Muntané, "Del *Iudicii* signum al Canto de la Sibila: primeros testimonios," in *Hispania Vetus: Manuscritos litúrgico-musicales: de los orígenes visigóticos a la transición francorromana (siglos X–XII)*, ed. Susana Zapke (Madrid: Fundación BBVA, 2007), 159–73.

49. Vic, Archivo y Biblioteca Episcopal, Frag. XI/I, described most recently by Maricarmen Gómez Muntané and Susana Zapke, "Breviary (fragmentum)," in *Hispania Vetus*, 328.

50. For the complete text of the sermon, see Braun, *Opera Quodvultdeo Carthaginiensi episcopo tributa*, 227–58.

51. For overviews of the tradition, with transcriptions of melodies, see Anglès, *La música a Catalunya*, 288–302; Colette, "Le chant de la Sibylle," 165–76; Corbin, "Le Cantus Sibyllae," 1–10; Gómez Muntané, *El canto de la Sibila*; Gómez Muntané, "El Canto de la Sibila," 35–70; Gómez Muntané, *La música medieval*, 70–82.

52. Although one cannot draw any firm conclusions on the basis of these adiastematic neumes, the melody they transmit appears to resemble those preserved in Iberian manuscripts of the eleventh century.

53. Brou, "Notes," 23–29.

54. Boynton, "Orality," 124–32 (instances of partial notation in other types of manuscripts are described on 124–25).

55. On liquescence, see Betteray, *Quomodo cantabimus canticum*; Freistedt, *Die liqueszierenden Noten*; Haug, "Zur Interpretation der Liqueszenzneumen," 85–100.

56. This discussion of the Escorial Augustine and Palomares's copy of it builds on my earlier brief study, "An Early Notated Song of the Sibyl," 47–56.

57. Palomares, *Polygraphia*, 20: "La muestra o Lamina 43 representa al vivo otros dos generos de puntos, ò notas musicales, que parecen diferentes de los que se dan en la Lamina 28. El primero, y segundo numero representan los puntos que se hallan à cada paso en los Misales, y otros Libros Gothicos, que se guardan en la Libreria de la Santa Iglesia de Toledo."

58. On Madrid, BN 10001 and its flyleaves, see, most recently, the description with full-color illustration by Eliza Ruíz García, "Psalterium, Liber canticorum, Liber hymnorum," in *Hispania Vetus*, 310–11.

59. This was also the case in Palomares's copy of New York, HSA, B2916, *olim* Toledo, BC 33.2 (discussed in chapter 2).

60. On the parchment facsimile, see chapter 3.

61. C. U. Clark, *Collectanea Hispanica*, 100.

62. Palomares, *Polygraphia*, 19.

63. Palomares copied part of the right column of Madrid, BN 10001, fol. 1v in Madrid, BN 13054.

64. *Soni* in the Old Hispanic rite are melismatic chants sung at Matins and Vespers. See Randel and Nadeau, "Mozarabic Chant."

65. Antolín, *Catálogo*, 2:33–34, states that the manuscript was copied in England in the late eleventh century and later made its way to France.

66. Palomares, *Polygraphia*, 20.

67. According to Sam Barrett, the neumes in the first twelve lines seem to have been copied by a single English scribe, and several different scribes (including the first one) added notation beginning in line 12. I am grateful to Dr. Barrett for confirming my initial impression that the first set of neumes is English and for sharing with me sections of his forthcoming edition, *The Melodic Tradition of Boethius's "De consolatione philosophiae."*

68. Escorial E.II.1, 100r–v.

69. The excerpt is taken from Escorial E.II.1, fol. 38r. For the dating of the neumes, see Barrett, *The Melodic Tradition*.

70. See, for instance, Huglo, "La notation wisigothique."

71. Palomares, *Polygraphia*, 20: "No serà muy facil averiguar si los Puntos, ò Notas musicales, que se hallan en los Missales y otros Codices antiquissimos semejantes à los que acabo de citar, los aprendieron los Godos de los Romanos, ò si San Isidoro, quando compuso ù ordenò la Liturgia Goda, los tomò de los que usaban en Espana, ò en Italia; ò finalmente si estos puntos eran los comunes, y usuales a toda la Iglesia Catholica."

72. Palomares, *Polygraphia*, 20.

73. Escorial M. III.3, fol. 92r. For the diverse contents of this manuscript see Antolín, *Catálogo*, 3:88–8. As Antolín observes, the last six folios, containing the mass of Saint Vincent, are a separate codicological unit, copied in the eleventh century.

74. Madrid, BN 13054, fol. 111r: "Exemplar caracterum, quibus conscriptum est fragmentum Codicis cujusdam gothico-muzarabici, continens partem Missae de Sancto Genesio Martyre Arelatensi, penes D. Petrum Camino Velasco, Toleti asservatum."

75. Madrid, BN 13054, fol. 110r: "Exemplar Caracterum, quibus conscriptum est fragmentum codicis cujusdam Gothico-Muzarabici, continens aliquot hymnos suis versiculis distinctos, penes D. Petrum Camino Velasco Toleti asservatum." On this manuscript see Janini and Serrano, *Manuscritos Litúrgicos*, 166–68.

76. *Polygraphia*, plate 33, number 1, caption: "Parte de un hymno Muzarabico en la festividad de los Santos Martyres Hadriano y Natalia. Saquè esta muestra de dos hojas que estaban en poder de Don Pedro Camino, Capellan Muzarabe de Toledo."

77. Madrid, BN 10001, right column of p. 29: *Beata gens cuius est dominus.*

78. Toledo, BC 35.3, fol. 67r: *Deus qui beatam eulaliam*, ed. in Férotin, *Le liber Mozarabicus*, 139 (number 298). Another, as yet unidentified manuscript was the source of the prayer written below: *Deus pater omnipotens qui in principio*, ed. José Vives, in Vives, *Oracional visigótico*, 830–31 (number 1024). In this study I follow the dates assigned to the manuscripts in Mundó, "La datación."

79. Toledo, BC 35.5 (thirteenth century), fol. 116v, beginning of first column, Galatians 1:3; Toledo, BC 35.7 (late eleventh or early twelfth century), fol. 65r, Isaiah 45:1.

80. Toledo, BC 35.8 (twelfth century), fol. 33r, second column, John 1:15. In the copy four lines are made into three longer ones, and the rubric is displaced to the left.

81. Toledo, BC 33.1 (mid-twelfth century), fol. 53r: "Erant adpropinquantes. . . . Homily: Pius dominus et misericors ac redemtor noster." Madrid, BN 13051, contains a complete transcription of the homiliary and Madrid, BN 13054, fol. 72–84 contains the incipit and explicit of all the homilies in the manuscript.

82. Toledo, BC 33.3 (late twelfth century), fol. 17r, Revelations 3:7; Toledo, BC 35.6 (late tenth or eleventh century), fol. 7r: *Quamuis domine plurima*, ed. Vives, in *Oracional visigótico*, 262 (number 819).

83. *Speciosa christe filius dei in oculis fidelium*, ed. Vives, in *Oracional visigótico*, 45 (umber 137). The text copied in p. 5 is Jeremiah 31:2–4.

84. Madrid, BN 13054, fol. 112r: "Exemplar caracterum quibus conscriptum est fragmentum codicis cuiusdam Gothico-muzarabici continens partem offici de sancta Leocadia martyre Toletana, penès D. Franciscum de Santiago, et Palomares."

85. Corbeto, "Eighteenth Century Spanish Type Design," 272–97.

86. Palomares, *Arte nueva de escribir*.

87. Madrid, BN 1677–1680.

88. Madrid, BN 1680, fol. 187r: "Quatro Estampas de las laminas del Codice Vigilano que se han grabado e iluminado conforme al original." Signed "Franciscus Asensio sculpsit Matriti" and "Franciscus Asensio sculpsit 1777."

89. A recent overview of Abad's life and works can be found in Nieto Callén and Sánchez Molledo, "Fray Manuel Abad y Lasierra," 371–89. See also García, "La labor intelectual," 101–107.

90. According to Paul Ewald, in "Reise nach Spanien im Winter 1878 auf 1879," 341, the first volume is from 1764, the second from 1781, but the title page of volume 1 refers to Lasierra as prior of Meyá (a position he held from 1773 to 1783): Abad y Lasierra, *Ensayo diplomatico*.

91. Lleida, Archivo Capitular, Roda 16 (now RC 0036), fol. 125r; see the description of this manuscript (illustrated with a detail of this page, incorrectly identified there as fol. 124v) by Màrius Bernadó, "Sacramentary, Ritual and Pontifical." in *Hispania Sacra*, 320. I am grateful to Màrius Bernadó for kindly confirming my identification of the original.

92. Lleida, Archivo Capitular, Roda 11 (now RC 0029), fol. 153v; see the description of this page by Màrius Bernadó, "Psalter, Hymnary, and Rhymed Office of Saint Raymond," in *Hispania Vetus*, 324.

In 1770 Francisco Antonio Lorenzana (1722–1804), archbishop of Mexico, published the *Missa Gothica*, an edition of the mass and office as celebrated in the Mozarabic chapel of Toledo Cathedral, introduced by explanatory material.[1] The proper texts of the mass are for Santiago, the patron saint of Spain. The symbolic association of Santiago and the Mozarabic rite with the idea of a transhistorical Spanish nation affirmed the link between the *Missa Gothica* and the Hispanic identity of the New World city in which it was printed.[2] This liturgical edition is just one of several major scholarly endeavors Lorenzana undertook during his years in Mexico (1766–71); another was a history of the Spanish colonies based in part on the *Noticia de la California* of Venegas, which had been revised by Burriel.[3] The introduction to the *Missa Gothica* refers to some of the eighteenth-century scholars of the Mozarabic rite, but surprisingly not to Burriel: perhaps the Jesuit's death in 1762 and the expulsion of the Jesuits from Spain and its dominions in 1767 were responsible for this curious omission. Once Lorenzana became a canon at Toledo in 1754, he must have had at least a passing acquaintance with Burriel, who spent his working days in the cathedral archives. As a member of the cathedral chapter that discussed the activities of the Commission on the Archives during their meetings, Lorenzana would presumably have been aware of Burriel's liturgical studies, but none of the archbishop's several editions make any mention of them. It is possible that Lorenzana never learned of Burriel's findings, because the latter retained his papers until his death, when the Jesuits gave them to the royal library.

One thing is certain: Lorenzana did not acknowledge that the medieval Mozarabic chant melodies were written in notation that could not be transcribed. His edition includes a section on chant performance with three grotesquely inaccurate likenesses of neumes accompanied by transcriptions. After Burriel's *Paleografía Española* of 1755, Lorenzana's 1770 *Missa Gothica* is the first mechanical reproduction of notation from a Toledan manuscript in Visigothic script, and it certainly does not signal any progress in the study either of paleography or of musical notation. The first two examples, both from Toledan manuscripts, are Old Hispanic chants in Visigothic script with Toledan neumes, both "transcribed" into black mensural notation. The idea of transcribing Visigothic neumes rhythmically seems to derive from the use of black mensural notation in the Ortiz *Missale Mixtum* of 1500 and the cantorales commissioned by Cisneros for the Mozarabic Chapel in Toledo Cathedral. If Lorenzana read Burriel's comments in the *Paleografía Española* on the illegibility of the staffless neumes in the Mozarabic liturgical manuscripts, there is no sign of it.

Although these musical examples may not come from Lorenzana's hand, they appear to have originated in the appendix to a letter he wrote seven years earlier to the papal nuncio in Madrid.[4] The first chant reproduced is the first phrase of the *ad confractionem panis* chant *Mediante die festo*. The source of the melody is identified and the commentary interprets each sign as indicating a note with a specific pitch and duration.[5] The text does not specify the source of the second example, the incipit of the Praelegendum *Alleluia Christi generatio*, but the attribution of the chant to the mass for the Virgin Mary composed by Ildefonsus of Toledo suggests that the transcription was made from Toledo, BC 35.7.[6] In the third example the incipit of the Gregorian introit *Suscepimus Deus* for the feast of the Purification (evidently copied from a manuscript with Aquitanian-style notation) is transcribed in square chant notation and described as "taken from an ancient Toledan service book."[7] No distinction is made between the two radically different styles of medieval neumatic notation represented in the examples—the adiastematic Visigothic neumes and the heighted Aquitanian ones—nor is it noted that the third chant is from the Roman rite, and thus completely out of place in the *Missa Gothica*. It is possible that the incipit of the Introit was confounded with that of an antiphon in Madrid, BN 10001, which was at Toledo Cathedral in the eighteenth century.[8] Such a mistake suggests ignorance of the fact that Old Hispanic chants, with very few exceptions, are not transmitted in Aquitanian-style neumes. When the crude notation and anachronistic commentary in the *Missa Gothica* are juxtaposed with the more sophisticated studies accomplished by Burriel and Palomares decades earlier, the disparity is striking. The comparison illuminates the irony in the fact that Lorenzana is considered by some to be a paradigm of Enlightenment liturgical scholarship, while Burriel's contribution to the field is largely ignored.

Lorenzana returned to Spain as archbishop of Toledo in 1772 and went on to publish more editions of the neo-Mozarabic rite. One of these was an edition of the Mozarabic breviary based on the one compiled by Ortiz for Cardinal Cisneros, but with the extraneous Roman rite elements introduced by Ortiz relegated to an appendix.[9] The only new features in Lorenzana's 1775 edition are his brief treatise on the Mozarabic liturgy (a philological introduction), an edition of the Mozarabic psalter and hymns, and an explanation of neumes by Jerónimo Romero, a priest of the cathedral.[10] Later Lorenzana reprinted the Mozarabic missal of Ortiz, leaving it essentially unchanged. The introductions to these editions show no awareness of the research carried out in Toledo Cathedral from 1750 to 1755 by the Commission on the Archives, and Burriel's work on the liturgy was all but forgotten until the twentieth century, when the rediscovery of his labors paved the way for modern scholars of the Mozarabic rite, such as Férotin and Janini, who made liberal use of his copies and transcriptions.[11]

Unlike Burriel and his twentieth-century counterparts, however, Lorenzana perpetuated the legendary character of the Mozarabic rite. The preface to the *Missa Gothica* edition recounts the stories of the duel and the trial by fire that had come to symbolize the contest between the old and new traditions in Castile (see chapter 5). To reinforce that point, the volume includes two engravings representing these events. Perhaps the optimistic, if inaccurate, decoding of the Old Hispanic neumes in Lorenzana's editions reveals the underlying meaning of the legend: there could be no truly silent music. Just as the Toledan book remained unharmed by the fire, so too did the Mozarabic chant survive as a cultural symbol through its reinvention in the early modern period. Even though the practice of the rite became ever more limited, over the centuries its prestige was renewed to the point of creating an impression of uninterrupted continuity.[12]

In the Mozarabic Chapel of Toledo Cathedral the performance of the neo-Mozarabic chant maintained its status as a revered tradition. Palomares and Burriel understood the power of this symbolism even as they analyzed the medieval manuscript sources in unprecedented detail. As we have seen, each of these men sought in his own way to balance modern historical methods with the exigencies of state-supported research. Along with their contemporaries they participated in the larger project of defining Spanish identity through study of the Middle Ages. What set them apart from most historians of the period was their shared realization that the silent music of the past is an integral part of history.

Notes

1. *Missa Gothica seù Mozarabica*. He was assisted in this project by a former canon of Toledo Cathedral, Francisco Fabián y Fuero (1719–1801), who was bishop of Puebla from 1764 to 1772.

2. I am grateful to Grayson Wagstaff for pointing this out.

3. Malagón-Barceló, "La obra escrita," 437–65.

4. Fernández Collado, "El Cardenal Lorenzana," 434–45. Eduardo Henrik Aubert brought this study to my attention.

5. *Missa Gothica*, 69–71. The chant is copied from Toledo, BC 35.3, fol. 92v.

6. *Missa Gothica*, 72. The Praelegendum in the Old Hispanic rite is an antiphon with a function comparable to that of the Gregorian Introit. This Praelegendum is found in Toledo, BC 35.7, fol. 35v, and also in other Old Hispanic manuscripts. See Randel, *An Index*, 400.

7. *Missa Gothica*, 72. I have not yet identified the source of this chant.

8. Madrid, BN 1001, fol. 23r.

9. *Breviarium Gothicum*.

10. *Breviarium Gothicum*, xxvii: "Cantus Eugeniani seu melodici explanatio." For a brief discussion of the discourses on notation in Lorenzana's edition, see the forthcoming monograph by Eduardo Henrik Aubert, *The Modern Life of "Medieval Neumes."* I am grateful to the author for sharing this study with me before its publication.

11. According to Janini and Gonzálvez, in *Catálogo*, 21–22, Férotin's edition of Toledo, BC 35.3 in *Le liber mozarabicus sacramentorum* took as a point of departure the transcription made for Burriel (Madrid, BN 13046), as Férotin himself had admitted. See also Janini, ed., *Liber missarum*, 2:lxxiii–lxxvii. Férotin also published Burriel's manuscript descriptions as his own. Janini published the transcription of Toledo 33.2 (now New York, Hispanic Society of America B2916) in Janini, ed., *Liber missarum*, 2:275–99.

12. As Casiano Rojo and Germán Prado affirm, "Without a doubt, the ancient Hispanic rite has never been entirely interrupted" ("Sin embargo, el antiguo rito hispano nunca ha sido enteramente interrumpido"; *El canto mozárabe*, 103). In the same vein, the new facsimile edition of the Cisneros cantorales suggestively frames the reproduction of each choirbook with details from medieval Toledan liturgical books in Visigothic script. See *Los Cantorales Mozárabes de Cisneros*, 1:xii, 1, 376–77, 1:376, 628; 2:639–40, 847–88. A separate appendix presents full-page photographs of the manuscripts, with their shelfmarks (*Los Cantorales*, 2:849–97).

BIBLIOGRAPHY

Manuscripts

Barcelona, Archivo de la Corona de Aragón, 106
Barcelona, Biblioteca de Catalunya, M. 1408/3 [80]
Florence, Biblioteca Nazionale, Banco Rari, 20
Lleida, Archivo Capitular, Roda 11 (now RC 0029)
Lleida, Archivo Capitular, Roda 16 (now RC 0036)
London, British Library, Egerton 588
Madrid, Biblioteca Nacional de España, 1677–80
Madrid, Biblioteca Nacional de España, 2924
Madrid, Biblioteca Nacional de España, 10001
Madrid, Biblioteca Nacional de España, 10069
Madrid, Biblioteca Nacional de España, 10110
Madrid, Biblioteca Nacional de España, 12992
Madrid, Biblioteca Nacional de España, 13015
Madrid, Biblioteca Nacional de España, 13016
Madrid, Biblioteca Nacional de España, 13017
Madrid, Biblioteca Nacional de España, 13046
Madrid, Biblioteca Nacional de España, 13047
Madrid, Biblioteca Nacional de España, 13048
Madrid, Biblioteca Nacional de España, 13049
Madrid, Biblioteca Nacional de España, 13050
Madrid, Biblioteca Nacional de España, 13053
Madrid, Biblioteca Nacional de España, 13054
Madrid, Biblioteca Nacional de España, 13055
Madrid, Biblioteca Nacional de España, 13058
Madrid, Biblioteca Nacional de España, 13059
Madrid, Biblioteca Nacional de España, 13060
Madrid, Biblioteca Nacional de España, 13061
Madrid, Biblioteca Nacional de España, 13127
Madrid, Biblioteca Nacional de España, 13413

Madrid, Palacio Real, Biblioteca, II/482

Madrid, Palacio Real, Biblioteca, II/483

Madrid, Palacio Real, Biblioteca, II/2838

Madrid, Real Academia de la Historia, 29

Madrid, Real Academia de la Historia, 56

Madrid, Real Academia de la Historia, 9/3535

Madrid, Real Academia de la Historia, 9/4752

Madrid, Real Academia de la Historia, 9/4754

Madrid, Real Academia de la Historia, 9/5921

New York, Hispanic Society of America, B2916

Paris, Bibliothèque Nationale de France, lat. 1154

Paris, Bibliothèque Nationale de France, lat. 2832

Paris, Bibliothèque Nationale de France, lat. 8093

San Lorenzo El Escorial, Real Biblioteca, E.II.1

San Lorenzo El Escorial, Real Monasterio de San Lorenzo, S.I.16

San Lorenzo El Escorial, Biblioteca del Real Monasterio de San Lorenzo, B.I.2

San Lorenzo El Escorial, Biblioteca del Real Monasterio de San Lorenzo, T.I.1

San Lorenzo El Escorial, Biblioteca del Real Monasterio de San Lorenzo, M.III.3

Toledo, Archivo Capitular, Actas Capitulares, vol. 68

Toledo, Archivo Capitular, Actas Capitulares, vol. 70

Toledo, Biblioteca Capitular, 14.23

Toledo, Biblioteca Capitular, 33.1

Toledo, Biblioteca Capitular, 33.3

Toledo, Biblioteca Capitular, 35.3

Toledo, Biblioteca Capitular, 35.5

Toledo, Biblioteca Capitular, 35.6

Toledo, Biblioteca Capitular, 35.7

Toledo, Biblioteca Capitular, 35.8

Toledo, Biblioteca Capitular, 44.2

Toledo, Biblioteca Capitular, 44.11

Toledo, Biblioteca Capitular, 48.1

Toledo, Biblioteca Capitular, 48.11

Vic, Archivo y Biblioteca Episcopal, Frag XI/I

EIGHTEENTH-CENTURY TREATISES IN MANUSCRIPT

Abad y Lasierra, Manuel. *Ensayo diplomático*. Madrid, Real Academia de la Historia, 9/4754.

Camino y Velasco, Pedro. *Defensa de los Privilegios de los Nobles Mozárabes de Toledo*. Madrid, BN MS 13059, fols. 208–223v.

Palomares [Santiago y Palomares], Francisco Xavier. *Polygraphia Gothico-Española*. Madrid, Real Academia de la Historia, 9/4752.

Published Primary Sources

Aldrete, Bernardo. *Del origen y principio de la lengua castellana ò romance que oi se usa en España*. Rome, 1606. 2 vols. Facsimile edition by Lidio Nieto Jiménez. Madrid: Consejo Superior de Investigaciones Científicas, 1972–75.

Alfonso X, el Sabio. *Cantigas de Santa María*. Ed. Walter Mettmann. 3 vols. Madrid: Clásicos Castalia, 1986.

Alleluia-Melodien II, ab 1100. Ed. Karlheinz Schlager. Monumenta Monodica Medii Aevi, 8. Kassel: Bärenreiter, 1987.

Antiphonale Silense. British Library Mss. Add. 30.850. Ed. Ismael Fernández de la Cuesta. Madrid: Sociedad Española de Musicología, 1985.

Antonio, Nicolás. *Censura de historias fabulosas*, ed. Gregorio Mayans y Siscar. Valencia: Antonio Bordázar, 1742.

Augustine of Hippo. *Sancti Aurelii Augustini Episcopi de Civitate Dei Libri XXII*. Ed. Bernard Dombart and Alfons Kalb. 5th revised edition. Stuttgart: Teubner, 1981.

Augustine: The City of God against the Pagans. Ed. and trans. R. W. Dyson. Cambridge: Cambridge University Press, 1998.

Bianchini, Giuseppe. "Adnotationes in sequentem libellum orationum antiquissimi ritùs gothico-hispani." In *Liturgia antiqua, Hispanica, Gothica, Isidoriana, Mozarabica Toletana Mixta illustrata*. Rome: H. Mainardi, 1746.

———. *Josephi Mariae . . . Thomasii Opera omnia: Quà edita, quà nondum vulgata, nunc primùm in unum collecta*. Rome: Mainardi, 1741.

Bona, Giovanni. *Rerum liturgicarum libri duo*. Paris: Martin and Boudot, 1658.

Braun, René, ed. *Opera Quodvultdeo Carthaginiensi episcopo tributa*. Corpus Christianorum Series Latina, 60. Turnhout: Brepols, 1976.

Breviarium Gothicum Secundum Regulam Beatissimi Isidori. Madrid, 1775.

Breviarium secundum regulam Beati Isidori. Toledo: Petrus Hagenbach, 1502.

Burriel, Andrés Marcos. *Cartas eruditas y criticas del P. Andrés Marcos Burriel, de la extinguida Compañía de Jesús*. Ed. Antonio Valladares de Sotomayor. Madrid: Marin, 1775.

———. "Memorias auténticas de las santas vírgenes y mártires sevillanas Justa y Rufina." In *Colección de algunas obras inéditas, eruditas, históricas y políticas de nuestros mejores autores antiguos y modernos, recogidas y publicadas por D.A.V.D.S.* [D. Antonio Valladares de Sotomayor]. 2 vols. Madrid: Imprenta de la calle de Relatores, 1806–7.

———. *Memorias para la vida del santo Rey Don Fernando III*, anotadas y editadas por Miguel de Manual Rodríguez. Madrid: Viuda de Don Joaquin Ibarra, 1800. Rpt. Barcelona: El Albir, 1974.

———. *Paleografía Española, que contiene todos los modos conocidos, que ha habido de escribir en España . . . substituida en la obra del Espectáculo de la Naturaleza, en vez de la Paleografía Francesa, Por el P. Estevan de Terreros y Pando, Maestro de Mathematicas en el Colegio Imperial de la Compañia de Jesus de esta Corte: y la dedica a la reyna nuestra Señora Doña Maria Barbara*. Madrid: Joachin Ibarra, 1758.

Camino y Velasco, Pedro. *Noticia historico-chronologica de los privilegios de las nobles familias de los mozarabes, de la imperial ciudad de Toledo*. Toledo, 1740.

Los Cantorales Mozárabes de Cisneros. Ed. Férnandez Collado, Alfredo Rodríguez González and Isidoro Castañeda Tordera. 2 vols. Toledo: Cabildo de la Catedral Primada de Toledo, 2011.

Cenni, Gaetano. *De antiquitate Ecclesiae hispanae dissertationes*. 2 vols. Rome: Apud fratres Palearinos, 1741.

Chronica Naierensis, ed. Juan A. Estéves Sola. Corpus Christianorum Continuatio Mediaeualis 71A. Turnhout: Brepols, 1995.

Corpus scriptorum muzarabicorum. Ed. Juan Gil. 2 vols. Madrid: Instituto "Antonio de Nebrija," 1973.

Correspondência de D. João V e D. Bárbara de Bragança raínha de España (1746–1747). Ed. J. A. Pinto Ferreira. Coimbra: Livraria Gonçalves, 1945.

De Rueda, Manuel. *Instrucción para grabar en cobre.* Madrid: Joaquín Ibarra, 1761. Facsimile edition by Antonio Moreno Garrido. Granada: Universidad de Granada, 1991.

Espectáculo de la Naturaleza, o conversaciones a cerca de las particularidades de la historia natural, que han parecido mas a proposito para excitar una curiosidad util, y formarlas la razon a los Jovenes Lectores 13 vols. Trans. Estevan de Terreros y Pando. Madrid: Gabriel Ramirez, 1755.

Ewald, Paul. "Reise nach Spanien im Winter 1878 auf 1879." *Neues Archiv der Gesellschaft für ältere Deutsche Geschichtskunde* 6 (1881): 217–398.

Feijoo y Montenegro, Benito Jerónimo. *Teatro Crítico Universal.* 9 vols. Madrid, 1726–40.

Férotin, Marius. *Le Liber Mozarabicus Sacramentorum et les manuscrits mozarabes.* Ed. Anthony Ward. Bibliotheca Ephemerides Liturgicae Subsidia. Rome: Ephemerides Liturgicae, 1995.

———. *Le Liber Ordinum en usage dans l'église wisigothique et mozarabe d'Espagne du cinquième au onzième siècle.* Monumenta Ecclesiae Liturgica, v. Paris: Firmin-Didot, 1904.

Flórez, Enrique. *España Sagrada.* Vol. 3. *Predicación de los apóstoles en España.* Madrid: Antonio Marin, 1748.

———. *España Sagrada.* Vol. 4. *Origen y progresos de los obispados . . .* Madrid: Antonio Marin, 1749.

———. *España Sagrada.* Vol. 5. *Trata de la Provincia Cartaginense.* Madrid: Antonio Marin, 1750.

———. *España Sagrada.* Vol. 6. *De la santa Iglesia de Toledo . . .* Madrid: Antonio Marin, 1751.

Gerbert, Martin. *De Cantu et Musica Sacra a Prima Ecclesiae Aetate usque ad Praesens Tempus.* 2 vols. Sankt Blasien, 1774. Reprint edition with indices by Othmar Wessely. Graz: Akademische Druck-u. Verlagsanstalt, 1968.

Gregorio Mayans y Siscar. Epistolario. II. Mayans y Burriel. Ed. Antonio Mestre. Valencia: Artes Gráfigas Soler, 1972.

Ildefonsus of Toledo. *Ildefonsi Toletani Episcopi De virginitate Sanctae Mariae.* Ed. Valeriano Yarza Urquiola. Corpus Christianorum Series Latina 114A. Turnhout: Brepols, 2007, 147–263.

Janini, José, ed. *Liber missarum de Toledo y libros místicos.* 2 vols. Ed. José Janini. Toledo: Instituto de Estudios Visigótico-Mozárabes, 1982–83.

———. *Liber misticus de cuaresma (Cod. Toled. 35.2, hoy en Madrid, Bibl. Nac. 10.110).* Toledo: Instituto de Estudios Visigótico-Mozárabes, 1979.

———. *Liber misticus de cuaresma y Pascua (Cod. Toledo, Bibl. Capit. 35.5).* Toledo: Instituto de Estudios Visigótico-Mozárabes, 1980.

Jiménez de Rada, Rodrigo. *Historia de rebus Hispanie sive Historia Gothica.* Ed. Juan Fernández Valverde. Corpus Christianorum Continuatio Mediaeualis, 72. Turnhout: Brepols, 1987.

Libros del saber de astronomia del rey D. Alfonso X de Castilla. 5 vols. Ed. Manuel Rico y Sinobas. Madrid: Tipografía de Don Eusebio Aguado, 1863–67.

Mabillon, Jean. *De liturgia gallicana libri III*. Paris: Martin and Boudot, 1685.

————. *De re diplomatica libri VI in quibus quidquid ad veterum instrumentorum antiquitatem, materiam, scripturam, et stilum; quidquid ad sigilla, monogrammata, subscriptiones, ac notas chronologicas; quidquid inde ad antiquiariam, historicam, forensemque disciplinam pertinet, explicatur et illustratur*. Paris: Louis Billaine, 1681.

Mariana, Juan de. *Historia General de España*. Madrid: Andres Garcia de la Iglesia, 1699. [First edition: Toledo: Pedro Rodríguez, 1601.]

Missa Gothica seù Mozarabica, et Officium itidèm Gothicum, diligentèr ac dilucidè explanata ad usum percelebris Mozárabum Sacelli Toleti á munificentissimo Cardinali Ximenio erecti. Angelopoli: Typis Seminarii Palafoxiani, 1770.

Missale Gothicum. 2 vols. Ed. Henry Marriott Bannister. Henry Bradshaw Society 52, 54. London: Henry Bradshaw Society, 1917–19.

Missale Gothicum. Rome, 1804.

Missale Gothicum: E codice Vaticano Reginensi Latino 317 editum. Ed. Els Rose. Corpus Christianorum Series Latina, 159D. Turnhout: Brepols, 2005.

Missale mixtum secundum regulam Beati Isidori, dictum Mozarabes. Toledo: Petrus Hagenbach, 1500.

Missale mixtum secundum regulam Beati Isidori dictum Mozarabes. Rome: Monaldini, 1755.

Muratori, Lodovico Antonio, ed. *Liturgia romana vetus tria sacramentaria complectens, Leonianum scilicet, Gelasianum, et antiquum Gregorianum . . . Denique accedunt missale Gothicum, missale Francorum, duo Gallicana, et duo omnium vetustissimi Romanae Ecclesiae rituales libri*. 2 vols. Venice: Giovanni Baptista Pasquali, 1748.

Obras Californianas del Padre Miguel Venegas, S.J. 5 vols. Ed. W. Michael Mathes. La Paz, Baja California: Universidad Autónoma de Baja California Sur, 1979.

Oxford Cantigas de Santa Maria Database, http://csm.mml.ox.ac.uk/index.php?p=poemdata_view&rec=2.

Patrologiae cursus completus, series latina. Ed. Jacques-Paul Migne. 221 vols. Paris: Migne, 1844-1866.

Palomares [Santiago y Palomares], Francisco Xavier. *Arte nueva de escribir, inventada por el insigne maestro Pedro Diaz de Morante, e ilustrada con muestras nuevas, y varios discursos conducentes al verdadero magisterio de primeras letras, por D. Francisco X. de Santiago Palomares*. Madrid, 1776.

Pinius, Joannes. *Liturgia Mozarabica: Tractatus historico-chronologicus de liturgia antiqua Hispanica, Gothica, Isidoriana, Mozarabica, Toletana, mixta*. Antwerp, 1729. Reprint edition, Rome, 1740.

Porcel y Salablanca, José Antonio. "Canción Heroica." In *Poesía del siglo XVIII*, ed. John H. R. Polt. Madrid: Castalia, 1975.

Rodríguez, Cristóbal. *Bibliotheca Universal de la Polygraphia Española publicada por D. Blas Nassarre*. Madrid, 1738.

Sarmiento, Martín. *Obras posthumas del Reverendísimo P. Maestro Fr. Martín Sarmiento*. Vol. 1. *Memorias para la historia de la poesía y de los poetas españoles*. Madrid: Joaquin Ibarra, 1775.

————. *Sistema de adornos del Palacio Real de Madrid*. Ed. Joaquín Álvarez Barrientos and Concha Herrero Carretero. Madrid: Sociedad Estatal de Conmemoraciones Culturales, 2002.

The Songs of Holy Mary of Alfonso X, the Wise: A Translation of the Cantigas de Santa Maria. Trans. Kathleen Kulp-Hill. Tempe: Arizona Center for Medieval and Renaissance Studies, 2000.

Storia della Musica / Tomo Primo Alla Sacra Reale Cattolica Maestà Maria Barbara Infanta di Portogallo, Regina delle Spagne ec. ec. ec. Umiliato, e dedicato da Fr. Giambatista Martini de' Minori Conventuali Accademico nell'Instituto delle Scienze, e Filarmonico. Bologna: Lelio dalla Volpe, 1757.

Vives, José, ed. Oracional visigótico. Barcelona: Consejo Superior de Investigaciones Científicas, Escuela de Estudios Medievales, Sección de Barcelona, Balmesiana, Biblioteca Balmes, 1946.

Studies

Abadal y Vinyals, Ramón de. La batalla del adopcionismo en la desintegración de la Iglesia visigoda. Barcelona, 1939.

Aguilar Piñal, Francisco. "Las Academias." In La época de los primeros Borbones, II. La cultura española entre el Baroco y la ilustración (circa 1680–1759), 151–93. Historia de España 29:2. Madrid: Espasa-Calpe, 1985.

Aillet, Cyrille. Les mozarabes: Christianisme, islamisation et arabisation en péninsule ibérique (IXe–XIIe siècle). Bibliothèque de la Casa de Velázquez 45. Madrid: Casa de Velázquez, 2010.

Alcaraz Gómez, José F. Jesuitas y Reformismo: El Padre Francisco de Rávago (1747–1755). Facultad de Teología San Vicente Ferrer, Series Valentina 35. Valencia: Facultad de Teología, 1995.

Álvarez Barrientos, Joaquín. Los hombres de letras en la España del siglo XVIII: Apóstoles y arribistas. Madrid: Editorial Castalia, 2006.

———. "Monarquía y 'Nación Española' en el Sistema de adornos del Palacio Real de Madrid, de Martín Sarmiento." In Fénix de España: Modernidad y cultura propia en la España del siglo XVIII (1737–1766), Actas del congreso internacional celebrado en Madrid, noviembre de 2004, Homenaje a Antonio Mestre Sanchís, ed. Pablo Fernández Albaladejo, 191–213. Madrid: Marcial Pons Historia, Universidad Autónoma de Madrid, Universitat d'Alacant, Casa de Velázquez, 2006.

Álvarez, Maria-Salud. José de Nebra Blasco: vida y obra. Saragossa: Institución "Fernando el Católico," Sección de Música Antigua, Diputación de Zaragoza, 1993.

Andrew, Edward G. Patrons of Enlightenment. Toronto: University of Toronto Press, 2006.

Anglès, Higinio. La música a Catalunya fins al segle XIII. Barcelona: Institut d'Estudis Catalans y Biblioteca de Catalunya, 1935.

———. La música de las Cantigas de Santa Maria del Rey Alfonso X el Sabio. 3 vols. Barcelona: Diputación Provincial de Barcelona, Biblioteca Central, 1943–64.

Anglès, Higinio, and José Subirá. Catálogo Musical de la Biblioteca Nacional de Madrid. Manuscritos. Barcelona: Consejo Superior de Investigaciones Científicas, 1946.

Antolín, Guillermo. Catálogo de los códices latinos de la Real Bibliotheca del Escorial. 5 vols. 4. Madrid: Imprenta Helénica, 1910–23.

Arellano Garcia, Mario. La Capilla Mozárabe o del Corpus Christi. Toledo: Instituto de Estudios Visigóticos-Mozárabes de San Eugenio, 1980.

Atkinson, Charles M. *The Critical Nexus: Tone-System, Mode, and Notation in Early Medieval Music.* New York: Oxford University Press, 2009.

———. "*De Accentibus Toni Oritur Nota Quae Dicitur Neuma*: Prosodic Accents, the Accent Theory, and the Paleofrankish Script." In *Essays on Medieval Music in Honor of David G. Hughes,* ed. Graeme M. Boone, 17–42. Isham Library Papers 4. Cambridge, MA: Harvard University Department of Music, 1995.

———. "Glosses on Music and Grammar and the Advent of Music Writing in the West." In *Western Plainchant in the First Millennium: Studies in the Medieval Liturgy and Its Music,* ed. Sean Gallagher, James Haar, John Nádas, and Timothy Striplin, 199–215. Aldershot, UK: Ashgate, 2003.

Aubert, Eduardo Henrik. *The Modern Life of "Medieval Neumes": An Archeology of Medieval Notation (1600–1880).* Unpublished manuscript.

Aubrey, Elizabeth. "Medieval Melodies in the Hands of Bibliophiles of the Ancien Régime." In *Essays on Music and Culture in Honor of Herbert Kellman,* ed. Barbara Haggh, 17–34. Paris: Minerve, 2001.

Ayuso Marzuela, Teófilo. "Algunos problemas del texto biblico de Isidoro." In *Isidoriana,* ed. Manuel C. Díaz y Díaz, 143–91. León: Centro de Estudios "San Isidoro," 1961.

Barrett, Sam. *The Melodic Tradition of Boethius' "De Consolatione Philosophiae."* Monumenta monodica medii aevi, subsidia. Kassel: Bärenreiter, 2011.

———. "Music and Writing: On the Compilation of Paris, Bibliothèque Nationale Ms. Latin 1154." *Early Music History* 16 (1997): 55–96.

Barret-Kriegel, Blandine. *Les Académies de l'histoire.* Les historiens et la monarchie 3. Paris: Presses Universitaires de France, 1988.

Barrio Moya, José Luis. "Noticias familiares de D. Francisco Javier e Santiago Palomares, calígrafo toledano del siglo XVIII." *Anales toledanos* 43 (2007): 165–86.

Barton, Simon. *A History of Spain.* New York: Palgrave Macmillan, 2004.

Baumstark, Anton. *Comparative Liturgy.* Revised by Bernard Botte; English edition by F.L. Cross. Westminster: Newman Press, 1958.

Bernadó, Màrius. "The Hymns of the Intonarium Toletanum (1515): Some Peculiarities." In *Cantus Planus: Papers Read at the 6th Meeting, Eger, Hungary, 1993,* ed. Laszló Dobszay. 2 vols. Budapest: Hungarian Academy of Sciences, 1995. Published in Spanish as "Sobre el origen y la procedencia de la tradición himnódica hispánica a fines de la edad media." *Revista de musicología* 16 (1993): 2335–53.

Bertolucci Pizzorusso, Valeria. "Primo contributo all'analisi delle varianti redazionali nelle *Cantigas de Santa Maria.*" In *Cobras e son: Papers on the Text, Music and Manuscripts of the "Cantigas de Santa Maria,"* ed. Stephen Parkinson, 106–18. Oxford: Legenda, 2000.

Betteray, Dirk van. *Quomodo cantabimus canticum Domini in terra aliena. Liqueszenzen als Schlüssel zur Textinterpretation.* Studien und Materialien zur Musikwissenschaft 45. Hildesheim: Georg Olms, 2007.

Bobeth, Gundela. *Antike Verse in mittelalterlicher Vertonung. Neumierungen in Vergil-, Statius-, Lucan- und Terenz-Handschriften.* Monumenta Monodica Medii Aevi, Subsidia 5. Kassel: Bärenreiter, 2007.

———. "'Cantare Virgilium': Neumierte Vergilverse in karolingischen und postkarolingischen Handschriften." *Schweizer Jahrbuch für Musikwissenschaft* 23 (2003): 111–37.

Bonet Correa, Antonio. "Introducción." In *Un reinado bajo el signo de la paz: Fernando VI y Bárbara de Braganza, 1746–1759*, 2–3. Madrid: Real Academia de Bellas Artes de San Fernando, 2002.

Bosch, Lynette. *Art, Liturgy, and Legend in Renaissance Toledo: The Mendoza and the Iglesia Primada*. University Park: Penn State University Press, 2000.

Boynton, Susan. "An Early Notated Song of the Sibyl." In *Hortus troporum: Florilegium in honorem Gunillae Iversen*, ed. Alexander Andrée and Erika Kihlman, 47–56. Stockholm: Almqvist and Wiksell, 2008.

———. "A Lost Mozarabic Liturgical Manuscript Rediscovered: New York, Hispanic Society of America, B2916, olim Toledo, Biblioteca Capitular, 33.2." *Traditio* 57 (2002): 189–219.

———. "Orality, Literacy, and the Early Notation of the Office Hymns." *Journal of the American Musicological Society* 56 (2003): 99–167.

———. "Reconsidering the Toledo Codex of the Cantigas de Santa Maria in the Eighteenth Century." *In Quomodo Cantabimus Canticum? Studies in Honor of Edward H. Roesner*, ed. Rena Charnin Mueller, John Nadas, David Cannata, and Gabriela Ilnitchi, 209–22. Stuttgart: American Institute of Musicology, 2008.

———. "Writing History with Liturgy." In *Representing History, 900–1300: Art, Music, History*, ed. Robert A. Maxwell, 187–99. University Park: Penn State University Press, 2010.

Bradshaw, Paul. *The Search for the Origins of Christian Worship: Sources and Methods for the Study of Early Liturgy*. 2nd ed. New York: Oxford University Press, 2002.

Brockett, Clyde Waring. *Antiphons, Responsories, and Other Chants of the Mozarabic Rite*. Musicological Studies, no. 15. New York: Institute of Mediaeval Music, 1968.

Brou, Louis. "Deux mauvaises lectures du chanoine Ortiz dans l'édition du bréviaire mozarabe de Ximines: Lauda, capitula." In *Miscelánea en homenaje a Monseñor Higinio Anglés*, 2 vols., 1:175–202. Barcelona: Consejo superior de investigaciones científicas, 1958–61.

———. "Etudes sur le Missel et le Bréviaire 'mozarabes' imprimés." *Hispania Sacra* 11 (1958): 349–98.

———. "Notes de Paléographie Musicale Mozarabe." *Anuario Musical* 10 (1955): 23–29.

———. "Séquences et tropes dans la liturgie mozarabe." *Hispania Sacra* 4 (1951): 27–41.

Burman, Thomas E. *Religious Polemic and the Intellectual History of the Mozarabs, c. 1050–1200*. Leiden: E. J. Brill, 1994.

Burson, Jeffrey D. "The Crystallization of Counter-Enlightenment and Philosophe Identities: Theological Controversy and Catholic Enlightenment in Pre-Revolutionary France." *Church History* 77 (2008): 955–1002.

———. "Towards a New Comparative History of European Enlightenments: The Problem of Enlightenment Theology in France and the Study of Eighteenth-Century Europe." *Intellectual History Review* 18 (2008): 173–87.

Campos y Fernández de Sevilla, Francisco Javier. "Estudio preliminar: El P. Enrique Flórez y la *España Sagrada*." In *España Sagrada*, vol. 1, ix–lx. Madrid: Editorial Revista Agustiniana, 2000.

Cañizares-Esguerra, Jorge. *How to Write the History of the New World: Histories, Epistemologies, and Identities in the Eighteenth-Century Atlantic World*. Stanford: Stanford University Press, 2001.

Cárdenas, Anthony J. "Alfonso's Scriptorium and Chancery: Role of the Prologue in Bonding the *Translatio Studii* to the *Translatio Potestatis*." In *Emperor of Culture: Alfonso X the Learned of Castile and His Thirteenth-Century Renaissance*, ed. Robert I. Burns, 90–108. Philadelphia: University of Pennsylvania Press, 1990.

Carreras, Juan José. "From Literes to Nebra: Spanish Dramatic Music between Tradition and Modernity." In *Music in Spain during the Eighteenth Century*, ed. Malcolm Boyd and Juan José Carreras, 7–16. Cambridge: Cambridge University Press, 1998.

———. "Entre la zarzuela y la ópera de corte: Representaciones cortesanas en el Buen Retiro entre 1720 y 1724." In *Teatro y Música en España (siglo XVIII), Actas del Simposio Internacional Salamanca*, ed. Rainer Kleinertz, 49–77. Kassel: Reichenberger, 1996.

Carrete Parrondo, Juan. "El grabado en el siglo XVIII. Triunfo de la estampa ilustrada." In *El grabado en España (siglos XV al XVIII)*, ed. Juan Carrete Parrondo, Fernando Checa Cremades, and Valeriano Bozal, 395–644. Summa artis: Historia general del arte 31. Madrid: Espasa Calpe, 2001.

Cavadini, John C. "Elipandus and His Critics at the Council of Frankfort." In *Das Frankfurter Konzil von 794: Kristallisationspunkt karolingischer Kultur*, ed. Rainer Berndt, 2 vols., 2:787–807. Quellen und Abhandlungen zur Mittelrheinischen Kirchengeschichte 80. Mainz: Selbstverlag der Gesellschaft fur Mittelrheinische Kirchengeschichte, 1997.

———. *The Last Christology of the West: Adoptionism in Spain and Gaul, 785–820*. Philadelphia: University of Pennsylvania Press, 1993.

Ceballos, Sara Gross. "Scarlatti and María Bárbara: A Study of Musical Portraiture." In *Domenico Scarlatti Adventures: Essays to Commemorate the 250th Anniversary of His Death*, ed. Massimiliano Sala and W. Dean Sutcliffe, 197–223. Bologna: Ut Orpheus, 2008.

Cioffi, Irene. "Corrado Giaquinto and the Dissemination of the Italian Style at the Bourbon Court in Madrid." In *Painting in Spain in the Age of Enlightenment: Goya and His Contemporaries*, ed. Ronda Kasl and Suzanne L. Stratton, 26–38. Indianapolis: Indianapolis Museum of Art, 1997.

———. "Corrado Giaquinto at the Spanish Court: 1753–1762: The Fresco Cycles at the New Royal Palace in Madrid." PhD diss., Institute of Fine Arts, New York University, 1992.

Clark, Charles Upson. *Collectanea Hispanica*. Transactions of the Connecticut Academy of Arts and Sciences 24. Paris: Champion, 1920.

Clark, Jane. "Farinelli as Queen of the Night." *Eighteenth-Century Music* 2 (2005): 321–33.

Colette, Marie-Noël. "Le chant de la Sibylle, composition, transmission et interprétation." In *La Sibylle: Parole et représentation*, ed. Monique Bouquet and Françoise Morzadec, 165–76. Rennes: Presses Universitaires de Rennes, 2004.

————. "La notation du demi-ton dans le manuscrit Paris, B.N. lat. 1139 et dans quelques manuscrits du Sud de la France." In *La tradizione dei tropi liturgici*, Atti dei convegni sui tropi liturgici, Parigi (15–19 ottobre 1985), Perugia (2–5 settembre 1987), ed. Claudio Leonardi and Enrico Menestò, 297–311. Spoleto: Centro italiano di studi sull'alto medioevo, 1990.

Collamore, Lila. "Aquitanian Collections of Office Chants: A Comparative Survey." PhD diss., Catholic University of America, 2000.

Collins, Roger. *Early Medieval Spain: Unity in Diversity, 400–1000*. London: Macmillan, 1995.

————. *Visigothic Spain, 409–711*. Oxford: Blackwell, 2004.

Colomina Torner, Jaime. "El cardenal Lorenzana y las circunstancias históricas que rodearon la renovación del rito hispano-mozárabe." In *El cardenal Lorenzana, arzobispo de Toledo: Ciclo de Conferencias en el II Centenario de su muerte (1804–2004)*, ed. Angel Fernández Collado, 125–39. Toledo: Instituto superior de estudios teológicos San Ildefonso, 2004.

Comparative Liturgy Fifty Years after Anton Baumstark (1872-1948): Acts of the International Congress, Rome, 25-29 September 1998. Ed. Robert F. Taft and Gabriele Winkler. Orientalia Christiana Analecta 265. Rome: Pontificio Istituto Orientale, 2001.

Connolly, Thomas. *Mourning into Joy: Music, Raphael, and Saint Cecilia*. New Haven: Yale University Press, 1995.

Corbeto, Albert. "Eighteenth Century Spanish Type Design." *The Library: The Transactions of the Bibliographical Society* 10 (2009): 272–97.

Corbin, Solange. "Le Cantus Sibyllae: Origine et premiers textes." *Revue de musicologie* 34 (1952): 1–10.

Cuesta Gutierrez, Luisa. "Jesuitas confesores de reyes y directores de la Biblioteca Nacional." *Revista de Archivos, Bibliotecas y Museos* 69 (1961): 129–75.

Deacon, Philip. "Early Enlightenment and the Spanish World." *Eighteenth-Century Studies* 37 (2004): 129–40.

Deswarte, Thomas. *De la destruction à la restauration: L'idéologie du royaume d'Oviedo-Léon, VIIIe–XIe siècles*. Turnhout: Brepols, 2003.

Díaz, José Simón. "Un erudito español, el P. Andrés Marcos Burriel." *Revista bibliográfica y documental* 3 (1949): 5–52.

————. "El reconocimiento de los archivos españoles en 1750–1756." *Revista bibliográfica y documental* 4 (1950): 131–70.

Díaz y Díaz, Manuel C. "Agustín entre los mozárabes: Un testimonio." *Augustinus* 5 (1980): 157–80.

————. "Consideraciones sobre el oracional visigótico de Verona." In *Petrarca Verona e l'Europa: Atti del Convegno internazionale di studi*, ed. Giuseppe Billanovich and Giuseppe Frasso, 13–29. Studi sul Petrarca 26. Padua: Antenore, 1997.

————. *Manuscritos visigóticos del sur de la Península: Ensayo de distribución regional*. Seville: Secretariado de Publicaciones de la Universidad de Sevilla, 1995.

Divjak, Johannes. *Die Handschriftliche Überlieferung der Werke des Heiligen Augustinus*. Vol. 4. *Spanien und Portugal*. Philosophisch-historische Klasse, Sitzungsberichte 292. Vienna: Österreichischen Akademie der Wissenschaften, 1974.

Dodds, Jerrilyn. "Rodrigo, Reconquest, and Assimilation: Some Preliminary Thoughts about San Román." In *Spanish Medieval Art: Recent Studies*, ed. Colum Hourihane, 215–44. Tempe: Arizona Center for Medieval and Renaissance Studies, 2008.

Domínguez Rodríguez, Ana. "Imágenes de un rey trovador de Santa María (Alfonso X en las *Cantigas*)." In *Il Medio Oriente e l'Occidente nell'arte del XIII secolo*. Atti del XXIV Congresso Internazionale di Storia dell'Arte, 2, ed. Hans Belting, 229–39. Bologna: CLUEB, 1982.

Dubuis, Michel. "Erudition et piété: La réception en Espagne du *Traité des études monastiques*, de Mabillon." In *Foi et Lumières dans l'Espagne du XVIIIe siècle*, ed. Joël Saugnieux, 113–65. Lyon: Presses Universitaires de Lyon, 1985.

———. "Mabillon et la réflexion historiographique en Espagne aux XVIIe et XVIIIe siècles." In *Erudition et commerce épistolaire: Jean Mabillon et la tradition monastique*, ed. Daniel-Odon Hurel, 185–202. Textes et Traditions 6. Paris: Vrin, 2003.

Duchez, Marie-Elisabeth. "Jean-Jacques Rousseau historien de la musique." In *La Musique du théorique au politique*, ed. Hugues Dufourt and Joël-Marie Fauquet, 39–111. Paris: Klincksieck, 1991.

Echánove Tuero, Alfonso. *La preparación intelectual del P. Andrés Marcos Burriel, S.J. (1731–1750)*. Madrid: Consejo Superior de Investigaciones Científicas, Instituto Enríque Flórez, 1971.

Egido, Teófanes. "El Regalismo y las relaciones Iglesia-Estado en el siglo XVIII." In *La Iglesia en la España de los siglos XVII y XVIII*, *Historia de la Iglesia en España*, vol. 4, ed. Antonio Mestre Sanchís, 123–249. Madrid: Biblioteca de Autores Cristianos, 1979.

Ellis, Katharine. *Interpreting the Musical Past: Early Music in Nineteenth-Century France*. New York: Oxford University Press, 2005.

Feldman, Martha. *Opera and Sovereignty: Transforming Myths in Eighteenth-Century Italy*. Chicago: University of Chicago Press, 2007.

Fernández Collado, Ángel. "Los cantorales mozárabes de Cisneros." *Toletana: Cuestiones de Teología e historia, Estudio Teológico de San Ildefonso, Toledo* 2 (2000): 145–68.

———. "El Cardenal Lorenzana y la pervivencia del rito hispano- mozárabe." In *España y América entre el Barroco y la Ilustración*, ed. Jesús Paniagua Pérez, 433–45. León: Universidad de León, 2005.

———. "Razones de la reforma litúrgica mozárabe del cardenal Lorenzana." *Hispania Sacra* 57 (2005): 429–38.

Ferreira, Manuel Pedro. "Alfonso X, Compositor." *Alcanate: Revista de Estudios Alfonsíes* 5 (2006–7): 117–37.

———. "Cluny at Fynystere: One Use, Three Fragments." In *Studies in Medieval Chant and Liturgy in Honour of David Hiley*, ed. Terence Bailey and László Dobszay, 179–228. Budapest: Institute for Musicology and Ottawa: Institute of Mediaeval Music, 2007.

———. "The Layout of the *Cantigas*: A Musicological Overview." *Galician Review* 2 (1998): 47–61.

———. "The Stemma of the Marian Cantigas: Philological and Musical Evidence." *Cantigueros* 6 (1994): 72–98.

———. "Understanding the *Cantigas*: Preliminary Steps." Unpublished manuscript.

Firey, Abigail. "Carolingian Ecclesiology and Heresy: A Southern Gallic Juridical Tract against Adoptionism." *Sacris Erudiri* 39 (2000): 253–316.

Fita Colomé, Fidel. "Noticia de la California: Obra anónima del P. Andrés Marcos Burriel, emprendida en 1750, impresa en 1757 y traducida después de varias lenguas de Europa. Datos inéditos e ilustrativos de su composición, aprobación y edición." *Boletín de la Real Academia de la Historia* 52 (1908): 396–438.

Freistedt, Heinrich. *Die liqueszierenden Noten des Gregorianischen Chorals: Ein Beitrag zur Notationskunde.* Veröffentlichungen der Gregorianischen Akademie zu Freiburg 14. Freiburg: St. Paulusdruckerei, 1929.

Galende Diaz, Juan Carlos. "Repertorio bibliográfico de la biblioteca del Padre Burriel." *Espacio, Tiempo y Forma, Revista de la Facultad de Geografía y Historia, Serie IV: Historia moderna* 8 (1994): 241–68.

Gambra, Andrés. *Alfonso VI: Cancilleria, curia e imperio.* Colleción "Fuentes y estudios de historia leonesa," nos. 62–63. León: Centro de Estudios e Investigación "San Isidoro," Caja España de Inversiones, Caja de Ahorros y Monte de Piedad, Archivo Historico Diocesano, 1997.

García, Natalia Juan. "La labor intelectual en los monasterios: Los monjes escritores y investigadores del monasterio de San Juan de la Peña (siglos XVI–XIX)." *Studium: Revista de humanidades* 11 (2005): 93–116.

García-Arenal, Mercedes, and Fernando Rodríguez Mediano. "Jerónimo Román de la Higuera and the Lead Books of Sacromonte." In *The Conversos and Moriscos in Late Medieval Spain and Beyond.* Vol. 1. *Departures and Changes*, ed. Kevin Ingram, 243–68. Studies in Medieval and Reformation Traditions 141. Converso and Morisco Studies 1. Leiden: Brill, 2009.

García Avilés, Alejandro. "Alfonso X y la tradición de la magia astral." In *El Scriptorium Alfonsí: De los libros de astrología a las "Cantigas de Santa María,"* ed. Jesús Montoya Martínez and Ana Domínguez Rodríguez, 83–103. Madrid: Editorial Complutense, 1999.

García Cuadrado, Amparo, and Juan Antonio Montalbán Jiménez. "Bibliotheca Universal de la Polygraphia Española: Una impresión de 1738 realizada por la Biblioteca Real." *Anales de Documentación* 10 (2007): 113–43.

Garrigosa i Massana, Joaquim. *Els manuscrits musicals a Catalunya fins al segle XIII: L'evolució de la notació musical.* Lleida: Institut d'estudis ilerdencs, 2003.

Godoy Alcántara, José. *Historia crítica de los falsos cronicones.* Madrid, 1868; reprint, Madrid: Editorial Tres Catorce Diecisiete, 1981; facsimile of the 1868 edition, Granada: Editorial Universal de Granada, 1999.

Gómez Muntané, Maricarmen. *El canto de la Sibila.* Vol. 1. *Castilla y León.* Vol. 2. *Cataluña y Baleares.* Madrid: Alpuerto, 1996–97.

———. "El Canto de la Sibila: Orígenes y Fuentes." In *Fuentes Musicales en la Península Ibérica / Fonts Musicals a la Península Ibèrica*, ed. Maricarmen Gómez and Màrius Bernadó, 35–70. Lleida: Edicions de la Universitat de Lleida, Institut d'Estudis Ilerdencs, 2001.

———. *La música medieval en España.* Kassel: Reichenberger, 2001.

Gómez-Ruiz, Raúl. "Mozarabic Rite." In *New Catholic Encyclopedia*, 2nd ed., 10:44–47. Washington, DC: Thomson Gale, 2000.

———. *Mozarabs, Hispanics, and the Cross.* Maryknoll, NY: Orbis Books, 2007.

González Barrionuevo, Herminio. "La música litúrgica de los mozárabes." In *Los mozárabes: Una minoría olvidada*, ed. Manuel González Jiménez and Juan del Río Martín, 151–200. Seville: Fundación "El Monte," 1998.

Gonzálvez Ruiz, Ramón. *Hombres y libros de Toledo, 1086–1300*. Madrid: Fundación Ramón Areces, 1997.

———. "The Persistence of the Mozarabic Liturgy in Toledo after A.D. 1080." In *Santiago, Saint-Denis, and Saint Peter: The Reception of the Roman Liturgy in León-Castile in 1080*, ed. Bernard F. Reilly, 157–85. New York: Fordham University Press, 1985.

Gorman, Michael. "A Survey of the Oldest Manuscripts of St. Augustine's *De ciuitate Dei*." *Journal of Theological Studies*, n.s. 33 (1982): 398–410.

Gossman, Lionel. *Medievalism and the Ideologies of the Enlightenment: The World and Work of La Curne de Sainte-Palaye*. Baltimore: Johns Hopkins University Press, 1968.

Grier, James. *The Musical World of a Medieval Monk: Adémar de Chabannes in Eleventh-Century Aquitaine*. Cambridge: Cambridge University Press, 2006.

Grieve, Patricia. *The Eve of Spain: Myths of Origins in the History of Christian, Muslim, and Jewish Contact*. Baltimore: Johns Hopkins University Press, 2009.

Haines, John. *Eight Centuries of Troubadours and Trouvères: The Changing Identity of Medieval Music*. Cambridge: Cambridge University Press, 2004.

Hainthaler, Theresia. "Von Toledo nach Frankfurt." In *Das Frankfurter Konzil von 794: Kristallisationspunkt karolingischer Kultur*, ed. Rainer Berndt, 809–60. Quellen und Abhandlungen zur Mittelrheinischen Kirchengeschichte 80. 2 vols. Mainz: Selbstverlag der Gesellschaft für Mittelrheinische Kirchengeschichte, 1997.

Harris, A. Katie. *From Muslim to Christian Granada: Inventing a City's Past in Early Modern Spain*. Baltimore: Johns Hopkins University Press, 2007.

Haskell, Francis. *History and Its Images: Art and the Interpretation of the Past*. New Haven: Yale University Press, 1993.

Haug, Andreas. "Zur Interpretation der Liqueszenzneumen." *Archiv für Musikwissenschaft* 50 (1993): 85–100.

Heartz, Daniel. "Farinelli Revisited: From the Sublime to the Ridiculous." *Early Music* 18 (1990): 430–48.

Hernández, Francisco J. "Language and Cultural Identity: The Mozarabs of Toledo." *Boletín Burriel* 1 (1989): 29–48.

———. "Los mozárabes del siglo XII en la ciudad y la iglesia de Toledo." *Toletum* 16 (1985): 57–124.

Hernández, Francisco J., and Peter Linehan. *The Mozarabic Cardinal: The Life and Times of Gonzalo Pérez Gudiel*. Florence: SISMEL, Edizioni del Galluzzo, 2004.

Hiley, David. *Western Plainchant: A Handbook*. Oxford: Oxford University Press, 1993.

Hill, Ruth. *Sceptres and Sciences in the Spains: Four Humanists and the New Philosophy (ca. 1680–1740)*. Liverpool: Liverpool University Press, 2000.

Hillgarth, Jocelyn N. *The Visigoths in History and Legend*. Studies and Texts 166. Toronto: Pontifical Institute of Mediaeval Studies, 2009.

Hispania Vetus: Musical-Liturgical Manuscripts from Visigothic Origins to the Franco-Roman Transition (9th–12th Centuries). Ed. Susana Zapke. Bilbao: Fundación BBVA, 2007.

Hitchcock, Richard. "An Examination of the Use of the Term 'Mozarab' in Eleventh- and Twelfth-Century Spain." PhD diss., University of St. Andrews, 1971.

————. "Mozarabs and Moriscos: Two Marginalized Communities in Sixteenth-Century Toledo." In *Historicist Essays on Hispano-Medieval Narrative: In Memory of Roger M. Walker*, ed. Barry Taylor and Geoffrey West, 171–84. London: Modern Humanities Research Association, 2005.

————. *Mozarabs in Medieval and Early Modern Spain: Identities and Influences*. Aldershot, UK: Ashgate, 2008.

————. "El rito hispánico, las ordalías y los mozárabes en el reinado de Alfonso VI." *Estudios orientales* 8 (1973): 19–41.

Hobsbawm, Eric. "Introduction: Inventing Traditions." In *The Invention of Tradition*, ed. Eric Hobsbawm and Terence Ranger, 1–14. Cambridge: Cambridge University Press, 1983.

Huglo, Michel. "La notation wisigothique est-elle plus ancienne que les autres notations européennes?" In *España en la Música de Occidente*, ed. Emilio Casares Rodicio, Ismael Fernández de la Cuesta, and José López-Calo, 19–26. Madrid: Instituto Nacional de las Artes Escénicas y de la Música, Ministerio de Cultura, 1987.

————. "La pénétration des manuscrits aquitains en Espagne." *Revista de musicología* 8 (1985): 249–56.

Humfrey, Peter. *The Altarpiece in Renaissance Venice*. New Haven: Yale University Press, 1993.

Imbasciani, Vito. "Cisneros and the Restoration of the Mozarabic Rite." PhD diss., Cornell University, 1979.

Israel, Jonathan. *Enlightenment Contested: Philosophy, Modernity, and the Emancipation of Man 1670–1752*. Oxford: Oxford University Press, 2006.

————. *Radical Enlightenment: Philosophy and the Making of Modernity 1650–1750*. Oxford: Oxford University Press, 2001.

Janini, José. "Misas mozárabes recompuestas por Ortiz." *Hispania Sacra* 34 (1982): 153–63.

————. "El oficio mozárabe de la Asunción." *Hispania Sacra* 28 (1975): 3–35.

————. "Las piezas litúrgicas del Toledo 35.7 editadas por Ortiz." *Escritos del Vedat* 8 (1978): 161–77.

Janini, José, and Ramón Gonzálvez. *Catálogo de los Manuscritos litúrgicos de la Catedral de Toledo*. Toledo: Diputación Provincial, 1977.

Janini, José, and José Serrano. *Manuscritos litúrgicos de la Biblioteca Nacional*. Madrid: Dirección General de Archivos y Bibliotecas, 1969.

Joncus, Berta. "One God, So Many Farinellis: Mythologising the Star Castrato." *Journal of Eighteenth-Century Studies* 28 (2005): 437–96.

Kagan, Richard L. *Clio and the Crown: The Politics of History in Medieval and Early Modern Spain*. Baltimore: Johns Hopkins University Press, 2009.

Kamen, Henry. *Imagining Spain: Historical Myth and National Identity*. New Haven: Yale University Press, 2008.

————. *Philip V of Spain: The King Who Reigned Twice*. New Haven: Yale University Press, 2001.

Kelly, Thomas Forrest, ed. *Oral and Written Transmission in Chant*. Burlington, VT: Ashgate, 2009.

Kendrick, Laura. "The Science of Imposture and the Professionalization of Medieval Occitan Literary Studies." In *Medievalism and the Modernist Temper*, ed. R. Howard

Bloch and Stephen G. Nichols, 95–126. Baltimore: Johns Hopkins University Press, 1996.

Kleinertz, Rainer. *Grundzüge des spanischen Musiktheaters im 18. Jahrhundert: Ópera, comedia und zarzuela.* 2 vols. Kassel: Reichenberger, 2003.

———. "Music Theatre in Spain." In *The Cambridge History of Eighteenth-Century Music,* ed. Simon P. Keefe, 402–19. Cambridge: Cambridge University Press, 2009.

———. "Ruler-Acclamation in Spanish Opera of the 1730s." In *Italian Opera in Central Europe.* Vol. 1. *Institutions and Ceremonies,* ed. Melania Bucciarelli, Norbert Dubowy, and Reinhard Strohm, 235–51. Berlin: Berliner Wissenschafts-Verlag, 2006.

———, ed. *Teatro y Música en España (siglo XVIII), Actas del Simposio Internacional Salamanca.* Kassel: Reichenberger, 1996.

Kruckenberg, Lori. "Neumatizing the Sequence: Special Performances of Sequences in the Central Middle Ages." *Journal of the American Musicological Society* 59 (2006): 243–317.

Lenain, Philippe. *Histoire Littéraire des Bénédictins de Saint-Maur.* Vol. 1 (1612–55). Bibliothèque de la Revue d'Histoire Eccésiastique, 88. Louvain-La-Neuve: La Revue d'Histoire Ecclésiastique, 2006.

Levesque de la Ravallière, Pierre-Alexandre. *Les Poësies du Roi de Navarre.* Paris: Hippolyte-Louis Guerin, 1742.

Levy, Kenneth. *Gregorian Chant and the Carolingians.* Princeton: Princeton University Press, 1998.

———. "On the Origin of Neumes." *Early Music History* 7 (1987): 59–90.

Leza, José-Máximo, and Tess Knighton. "Metastasio on the Spanish Stage: Operatic Adaptations in the Public Theatres of Madrid in the 1730s." *Early Music* 26 (1998): 623–31.

Linehan, Peter. "El concepto de capital del reino en la Edad Media española." *Boletín Burriel* 1 (1989): 21–27.

———. *History and the Historians of Medieval Spain.* Oxford: Clarendon Press, 1993.

———. "Religion, Nationalism and National Identity in Medieval Spain." In *Religion and National Identity: Papers Read at the Nineteenth Summer Meeting and the Twentieth Winter Meeting of the Ecclesiastical History Society,* ed. Stuart Mews, 161–99. Studies in Church History 18. Oxford: Boydell and Brewer, 1982.

———. "The Toledo Forgeries, c. 1150–c. 1300." In *Falschungen im Mittelalter,* 642–74. Schriften der Monumenta Germaniae Historica 33. Hannover: Hahnsche Buchhandlung, 1988.

López Vidriero, Maria Luisa. "Camino de perfección: La recuperación de fuentes manuscritas en la España ilustrada." *Reales sitios* 31, no. 121 (1994): 2–11.

Lynch, John. *Bourbon Spain 1700–1808.* Oxford: Basil Blackwell, 1989.

Malagón-Barceló, Javier. "La obra escrita de Lorenzana como arzobispo de México, 1766–1772." *Historia Mexicana* 23 (1974): 437–65.

Maldonado, Pedro Castillo. "*Angelorum Participes*: The Cult of the Saints in Late Antique Spain." In *Hispania in Late Antiquity: Current Perspectives,* ed. and trans. Kim Bowes and Michael Kulikowski, 151–88. The Medieval and Early Modern Iberian World 24. Leiden: Brill, 2005.

Martin, Céline. *La géographie du pouvoir dans l'Espagne visigothique.* Lille: Presses Universitaires du Septentrion, 2003.

Martín Patino, José Maria. "El Breviarium Mozárabe de Ortiz: Su valor documental para la historia del oficio catedralicio hispánico." *Miscelánea Comillas* 50 (1963): 207–97.

Martínez Gil, Carlos. *La Capilla de Música de La Catedral de Toledo (1700–1764), Evolución de un concepto sonoro.* Toledo: Junta de Comunidades de Castilla-La Mancha, Consejería de Cultura, Servicio de Publicaciones, 2003.

Mas, Josiane. "La notation catalane." *Revista de musicología* 11 (1988): 11–30.

Mecham, J. Lloyd. "The Origins of 'Real Patronato de Indias.'" *Catholic Historical Review* 14 (1928): 205–27.

Meseguer Fernández, Juan. "El Cardenal Jiménez de Cisneros, fundador de la Capilla Mozárabe." In *Historia mozárabe: Ponencias y comunicaciones presentadas al I Congreso Internacional de Estudios Mozárabes,* 149–245. Toledo: Instituto de Estudios Visigótico-Mozárabes de San Eugenio, 1975.

Mestre Sanchís, Antonio. "Clausura: Reflexiones de un historiador del siglo XVIII español." In *Fénix de España: Modernidad y cultura propia en la España del siglo XVIII (1737–1766), Actas del congreso internacional celebrado en Madrid, noviembre de 2004, Homenaje a Antonio Mestre Sanchís,* ed. Pablo Fernández Albaladejo, 349–53. Madrid: Marcial Pons Historia, Universidad Autónoma de Madrid, Universitat d'Alacant, Casa de Velázquez, 2006.

———. *Despotismo e ilustración en España.* Barcelona: Ariel, 1976.

———. "Historia crítica y reformismo en la ilustración española." In *La ilustración española: Actas del Coloquio Internacional celebrado en Alicante 1–4 octubre 1985,* ed. A. Alberola and E. La Parra. Alicante: Instituto Juan Gil-Albert, Diputación provincial de Alicante, 1986.

———. *Historia, fueros y actitudes políticas: Mayans y la historiografía del XVIII.* Valencia, 1970; revised edition, Valencia: Universitat de Valencia, 2000.

———. *Humanistas, políticos e ilustrados.* Alicante: Universidad de Alicante, 2002.

———. *La ilustración española: Actas del Coloquio Internacional celebrado en Alicante 1–4 octubre 1985,* ed. A. Alberola and E. La Parra. Alicante: Instituto Juan Gil-Albert, Diputación provincial de Alicante, 1986.

———. "Nueva dinastía e iglesia nacional." In *Los Borbones: Dinastía y memoría de nación en la España del siglo XVIII,* Actas del coloquio internacional celebrado en Madrid, mayo de 2000, ed. Pablo Fernández Albaladejo, 549–67. Madrid: Casa de Velázquez, 2002.

Mettmann, Walter. "Algunas observaciones sobre la génesis de la colección de las *Cantigas de Santa María* y sobre el problema del autor." In *Studies on the* Cantigas de Santa María*: Art, Music, and Poetry,* ed. Israel J. Katz and John E. Keller, 355–66. Madison, WI: Hispanic Seminary of Medieval Studies, 1987.

Michael, Ian. "From the Belles of St Clement's to the *Book of Good Love*: The Late Survival of Mozarabic Culture in Toledo." In *Cross, Crescent, and Conversion: Studies on Medieval Spain and Christendom in Memory of Richard Fletcher,* ed. Simon Barton and Peter Linehan, 277–92. Leiden: Brill, 2008.

Millares Carlo, Agustín. *Los codices visigóticos de la Catedral Toledana.* Madrid: Ignacio de Noreña, 1935.

———. *Corpus de códices visigóticos.* 2 vols. Ed. Manuel C. Díaz y Díaz, Anscari M. Mundó, José Maria Ruiz Asencio, B. Casado Quintanilla, and E. Lecuona Ribot. Las

Palmas de Gran Canaria: Fundación de Enseñanza Superio a Distancia de Las Palmas de Gran Canaria, 1999.

———. "El siglo XVIII español y los intentos de formación de un corpus diplomático." *Revista de la Biblioteca, Archivo y Museo* 2 (1925): 515–30.

———. *Tratado de Paleografía Española*. Ed. José Manual Ruiz Asencio. Madrid: Espasa-Calpe, 1983.

Monteagudo, Henrique. "'Cantares con sões saborosos de cantar': Apuntamentos para un proemio." In *Cantigas de Santa Maria: Códice Toledano*. Santiago de Compostela: Consello da Cultura Galega, 2003.

Moore, Liam. "Religious Language and the Construction of Royal Power: León, 1037–1126." PhD diss., Columbia University, 2009.

Mundó, Anscari M. "La datación de los códices litúrgicos visigóticos toledanos." *Hispania Sacra* 38 (1965): 1–25.

Muniain Ederra, Sara. *El programa escultórico de Palacio Real de Madrid y la ilustración española*. Madrid: FUE, 2000.

Navarro Brotóns, Víctor. "Science and Enlightenment in Eighteenth-Century Spain: The Contribution of the Jesuits before and after the Expulsion." In *The Jesuits II: Cultures, Sciences, and the Arts, 1540–1773*, ed. John W. O'Malley, Gauvin Alexander Bailey, Steven J. Harris, and T. Frank Kennedy, 390–404. Toronto: University of Toronto Press, 2006.

Nieto Callén, Juan José, and José María Sánchez Molledo. "Fray Manuel Abad y Lasierra, un aragonés de la ilustración." *Argensola: Revista de Ciencias Sociales del Instituto de Estudios Altoaragoneses* 114 (2004): 371–89.

Noel, Charles C. "Clerics and Crown in Bourbon Spain, 1700–1808: Jesuits, Jansenists, and Enlightened Reformers." In *Religion and Politics in Enlightenment Europe*, ed. James E. Bradley and Dale K. Van Kley, 119–53. Notre Dame, IN: University of Notre Dame Press, 2001.

———. "In the House of Reform: The Bourbon Court of Eighteenth-Century Spain." In *Enlightened Reform in Southern Europe and its Atlantic Colonies, c. 1750–1830*, ed. Gabriel Paquette, 145–65. Aldershot, UK: Ashgate, 2009.

Noone, Michael, and Graeme Skinner. "Toledo Cathedral's Collection of Manuscript Plainsong Choirbooks: A Preliminary Report and Checklist." *Notes: Quarterly Journal of the Music Library Association*, 63 (2006): 289–328.

O'Callaghan, Joseph F. *A History of Medieval Spain*. Ithaca, NY: Cornell University Press, 1975.

———. "Image and Reality: The King Creates His Kingdom." In *Emperor of Culture: Alfonso X the Learned of Castile and His Thirteenth-Century Renaissance*, ed. Robert I. Burns, 14–32. Philadelphia: University of Pennsylvania Press, 1990.

———. "The Integration of Christian Spain into Europe: The Role of Alfonso VI of León-Castile." In *Santiago, Saint-Denis, and Saint Peter: The Reception of the Roman Liturgy in León-Castile in 1080*, ed. Bernard F. Reilly, 101–20. New York: Fordham University Press, 1985.

———. *Learned King: The Reign of Alfonso X of Castile*. Philadelphia: University of Pennsylvania Press, 1993.

Octavio de Toledo, José María. *Catálogo de la Libreria del Cabildo Toledano*. Part 2. *Impresos*. Madrid: Tipografía de la Revista de Archivos, Bibliotecas y Museos, 1906.

Olaechea, Rafael. "La Política eclesiástica del gobierno de Fernando VI." In *La época de Fernando VI: Ponencias leídas en el coloquo conmemorativo de los 25 años de la fundación de la Cátedra Feijoo*, 139–226. Oviedo: Facultad de filosofía y letras, Universidad de Oviedo, 1981.

Olds, Katrina Beth. "'The False Chronicles' in Early Modern Spain: Forgery, Tradition, and the Invention of Texts and Relics, 1595–c. 1670." PhD diss., Princeton University, 2008.

Olstein, Diego Adrián. *La era mozárabe: Los mozárabes de Toledo (siglos XI y XIII) en la historiografía, las fuentes y la historia*. Salamanca: Ediciones universidad de Salamanca, 2006.

Orlandis, José. "La circunstancia histórica del adopcionismo español." *Scripta theologica* 26 (1994): 1074–91.

———. "Toletanae illusionis superstitio." *Scripta Theologica* 18 (1986): 197–213.

Parkes, Malcolm, and Sonia Scott-Fleming. "Round Table: The Manuscripts of the *Cantigas de Santa Maria*." In *Cobras e son: Papers on the Text, Music and Manuscripts of the "Cantigas de Santa Maria*," ed. Stephen Parkinson, 214–20. Oxford: Legenda, 2000.

Parkinson, Stephen. "Layout and Structure of the Toledo Manuscript of the *Cantigas de Santa Maria*." In *Cobras e son: Papers on the Text, Music and Manuscripts of the "Cantigas de Santa Maria*," ed. Stephen Parkinson, 133–53. Oxford: Legenda, 2000.

Parkinson, Stephen, and Deirdre Jackson. "Collection, Composition, and Compilation in the *Cantigas de Santa Maria*." *Portuguese Studies* 22 (2006): 159–72.

Peñas García, María Concepción. "De los cantorales de Cisneros y las melodías de tradición mozárabe." *Nassarre: Revista aragonesa de musicología* 12 (1996): 413–34.

Peñas García, María Concepción, and María Carmen Casas Gras. "Los cantorales de Cisneros: Estudio y presentación del Cantoral I." *Nassarre: Revista aragonesa de musicología* 20 (2004): 261–402.

Pérez Higuera, Teresa. "Escenas de la vida, muerte y hallazgo de las reliquias de San Ildefonso en la Puerta del Reloj de la Catedral de Toledo." *En la España medieval* 5 (1984): 797–811.

Pérez Magallón, Jesús. *Construyendo la modernidad: La cultura española en el tiempo de Los Novatores*. Madrid: Consejo Superior de Investigaciones Científicas, Instituto de la Lengua Española, 2002.

Pérez Sánchez, Alfonso E., ed. *Corrado Giaquinto y España*. Madrid, Palacio Real 5 abril–25 junio 2006. Madrid: Patrimonio Nacional, 2006.

Pick, Lucy K. *Conflict and Coexistence: Archbishop Rodrigo and the Muslims and Jews of Medieval Spain*. Ann Arbor: University of Michigan Press, 2004.

Pinell, Jordi. *Liturgia Hispánica*. Biblioteca litúrgica. Barcelona: Centre de Pastoral Litúrgica, 1998.

———. "El problema de las dos tradiciones del antiguo rito hispánico: Valoración documental de la tradición B, en vistas a una eventual revision del Ordinario de la Misa Mozárabe." In *Liturgia y música mozárabes: I Congreso Internacional de Estudios Mozárabes*, 3–44. Toledo: Instituto de Estudios Visigótico-Mozárabes de San Eugenio, 1978.

———. "Los textos de la Antigua liturgia hispánica." In *Estudios sobre la liturgia mozárabe*, ed. Juan Francisco Rivera Recio, 209–64. Toledo: Diputación Provincial, 1965.

————. *Los Plomos del Sacromonte. Invención y Tesoro.* Ed. Manuel Barrios Aguilera and Mercedes García-Arenal. Valencia: University of Valencia, 2006.

Polt, John H. R. *Poesia del siglo XVIII.* Madrid: Castalia, 1975.

Porres Martín-Cleto, Julio. "La iglesia mozárabe de Santa María de Alficén." In *Historia mozárabe: Ponencias y comunicaciones presentadas al I Congreso Internacional de Estudios Mozárabes,* 29–42. Toledo: Instituto de Estudios Visigótico-Mozárabes de San Eugenio, 1975.

Raizman, David. "A Rediscovered Illuminated Manuscript of St. Ildefonsus's *De Virginitate Beatae Mariae* in the Biblioteca Nacional in Madrid." *Gesta* 26 (1987): 37–46.

Ramos López, Pilar. "*Pastorelas* and the Pastoral Tradition in 18th-Century Spanish Villancicos." In *Devotional Music in the Iberian World, 1450–1800: The Villancico and Related Genres,* ed. Tess Knighton and Alvaro Torrente, 283–306. Aldershot, UK: Ashgate, 2007.

Randel, Don. *An Index to the Chant of the Mozarabic Rite.* Princeton Studies in Music 6. Princeton: Princeton University Press, 1973.

————. *The Responsorial Psalm Tones for the Mozarabic Office.* Princeton Studies in Music 3. Princeton: Princeton University Press, 1969.

Randel, Don M., and Nils Nadeau. "Mozarabic Chant." In *Grove Music Online, Oxford Music Online.* www.oxfordmusiconline.com/subscriber/article/grove/music/19269. Accessed March 19, 2009.

Rees, Owen. "Adventures of Portuguese 'Ancient Music': Oxford, London, and Paris: Duarte Lobo's 'Liber Missarum' and Musical Antiquarianism, 1650–1850." *Music and Letters* 85 (2005): 42–73.

Reilly, Bernard F. *The Kingdom of León-Castilla under King Alfonso VI.* Princeton: Princeton University Press, 1988.

Un reinado bajo el signo de la paz: Fernando VI y Bárbara de Braganza, 1746–1759. Madrid: Real Academia de Bellas Artes de San Fernando, 2002.

Reynolds, Roger. "Baptismal Rite and Paschal Vigil in Transition: A New Text in Visigothic Script." *Mediaeval Studies* 55 (1993): 257–72.

————. "The Ordination Rite in Medieval Spain: Hispanic, Roman, and Hybrid." In *Santiago, Saint-Denis, and Saint Peter: The Reception of the Roman Liturgy in León-Castile in 1080,* ed. Bernard F. Reilly, 131–55. New York: Fordham University Press, 1985.

————. "The Visigothic Liturgy in the Realm of Charlemagne." In *Das Frankfurter Konzil von 794: Kristallisationspunkt karolingischer Kultur,* ed. Rainer Berndt, 919–45. Quellen und Abhandlungen zur Mittelrheinischen Kirchengeschichte, 80. 2 vols. Mainz: Selbstverlag der Gesellschaft für Mittelrheinische Kirchenge-schichte, 1997.

Rincón García, Wilfredo, and Emilio Quintanilla Martínez. *Iconografía de San Ildefonso, Arzobispo de Toledo.* Madrid: Real Cuerpo de la Nobleza de Madrid, 2005.

Ríos Saloma, Martín. "De la Restauración a la Reconquista: La construcción de un mito nacional (Una revisión historiográfica. Siglos XVI–XIX)." *En la España Medieval* 28 (2005): 379–414.

————. *La Reconquista: Génesis y desarrollo de una construcción historiográfica (s. XVI–XIX).* Madrid: Marcial-Pons–UNAM, 2011.

Ripa, Cesare. *Iconologia, overo descrittione di diverse imagini cavate dall'antichità, e di propria inventione.* Reprint of the 1603 Rome edition with an introduction by Erna Mandowsky. Hildesheim: Georg Olms, 1970.

Rivera Recio, Juan Francisco. *El adopcionismo en España—siglo VIII—Historia y Doctrina.* Toledo: Seminario Conciliar, 1980.

———. "La controversia adopcionista del siglo VIII y la ortodoxia de la Liturgia Mozárabe." *Ephemerides liturgicae* 47 (1933): 506–36.

———. *San Ildefonso de Toledo: Biografía, época y posteridad.* Toledo: Estudio Teológico de San Ildefonso, 1985.

Rodríguez G. de Ceballos, A. "La piedad y el sentimiento de la muerte en el reinado de Fernando VI y Bárbara de Braganza." In *Un reinado bajo el signo de la paz: Fernando VI y Bárbara de Braganza, 1746–1759,* 361–74. Madrid: Real Academia de Bellas Artes de San Fernando, 2002.

Rodríguez-Moñino Soriano, Rafael. *El Cardenal Cisneros y la España del XVII.* Valencia: Castalia, 1978.

Rojo, Casiano, and Germán Prado. *El canto mozárabe: Estudio histórico-crítico de su antigüedad y estado actual.* Barcelona: Diputación provincial, 1929.

Sánchez Blanco, Francisco. *El absolutismo y las luces en el reinado de Carlos III.* Madrid: Marcial Pons, 2002.

———. *La mentalidad ilustrada.* Madrid: Taurus, 1999.

Sánchez Candeira, Alfonso. *Castilla y León en el Siglo XI: Estudio del Reinado de Fernando I.* Ed. Rosa Montero Tejada. Madrid: Real Academia de la Historia, 1999.

Sancho, José Luis. "Francesco Sabatini, *primer arquitecto,* director de la decoración interior en los palacios reales." In *Francisco Sabatini, 1721–1797: La arquitectura como metáfora del poder,* 143–65. Madrid: Electa, 1993.

———. *The Royal Palace of Madrid.* Trans. Laura Suffield. Madrid: Reales Sitios de España, 2004.

Saugnieux, Joël. "Ilustración católica y religiosidad popular: El culto mariano en la España del siglo XVIII." In *La época de Fernando VI, Ponencias leídas en el coloquo conmemorativo de los 25 años de la fundación de la Cátedra Feijoo,* 275–95. Oviedo: Facultad de filosofía y letras, Universidad de Oviedo, 1981.

Savage, Roger. "Getting By with a Little Help from my Twin: Farinelli with Metastasio at His Right Hand, 1747–1759." *Journal of Eighteenth-Century Studies* 28 (2005): 387–409.

Scarborough, Connie. "Autoría o autorías." In *El Scriptorium Alfonsí: De los libros de astrología a las "Cantigas de Santa María,"* ed. Jesús Montoya Martínez and Ana Domínguez Rodríguez, 331–37. Madrid: Editorial Complutense, 1999.

Schaffer, Martha E. "Los códices de las 'Cantigas de Santa María': Su problemática." In *El Scriptorium Alfonsí: De los libros de astrología a las "Cantigas de Santa María,"* ed. Jesús Montoya Martínez and Ana Domínguez Rodríguez, 127–48. Madrid: Editorial Complutense, 1999.

———. "The 'Evolution' of the *Cantigas de Santa Maria*: The Relationships between Manuscripts T, F, and E." In *Cobras e son: Papers on the Text, Music and Manuscripts of the "Cantigas de Santa Maria,"* ed. Stephen Parkinson, 186–213. Oxford: Legenda, 2000.

————. "Marginal Notes in the Toledo Manuscript of Alfonso el Sabio's *Cantigas de Santa Maria*." *Cantigueiros* 7 (1995): 65–84.

————. "Questions of Authorship: The Cantigas de Santa María." In *Proceedings of the Eighth Colloquium*, ed. Andrew M Beresford and A. D. Deyermond, 17–30. Papers of the Medieval Hispanic Research Seminar 5. London: Department of Hispanic Studies, Queen Mary and Westfield College, 1997.

Schechner Genuth, Sara. "Armillary Sphere." In *Instruments of Science: An Historical Encyclopedia*, ed. Robert Bud and Debra Jean Warner, 28–31. New York: Garland, 1998.

Schulz, Andrew. "Spaces of Enlightenment: Art, Science, and Empire in Eighteenth-Century Spain." In *Spain in the Age of Exploration, 1492–1819*, ed. C. Ishikawa, 189–227. Seattle: Seattle Art Museum, 2004.

Seniff, Dennis P., ed. *Francisco Javier de Santiago y Palomares: Selected Writings, 1776–95.* Exeter: University of Exeter Press, 1984.

Shailor, Barbara. "The Scriptorium of San Sahagún: A Period of Transition." In *Santiago, Saint-Denis and Saint Peter: The Reception of the Roman Liturgy in León-Castile in 1080*, ed. Bernard F. Reilly, 41–61. New York: Fordham University Press, 1985.

Shiels, W. Eugene. *King and Church: The Rise and Fall of the Patronato Real.* Chicago: Loyola University Press, 1961.

Sloane, Carl. "An End Date for the Scarlatti Sonatas." *Studi Musicali* 38 (2009): 55–60.

Snow, Joseph T. "Alfonso as Troubadour: The Fact and the Fiction." In *Emperor of Culture: Alfonso X the Learned of Castile and His Thirteenth-Century Renaissance*, ed. Robert I. Burns, 126–40. Philadelphia: University of Pennsylvania Press, 1990.

————. "Alfonso X y las 'Cantigas': Documento personal y poesía colectiva." In *El Scriptorium Alfonsí: De los libros de astrología a las "Cantigas de Santa María,"* ed. Jesús Montoya Martínez and Ana Domínguez Rodríguez, 159–72. Madrid: Editorial Complutense, 1999.

Stiffoni, Giovanni. "Alcune tematiche del Settecento." In *La Guida della ragione e il labirinto della politica: Studi di storia di Spagna*, 9–42. Biblioteca di Cultura 279. Rome: Bulzoni, 1984.

Stocking, Rachel. *Bishops, Councils, and Consensus in the Visigothic Kingdom, 589–633.* Ann Arbor: University of Michigan Press, 2000.

Strohm, Reinhard. "Francesco Corselli's Operas for Madrid." In *Teatro y Música en España (siglo XVIII), Actas del Simposio Internacional Salamanca*, ed. Rainer Kleinertz, 49–77. Kassel: Reichenberger, 1996.

Sutcliffe, W. Dean. *The Keyboard Sonatas of Domenico Scarlatti and Eighteenth-Century Musical Style.* Cambridge: Cambridge University Press, 2003.

Taylor, Andrew. *Textual Situations: Three Medieval Manuscripts and Their Readers.* Philadelphia: University of Pennsylvania Press, 2002.

————. *The Whole Book: Cultural Perspectives on the Medieval Miscellany.* Ed. Stephen G. Nichols and Siegfried Wenzel. Ann Arbor: University of Michigan Press, 1996.

Téllez Alarcia, Diego. "Literatos, intelectuales y poder político en el reinado de Fernando VI (1746–59)." *Dieciocho: Hispanic Enlightenment* 26 (2003): 53–70.

Torrente, Álvaro. "Italianate Sections in the Villancicos of the Royal Chapel, 1700–40." In *Music in Spain during the Eighteenth Century*, ed. Malcolm Boyd and Juan José Carreras, 72–79. Cambridge: Cambridge University Press, 1998.

Torrione, Margarita ed. *Crónica festiva de dos reinados en la Gaceta de Madrid: 1700–1759.* Paris: CRIC and Ophrys, 1998.

———. "La sociedad de Corte y el ritual de la ópera." In *Un reinado bajo el signo de la paz: Fernando VI y Bárbara de Braganza, 1746–1759,* ed. Antonio Bonet Correa; Beatriz Blasco Esquivias, 165–95. Madrid: Real Academia de Bellas Artes de San Fernando, 2002.

Treitler, Leo. "Oral, Written, and Literate Process in the Transmission of Medieval Music." *Speculum* 56 (1981): 471–91.

———. "Reading and Singing: on the Genesis of Occidental Music-Writing." *Early Music History* 4 (1984): 135–208.

———. "The 'Unwritten' and 'Written Transmission' of Medieval Chant and the Start-up of Musical Notation." *Journal of Musicology* 10 (1992): 131–91.

Trinkle, D. "Noël-Antoine Pluche's *Le Spectacle de la nature*: An encyclopaedic best seller." *Studies on Voltaire and the Eighteenth Century* 358 (1997): 93–134.

Urvoy, Dominique. "Les conséquences christologiques de la confrontation islamo-chrétienne en Espagne au VIIIe siècle." In *Das Frankfurter Konzil von 794: Kristallisationspunkt karolingischer Kultur,* ed. Rainer Berndt, 981–92. Quellen und Abhandlungen zur Mittelrheinischen Kirchengeschichte, 80. 2 vols. Mainz: Selbstverlag der Gesellschaft für Mittelrheinische Kirchengeschichte, 1997.

Vadillo Romero, Eduardo, and Angel Fernández Collado. "El breviario mozárabe de Lorenzana." In *El cardenal Lorenzana, arzobispo de Toledo: Ciclo de Conferencias en el II Centenario de su muerte (1804–2004),* ed. Angel Fernández Collado, 141–52. Toledo: Instituto superior de estudios teológicos San Ildefonso, 2004.

Valero, José Antonio. "Razón y nación en la política cultural del primer dieciocho." *Espéculo: Revista de estudios literarios,* 2002. www.ucm.es/info/especulo/numero22/razon18.html. Accessed March 19, 2009.

Van Kley, Dale K. "Piety and Politics in the Century of Lights." In *The Cambridge History of Eighteenth-Century Political Thought,* ed. Mark Goldie and Robert Wokler, 110–43. Cambridge: Cambridge University Press, 2006.

Villacorta Rodríguez, Tomás. *El Cabildo Catedral de León: Estudio histórico-jurídico: Siglos XII–XIX.* Fuentes y estudios de historia leonesa 12. León: Centro de Estudios e Investigación "San Isidoro," 1974.

Viñayo González, Antonio. *Fernando I, El Magno, 1035–1065.* Corona de España. Serie de Reyes de León y Castilla 16. Burgos: La Olmeda, 1999.

Vismara, Paola. "Muratori alla 'Scuola Mabillona': Dalle Riflessioni sopra il buon gusto agli Annali d'Italia." In *Erudition et commerce épistolaire: Jean Mabillon et la tradition monastique,* ed. Daniel-Odon Hurel, 135–52. Textes et Traditions 6. Paris: Librairie Philosophique J. Vrin, 2003.

Vivancos, Manuel C. "El oracional visigótico de Verona: Notas codicológicas y paleográficas." *Cuadernos de Filologia Clásica: Estudios Latinos* 26 (2006): 121–44.

Vones, Ludwig. "The Substitution of the Hispanic Liturgy by the Roman Rite in the Kingdoms of the Iberian Peninsula." In *Hispania Vetus: Musical-Liturgical Manuscripts from Visigothic Origins to the Franco-Roman Transition (9th–12th Centuries),* ed. Susana Zapke, 43–59. Bilbao: Fundación BBVA, 2007.

Vones-Liebenstein, Ursula. "Katalonien zwischen Maurenherrschaft und Frankenreich: Probleme um die Ablösung westgotisch-mozarabischer Kirchenstrukturen." In

Das Frankfurter Konzil von 794: Kristallisationspunkt karolingischer Kultur, ed. Rainer Berndt. 2 vols. 1:453–505. Quellen und Abhandlungen zur Mittelrheinischen Kirchengeschichte 80. Mainz: Selbstverlag der Gesellschaft für Mittelrheinische Kirchengeschichte, 1997.

Walker, Rose. *Views of Transition: Liturgy and Illumination in Medieval Spain*. London: British Library, 1998.

Wälli, Silvia. *Melodien aus mittelalterlichen Horaz-Handschriften: Edition und Interpretation der Quellen*. Monumenta Monodica Medii Aevi, Subsidia 2. Kassel: Bärenreiter, 2002.

Whistler, Catherine. "On the Margins in Madrid: Some Questions of Identity at the Real Academia de Bellas Artes de San Fernando, 1744–1792." In *Art and Culture in the Eighteenth Century: New Dimensions and Multiple Perspectives*, ed. Elise Goodman, 76–89. Newark: University of Delaware Press, 2001.

Wilmart, André. "La tradition des grands ouvrages de Saint Augustin. III. *La Cité de Dieu*." In *Miscellanea agostiniana: Testi e studi, pubblicati a cura dell'Ordine eremitano di s. Agostino nel XV centenario dalla morte del santo dottore*, 2:279–92. Rome: Tipografia poliglotta vaticana, 1931.

Wulstan, David. "The Composition of the *Cantigas* of Alfonso el Sabio." In *Cobras e son: Papers on the Text, Music and Manuscripts of the "Cantigas de Santa Maria*," ed. Stephen Parkinson, 214–20. Oxford: Legenda, 2000.

Wunder, Amanda Jaye. "The Search for Sanctity in Baroque Seville: The Canonization of San Fernando and the Making of Golden-Age Culture, 1624–1729." PhD diss., Princeton University, 2002.

Zanardi, Tara. "Preservation and Promotion: The State of the Arts in Eighteenth-Century Spain." *Dieciocho: Hispanic Enlightenment* 27 (2004): 303–20.

Zapke, Susana. "Liber ordinum." In *Hispania Vetus, Musical-Liturgical Manuscripts from Visigothic Origins to the Franco-Roman Transition (9th–12th Centuries)*, ed. Susan Zapke, 260–61. Bilbao: Fundación BBVA, 2007.

———. "Notation Systems in the Iberian Peninsula." In *Hispania Vetus, Musical-Liturgical Manuscripts from Visigothic Origins to the Franco-Roman Transition (9th–12th Centuries)*, ed. Susana Zapke, 199–243. Bilbao: Fundación BBVA, 2007.

———. "The Visigothic Dream: The Hispanic Rite in the Eras of Humanism and Enlightenment." *Goldberg: Early Music Magazine* 53 (2008): 66–73.

Ziolkowski, Jan. *Nota Bene: Reading Classics and Writing Melodies in the Early Middle Ages*. Publications of the Journal of Medieval Latin 7. Turnhout: Brepols, 2007.

cantorales, Mozarabic, 8–9, 11, 85–86, 176
Caroline minuscule, 4, 149, 151, 166
Carrillo de Acuña, Alonso, 8
Carvajal y Lancaster, José de, xi, xiii, 15, 52
Castilian language, xii, 29, 39, 41–42, 45n50
Castro, Pedro de, 10, 21, 89
Cavadini, John, 74, 75
Cenni, Gaetano, 12, 32–33, 88
Chansonniers, 116–17
Charlemagne, 73
Charles III of Spain (Carlos III), 27, 44n7, 141–43, 165
church history
   in France, 35
   in Spain, 25–27, 31, 35, 51
   and Spanish nationalism, 22–23
   Spanish royal academy of, xiii, 31
Cisneros, Francisco Ximénez de
   and the Virgin Mary, 9
   founding of Mozarabic chapel
comparative liturgy, 55
Concordat of 1753, 15, 98
Constanza of Burgundy, 149–50, 151
Council of Frankfurt (794), 73, 75
Council of Trent, 11, 54–55
councils, Visigothic, 26, 30, 33, 52, 103
Courcelle, Francisco (Corselli), xi
critical history and official history, 22
cultural nationalism (in Spain), xii, 13, 38

Elipandus of Toledo, 73–76, 105
Elisabeth of Parma. See Isabella Farnese
engraving in Spain, 38, 48n99
Enlightenment, 44n11
   in France, 23, 24
   in Spain, 16, 23–26, 44n7
Ensenada, Marques de la (Cénon de Somodevilla), xi, xiii, 15, 99
España Sagrada, 29–31, 51, 74. See also Flórez, Enrique
Eugenius of Toledo, 75

Falconnet, Camille, 35
false chronicles (falsos cronicones), 23, 44n20
Farinelli, xi–xii, 125
Feijoo y Montenegro, Benito, 23–24, 26
Felix of Urgell, 73
Ferdinand of Aragón, xiii, 8
Ferdinand I of Castile, 28, 120

Ferdinand III of Castile, 29
   Burriel's biography of, 22
   depicted by Giaquinto Corrado, 124–25
   in Sarmiento's Sistema, 28
Ferdinand VI of Spain, x–xiii
   association with Mercury, 121–22
   name of, 28, 29
   portrait of, xi, 122
Ferreira, Manuel Pedro, 115
Flórez, Enrique, 15, 21, 25, 29, 77n6
   on adoptionistm, 74
   on liturgical history, 32, 33, 105, 148
   and Mayans, 25

Gaceta de Madrid, 102, 125
"Gallican" liturgy, 10, 14, 88, 96
Giaquinto, Corrado, 122–25
González de Mendoza, Pedro, 8
González Ruiz, Antonio, xi, 122
Gothic. See Visigothic.
Goths. See Visigoths.
Granada, plomos. See plomos de Granada
Gregory VII, Pope, 4, 74, 149
Gudiel, Gonzálo Pérez, 7, 135n2

Hermengild, saint, 28, 45n26, 102
Hispanic rite. See Old Hispanic rite
hispanismo, xi–xii
historiography in eighteenth-century Spain, 13–14, 23, 26, 30, 34, 36
Hitchcock, Richard, 7, 44n20
hymns, office, 157

Ildefonsus of Toledo, 30, 94
   in the Cantigas de Santa María, 114
   and the liturgy, 43, 71, 75, 104
   representations in art, 113–14
   treatise on the perpetual virginity of Mary, 104–6, 113–14, 176
Imbasciani, Vito, 18n48, 86–87
Infantas, Juan Antonio de las, 13, 51, 52, 59
invention of tradition, 13–14
Isabella of Castile, xiii, 8, 55
Isabella Farnese (Elisabeth of Parma), x, 13
Isidore of Seville, 14, 42
   and the Latin Psalter, 68
   and the liturgy, 71, 74, 149, 163
   and neumes, 163
   De uiris illustribus, 30

Pluche, Nöel-Antoine, *Spectacle de la Nature*, 37
Porcel, José Antonio, 28, 121

Quintano y Bonifaz, Manuel, 15

Rávago, Francisco, xi, 15, 30, 32
Real Academia de la Lengua Española, 29
Reccared, 102
Reconquista, 40
Reynolds, Roger, 4
Rodríguez, Cristóbal. *See* Bibliotheca Universal de la Polygraphia Española
Roman rite
    Burriel's chronology of, 54–55
    in León and Castile, 4, 5, 8, 33, 34,148
    in Toledo, 54–55, 58–59, 88, 149–51
Romero, Jerónimo, 177
Rousseau, Jean-Jacques, 116
Royal Academy of Fine Arts (Real Academia de Bellas Artes de San Ferdando), xi, 38
Royal Academy of the Spanish Language. *See* Real Academia de la Lengua Española
Royal Commission on the Archives, xii–xiv, 15, 22–23, 29–30, 36, 46n66, 51–52. *See also* Pérez Bayer; Burriel; Palomares; Toledo cathedral chapter
Royal Library, Madrid, x, 26, 142, 165
Royal Palace, Madrid, 27, 165. *See also* Sarmiento

Sabatini, Francisco, 27
Santa María de Alficén, Toledo, 6
Santiago (Saint James the Greater), 22, 24, 26, 31, 33, 175
Sarmiento, Martín, 24
    Memorias para la historia de la poesía y poetas españoles, 29, 38–39, 139n81
    Sistema de adornos, 27–28, 121, 122, 135
Scarlatti, Domenico, xi, 118
Schaffer, Martha, 126, 130, 134
script, Visigothic. *See* Visigothic script

Seminary of Nobles (Seminario de Nobles), xiii–xiv, 121
Sistema de adornos. *See* Sarmiento
Somodevilla, Cénon de *See* Ensenada, Marques de la
Song of the Sibyl, 154–58

Teatro crítico universal. *See* Feijoo
Terreros y Pando, Esteban, 37, 39
Toledo, 6, 39, 41
    cathedral chapter, 7, 51–53, 94
    Mozarabic chapel, 8, 13–14, 91–92, 104, 175
    as primatial see 6, 30, 41, 53, 75, 101
Toledo Codex of the *Cantigas de Santa María*. *See under* Manuscripts: Madrid, Biblioteca Nacional de España, 10069
Tomasi, Giuseppe Maria, 12, 32, 33, 89
tradiciones jacobeas. *See* Santiago
Trent, Council of. *See* Council of Trent

Vázquez de Cepeda, Juan, 8
Venegas, Miguel, *Noticia de la California*, xiv, 175
Verona, visigothic *orationale*. *See under* manuscripts: Verona, Biblioteca Capitolare
villancico, xii
Virgin Mary *See* Mary, Virgin
Visigothic councils. *See* councils, Visigothic
Visigothic church, 30
Visigothic liturgy, 14, 135
Visigothic script
    continued use by Toledan Mozarabs, 4, 6, 10, 41–42, 97, 151
    eighteenth-century knowledge of, 12, 37–38, 56, 143
Visigoths (as represented in the eighteenth century), 28, 103

Wall, Ricardo, 15
War of Spanish Succession, x, xii, 12, 24

zarzuela, xiv

MANUSCRIPTS CITED